LIGHT & EA
WEEKNIGHT
COOKING

TASTE OF HOME BOOKS • RDA ENTHUSIAST BRANDS, LLC • MILWAUKEE, WI

© 2022 RDA Enthusiast Brands, LLC.
1610 N. 2nd St., Suite 102, Milwaukee, WI 53212-3906
All rights reserved. Taste of Home is a registered trademark of
RDA Enthusiast Brands, LLC.

Visit us at **tasteofhome.com** for other Taste of Home books
and products.

International Standard Book Number:
978-1-62145-756-5

Executive Editor: Mark Hagen
Senior Art Director: Raeann Thompson
Editor: Amy Glander
Art Director: Maggie Conners
Deputy Editor, Copy Desk: Dulcie Shoener
Copy Editor: Kara Dennison
Designer: Arielle Anttonen

Cover
Photographer: Dan Roberts
Set Stylist: Melissa Franco
Food Stylist: Shannon Norris

Pictured on front cover: Slow-Cooker Chicken Taco Salad, p. 151
Pictured on title page: Curried Chicken Skillet, p. 145
Pictured on back cover: Salmon with Horseradish Pistachio
Crust, p. 77; No-Guilt Brownies, p. 234; Stir-Fry Rice Bowl,
p. 105; Slow-Cooker Beef Barbacoa, 211.

INSTANT POT® is a trademark of Double Insight Inc.
This publication has not been authorized, sponsored
or otherwise approved by Double Insight Inc.

Printed in USA
1 3 5 7 9 10 8 6 4 2

Feta Mushroom
Burgers, p. 55

Table of Contents

Say Hello to Your Healthy Weeknight Dinner Inspiration!

Home cooks are often faced with the conundrum of creating nutritionally balanced meals that are a breeze to prepare and don't fall short on the flavor and fulfillment they know their families love.

Now it's easier than ever to cook from scratch and put delicious homemade foods on the table every night of the week without compromising quality, freshness, nutrition or time in the kitchen.

Light & Easy Weeknight Cooking brims with 307 flavorful recipes that are not only prepared with healthy wholesome ingredients, but can also be stirred up in a snap. With recipes that are as good for you as they are delectable, you'll always have a hot, satisfying meal within reach—even on your busiest nights!

At-A-Glance Icons

Refer to these 6 icons to easily locate recipes that suit your needs.

= Finished in 30 minutes or less

= Made in a pressure cooker

= Made in a slow cooker

= Made in an air fryer

= A nutritionally complete "power-packed" recipe that includes a lean protein, a whole grain, and at least 1 serving of fruits or vegetables

= Meatless recipe

MORE WAYS TO CONNECT WITH US:

Snacks & MUNCHIES

When a snack attack strikes, turn to these sweet and savory bites that won't weigh you down and come together in a jiffy.

BBQ Chicken Bites

Chicken bites wrapped in bacon get a kick from Montreal seasoning and sweetness from barbecue sauce. We love the mix of textures.
—Kathryn Dampier, Quail Valley, CA

- -

Takes: 25 min. • **Makes:** 1½ dozen

- 6 bacon strips
- ¾ lb. boneless skinless chicken breasts, cut into 1-in. cubes (about 18)
- 3 tsp. Montreal steak seasoning
- 1 tsp. prepared horseradish, optional
- ½ cup barbecue sauce

1. Preheat oven to 400°. Cut bacon crosswise into thirds. Place bacon on a microwave-safe plate lined with paper towels. Cover with additional paper towels; microwave on high 3-4 minutes or until partially cooked but not crisp.
2. Place chicken in a small bowl; sprinkle with steak seasoning and toss to coat. Wrap a bacon piece around each chicken cube; secure with a toothpick. Place on a parchment-lined baking sheet.
3. Bake 10 minutes. If desired, add horseradish to barbecue sauce; brush over wrapped chicken. Bake until the chicken is no longer pink and bacon is crisp, 5-10 minutes longer.
1 appetizer: 47 cal., 2g fat (0 sat. fat), 13mg chol., 249mg sod., 3g carb. (3g sugars, 0 fiber), 5g pro.

Triple Tomato Flatbread

I developed this recipe to show off my garden's plum, sun-dried and cherry tomatoes. The flatbread is easy to make and guaranteed to impress.
—Rachel Kimbrow, Portland, OR

- -

Takes: 20 min. • **Makes:** 8 pieces

- 1 tube (13.8 oz.) refrigerated pizza crust
  Cooking spray
- 3 plum tomatoes, finely chopped (about 2 cups)
- ½ cup soft sun-dried tomato halves (not packed in oil), julienned
- 2 Tbsp. olive oil
- 1 Tbsp. dried basil
- ¼ tsp. salt
- ¼ tsp. pepper
- 1 cup shredded Asiago cheese
- 2 cups yellow and/or red cherry tomatoes, halved

1. Unroll and press dough into a 15x10-in. rectangle. Transfer dough to an 18x12-in. piece of heavy-duty foil coated with cooking spray; spritz dough with cooking spray. In a large bowl, toss the plum tomatoes and sun-dried tomatoes with the oil and seasonings.
2. Carefully invert dough onto grill rack; remove foil. Grill, covered, over medium heat 2-3 minutes or until bottom is golden brown. Turn; grill 1-2 minutes longer or until second side begins to brown.
3. Remove from grill. Spoon plum tomato mixture over crust; top with cheese and cherry tomatoes. Return flatbread to grill. Grill, covered, 2-4 minutes or until crust is golden brown and the cheese is melted.
1 piece: 235 cal., 9g fat (3g sat. fat), 12mg chol., 476mg sod., 29g carb. (7g sugars, 3g fiber), 8g pro.
Diabetic exchanges: 1½ starch, 1½ fat, 1 vegetable.

Sundae Funday Bark

Any occasion is the right time to serve this easy-to-make bark. The fruits—packed with flavor but not overly sweet—go well with the white candy base. A dark chocolate drizzle makes this treat extra special.
—Kim Banick, Turner, OR

- -

Prep: 20 min. + chilling
Makes: 16 servings

- 1 pkg. (10 to 12 oz.) white baking chips
- ¼ cup freeze-dried pineapple
- ¼ cup dried banana chips, coarsely chopped
- ¼ cup freeze-dried strawberry slices
- ¼ cup dried cherries
- ⅓ cup salted peanuts, coarsely chopped
- ¼ cup dark chocolate chips, melted

1. Line a 15x10x1-in. pan with parchment. In a microwave, melt baking chips; stir until smooth. Spread into a 12x8-in. rectangle in prepared pan. Sprinkle with the pineapple, bananas, strawberries, cherries and peanuts; press into melted chips.
2. Refrigerate until firm, about 30 minutes. Break or cut bark into pieces. Drizzle dark chocolate over bark before or after dividing into pieces. Store between layers of waxed paper in an airtight container.
1 oz.: 152 cal., 9g fat (5g sat. fat), 4mg chol., 27mg sod., 17g carb. (16g sugars, 1g fiber), 2g pro.

TIMESAVING TIP

Feel free to use any type of dried fruits in place of the cherries and strawberries.

Asparagus Bruschetta

I like asparagus, so I'm always trying it in different things. This is a delicious twist on traditional bruschetta.
—Elaine Sweet, Dallas, TX

- -

Takes: 30 min. • **Makes:** 1 dozen

- 3 cups water
- ½ lb. fresh asparagus, trimmed and cut into ½-in. pieces
- 2 cups grape tomatoes, halved
- ¼ cup minced fresh basil
- 3 green onions, chopped
- 3 Tbsp. lime juice
- 1 Tbsp. olive oil
- 3 garlic cloves, minced
- 1½ tsp. grated lime zest
- ¼ tsp. salt
- ¼ tsp. pepper
- 12 slices French bread baguette (½ in. thick), toasted
- ½ cup crumbled blue cheese

1. In a large saucepan, bring water to a boil. Add the asparagus; cover and boil for 2-4 minutes. Drain and immediately place asparagus in ice water. Drain and pat dry.
2. In a large bowl, combine the asparagus, tomatoes, basil, onions, lime juice, oil, garlic, lime zest, salt and pepper. Using a slotted spoon, spoon asparagus mixture onto toasted bread. Sprinkle with the blue cheese.
1 piece: 88 cal., 3g fat (1g sat. fat), 4mg chol., 237mg sod., 13g carb. (1g sugars, 1g fiber), 3g pro.
Diabetic exchanges: 1 starch, ½ fat.

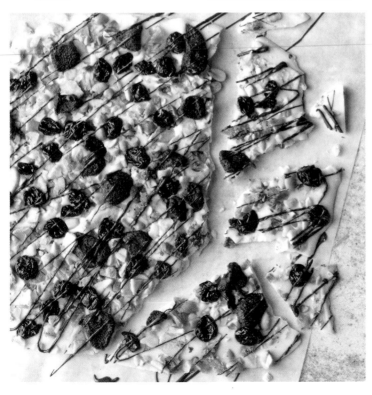

Almond-Pecan Date Truffles

My daughter and I came across a date candy recipe when she was learning about ancient Egypt. We changed some of the spices and nuts to suit our tastes.
—Lori Daniels, Beverly, WV

- -

Prep: 20 min. + chilling
Makes: about 1½ dozen

- ⅓ cup apple juice
- 1 pkg. (8 oz.) chopped dates
- 1 cup finely chopped pecans, toasted
- 1¼ tsp. ground cinnamon
- ¼ tsp. ground nutmeg
- 1 cup ground almonds, toasted

1. In a microwave, warm apple juice. Stir in dates; let stand 5 minutes to soften, stirring occasionally. Remove dates from apple juice; discard liquid. Transfer dates to the bowl of a food processor fitted with the blade attachment; process until smooth. Add pecans and spices; pulse just until combined (the mixture will be thick).
2. Shape mixture into 1-in. balls; place on a waxed paper-lined baking sheet. Refrigerate, covered, 30-60 minutes.
3. Roll date balls in almonds.
1 date ball: 109 cal., 7g fat (1g sat. fat), 0 chol., 0 sod., 12g carb. (9g sugars, 2g fiber), 2g pro.

Air-Fryer Potato Chips

I received an air fryer for Christmas one year. Potato chips are simple and healthy to make in this handy tool.
—Melissa Obernesser, Oriskany, NY

- -

Prep: 30 min. • **Cook:** 15 min./batch
Makes: 6 servings

- 2 large potatoes
  Olive oil-flavored
  cooking spray
- ½ tsp. sea salt
  Minced fresh parsley, optional

1. Preheat air fryer to 360°. Using a mandoline or vegetable peeler, cut potatoes into very thin slices. Transfer to a large bowl; add ice water to cover. Soak potatoes for 15 minutes; drain. Add more ice water and soak another 15 minutes.
2. Drain potatoes; place on towels and pat dry. Spritz potatoes with cooking spray; sprinkle with salt. In batches, place potato slices in a single layer on tray in greased air-fryer basket. Cook until crisp and golden brown, 15-17 minutes, stirring and turning potatoes every 5-7 minutes. If desired, sprinkle with minced parsley.
1 cup: 148 cal., 1g fat (0 sat. fat), 0 chol., 252mg sod., 32g carb. (2g sugars, 4g fiber), 4g pro.
Diabetic exchanges: 2 starch.

Try this easy way to make these truffles extra special. After they have chilled for 30 minutes, dip them in melted chocolate and chill until set.

Coconut Milk Strawberry-Banana Pops

These four-ingredient freezer pops are a delicious and refreshing way to use up a pint of fresh strawberries. You'll love the hint of tropical flavor from the coconut milk.
—*Taste of Home* Test Kitchen

- -

Prep: 10 min. + freezing
Makes: 12 servings

- 1 can (13.66 oz.) coconut milk
- 1 pint fresh strawberries, chopped, divided
- 1 medium banana, sliced
- 2 Tbsp. maple syrup
- 12 freezer pop molds or 12 paper cups (3 oz. each) and wooden pop sticks

Place the coconut milk, 1½ cups strawberries, banana and syrup in a blender; cover and process until smooth. Divide remaining berries among 12 molds or paper cups. Pour pureed mixture into molds or cups, filling ¾ full. Top the molds with holders. If using cups, top with foil and insert sticks through foil. Freeze until firm, at least 4 hours.

1 pop: 51 cal., 3g fat (3g sat. fat), 0 chol., 5mg sod., 7g carb. (5g sugars, 1g fiber), 1g pro.

Veggie Dill Dip

I keep this good-for-you dip and a variety of fresh cut-up veggies on hand for an easy snack.
—Hazel Baber, Yuma, AZ

Prep: 10 min. + chilling
Makes: 2½ cups

- 2 cups 1% cottage cheese
- 3 Tbsp. fat-free milk
- ¾ cup fat-free mayonnaise
- 1 Tbsp. dried minced onion
- 1 Tbsp. dried parsley flakes
- 1 tsp. dill weed
- 1 tsp. seasoned salt
- ¼ tsp. garlic powder

In a blender, blend cottage cheese and milk until smooth. Stir in the remaining ingredients and mix well. Chill dip overnight. Serve dip with raw vegetables.
2 Tbsp.: 37 cal., 0 fat (0 sat. fat), 2mg chol., 303mg sod., 3g carb. (2g sugars, 0 fiber), 5g pro.

Zippy Shrimp Skewers

These flavorful skewers deliver a mouthwatering kick with minimal effort. Fix them for your next party and watch them disappear.
—Jalayne Luckett, Marion, IL

Prep: 10 min. + marinating
Grill: 5 min. • **Makes:** 6 servings

- 2 Tbsp. brown sugar
- 2 tsp. cider vinegar
- 1½ tsp. canola oil
- 1 tsp. chili powder
- ½ tsp. salt
- ½ tsp. paprika
- ¼ tsp. hot pepper sauce
- ¾ lb. uncooked medium shrimp, peeled and deveined

1. In a large shallow dish, combine the first 7 ingredients; add shrimp. Turn to coat; cover and refrigerate for 2-4 hours.
2. Drain and discard marinade. Thread the shrimp onto 6 metal or soaked wooden skewers. Grill, uncovered, on a lightly oiled rack over medium heat or broil 4 in. from heat until shrimp turn pink, 2-3 minutes on each side.
1 skewer: 57 cal., 1g fat (0 sat. fat), 84mg chol., 199mg sod., 2g carb. (2g sugars, 0 fiber), 9g pro.
Diabetic exchanges: 1 lean meat.

So Easy Snack Mix

I enjoy this tasty treat just as much as the kids. Have fun with it by adding other goodies into the mix—nuts, cereal, pretzels and more.
—Jeff King, Duluth, MN

Takes: 5 min. • **Makes:** 4 qt.

- 4 cups Goldfish cheddar crackers
- 4 cups golden raisins
- 4 cups dried cherries
- 2 cups yogurt-covered raisins
- 2 cups miniature pretzels

Place all ingredients in a large bowl; toss to combine. Store in airtight containers.
½ cup: 195 cal., 3g fat (1g sat. fat), 1mg chol., 104mg sod., 42g carb. (29g sugars, 2g fiber), 2g pro.

Nutty Stuffed Mushrooms

Basil, Parmesan and mushrooms go together well, while buttery pecans give these appetizers unexpected crunch. Our children, grandchildren and great-grandchildren always ask for them!
—Mildred Eldred, Union City, MI

Takes: 30 min. • **Makes:** 20 servings

- 20 large fresh mushrooms
- 3 Tbsp. butter
- 1 small onion, chopped
- ¼ cup dry bread crumbs
- ¼ cup finely chopped pecans
- 3 Tbsp. grated Parmesan cheese
- ¼ tsp. salt
- ¼ tsp. dried basil
  Dash cayenne pepper

1. Preheat oven to 400°. Remove stems from mushrooms; set caps aside. Finely chop stems. In a large skillet, heat butter over medium heat. Add chopped mushrooms and onion; saute until the liquid has evaporated, about 5 minutes. Remove from heat; set aside.

2. Meanwhile, combine remaining ingredients; add mushroom mixture. Stuff firmly into mushroom caps. Bake, uncovered, in a greased 15x10x1-in. baking pan until tender, 15-18 minutes. Serve warm.

1 stuffed mushroom: 44 cal., 3g fat (1g sat. fat), 5mg chol., 67mg sod., 3g carb. (0 sugars, 0 fiber), 2g pro.

Pepperoni Stuffed Mushrooms: Prepare mushroom caps as directed. Omit pecans, salt, basil and pepper. Add 1 minced garlic clove to chopped mushrooms and onion when sauteing. Stir into mushroom mixture bread crumbs, Parmesan cheese, 3 oz. finely chopped pepperoni, 1 Tbsp. minced parsley and ⅛ tsp. pepper. Bake at 375° for 15-20 minutes or until tender. Serve warm.

Green Olive Tapenade

Here's a tasty tapenade for your next party. This recipe uses green olives instead of black. Besides serving it as an appetizer, you can also use it to punch up your favorite deli sandwich.
—Teresa Spencer, Oconomowoc, WI

Takes: 10 min. • **Makes:** 1¾ cups

- ⅓ cup olive oil
- 1½ tsp. lemon juice
- 2 anchovy fillets
- 1 garlic clove, peeled
- ¼ tsp. pepper
  Dash sugar
  Dash salt
- 2 cups pimiento-stuffed olives
- 14 slices French bread (½ in. thick), toasted

In a food processor, combine the first 7 ingredients; cover and process until smooth. Add olives; cover and pulse until coarsely chopped. Serve with toasted French bread.

2 Tbsp. with 1 piece bread: 116 cal., 9g fat (1g sat. fat), 0 chol., 512mg sod., 8g carb. (0 sugars, 0 fiber), 1g pro.

No-Bake Peanut Butter Oatmeal Bars

My daughter has food sensitivities, so I make these bars with certified gluten-free oats. Everyone loves the bars when we go to picnics or potlucks, and I feel confident knowing my daughter can enjoy the treat.
—Angela Lively, Conroe, TX

- -

Takes: 10 minutes + chilling
Makes: 9 servings

1   cup creamy peanut butter
¾   cup honey
3   cups old-fashioned oats

In a small saucepan, combine peanut butter and honey. Cook and stir over medium-low heat until melted and blended. Remove from heat; stir in oats. Spread into a greased 9-in. square pan; press lightly. Cool to room temperature; cover and chill for 1 hour.
1 bar: 355 cal., 17g fat (3g sat. fat), 0 chol., 122mg sod., 47g carb. (27g sugars, 4g fiber), 10g pro.

Greek Veggie Tartlets

The mixture in these tarts started as a salad I made after a trip to Greece. My husband suggested I bake it in phyllo cups for a tasty appetizer.
—Radelle Knappenberger, Oviedo, FL

- -

Takes: 25 min. • **Makes:** 45 tartlets

3   pkg. (1.9 oz. each) frozen miniature phyllo tart shells
¾   cup finely chopped seeded peeled cucumber
¾   cup finely chopped red onion
¾   cup finely chopped seeded plum tomatoes
¾   cup finely chopped pitted Greek olives
½   cup Greek vinaigrette
¾   cup crumbled feta cheese

1. Preheat oven to 350°. Place shells on two 15x10x1-in. pans. Bake until lightly browned, 7-10 minutes. Cool shells completely.
2. Toss vegetables and olives with vinaigrette. To serve, spoon about 1 Tbsp. mixture into each tart shell. Sprinkle with cheese.
1 tartlet: 43 cal., 3g fat (0 sat. fat), 1mg chol., 93mg sod., 3g carb. (0 sugars, 0 fiber), 1g pro.

Chocolate Hummus

This sweet twist on hummus is so easy to make with just a handful of healthy ingredients. I serve it with berries and pretzels for a quick snack.
—Catherine Ward, Mequon, WI

- -

Takes: 10 min. • **Makes:** 1½ cups

1   can (15 oz.) garbanzo beans or chickpeas, rinsed and drained
⅓   cup unsweetened vanilla almond milk
¼   cup baking cocoa
¼   cup honey
2   tsp. vanilla extract
    Assorted fresh fruit, crackers or pretzels

In a food processor, combine the first 5 ingredients; cover and process until smooth. Serve with fresh fruit, crackers or pretzels.
¼ cup: 124 cal., 2g fat (0 sat. fat), 0 chol., 102mg sod., 25g carb. (13g sugars, 3g fiber), 3g pro.

Easy Microwave Mint Fudge

This easy fudge tastes like it came from a confectionery. Try it for Christmas or St. Patrick's Day.
—Donna Roberts, Manhattan, KS

- -

Prep: 15 min. + chilling
Makes: about 3 lbs. (117 pieces)

- 2 tsp. butter
- 7½ cups confectioners' sugar
- 1 cup baking cocoa
- 15 Tbsp. butter, softened
- 7 Tbsp. 2% milk
- 2 tsp. vanilla extract
- 1 cup Andes creme de menthe baking chips

1. Line a 13x9-in. pan with foil; grease foil with 2 tsp. butter.
2. In a large microwave-safe bowl, sift together confectioners' sugar and cocoa. Add butter and milk (do not stir). Microwave on high 2-2½ minutes. Remove from the microwave; stir until blended. Stir in the vanilla. Spread into prepared pan.

Sprinkle with baking chips, pressing chips lightly into fudge. Refrigerate 1 hour or until firm.
3. Using foil, lift fudge out of pan. Remove foil; cut fudge into 1-in. squares. Store in an airtight container in the refrigerator.
Freeze option: Wrap fudge in waxed paper, then in foil. Place in freezer containers and freeze. To thaw, bring wrapped fudge to room temperature.
Note: This recipe was tested in a 1,100-watt microwave.
1 piece: 56 cal., 2g fat (2g sat. fat), 4mg chol., 14mg sod., 9g carb. (9g sugars, 0 fiber), 0 pro.

> **TIMESAVING TIP**
> Most fudge will last for 1-2 weeks when stored in an airtight container at room temperature. You can also prolong its life by storing it in the fridge or freezer. Fudge that has gone past its prime is typically rock hard or soft and gooey.

10 Minute Zesty Salsa

We have a great view of Pikes Peak from our mountain home, so we frequently eat on our wraparound porch in good weather. During family get-togethers, we savor this zippy salsa with chips while enjoying the natural beauty around us.
—Kim Morin, Lake George, CO

- -

Takes: 10 min. • **Makes:** 1½ cups

- 1 can (10 oz.) diced tomatoes and green chiles, undrained
- 1 Tbsp. seeded chopped jalapeno pepper
- 1 Tbsp. chopped red onion
- 1 Tbsp. minced fresh cilantro
- 1 garlic clove, minced
- 1 Tbsp. olive oil
-   Dash salt
-   Dash pepper
-   Tortilla chips

In a small bowl, combine tomatoes, jalapeno, onion, cilantro, garlic, oil, salt and pepper. Refrigerate until serving. Serve with tortilla chips.
Note: Wear disposable gloves when cutting hot peppers; the oils can burn skin. Avoid touching your face.
¼ cup: 29 cal., 2g fat (0 sat. fat), 0 chol., 214mg sod., 2g carb. (0 sugars, 1g fiber), 0 pro.
Diabetic exchanges: ½ fat.

Sides, Salads & BREADS

You'll have no guilt when you pile your plate high with these
light and colorful dinnertime sidekicks.

Couscous Tabbouleh with Fresh Mint & Feta

Using couscous instead of bulgur speeds up this colorful tabbouleh. Other quick-cooking grains, such as barley or quinoa, also work well.
—Elodie Rosinovsky, Brighton, MA

- -

Takes: 20 min. • **Makes:** 3 servings

¾ cup water
½ cup uncooked couscous
1 can (15 oz.) garbanzo beans or chickpeas, rinsed and drained
1 large tomato, chopped
½ English cucumber, halved and thinly sliced
3 Tbsp. lemon juice
2 tsp. grated lemon zest
2 tsp. olive oil
2 tsp. minced fresh mint
2 tsp. minced fresh parsley
¼ tsp. salt
⅛ tsp. pepper
¾ cup crumbled feta cheese
Lemon wedges, optional

1. In a small saucepan, bring water to a boil. Stir in couscous. Remove from the heat; cover and let stand until water is absorbed, 5-8 minutes. Fluff with a fork.
2. In a large bowl, combine beans, tomato and cucumber. In a small bowl, whisk lemon juice, lemon zest, oil and seasonings. Drizzle over bean mixture. Add couscous; toss to combine. Serve immediately or refrigerate until chilled. Sprinkle with cheese. If desired, serve with lemon wedges.
1⅔ cups: 362 cal., 11g fat (3g sat. fat), 15mg chol., 657mg sod., 52g carb. (7g sugars, 9g fiber), 15g pro.

TIMESAVING TIP

Make this refreshing main dish salad gluten-free by replacing the couscous with 1½ cups cooked quinoa.

Roasted Cauliflower

Roasting is a simple way to prepare cauliflower. Seasoned with a blend of herbs, this side dish is easy enough for weeknight dinners.
—Leslie Palmer, Swampscott, MA

- -

Takes: 30 min. • **Makes:** 4 servings

- 3 cups fresh cauliflowerets
- 2 Tbsp. lemon juice
- 4½ tsp. olive oil
- 1 garlic clove, minced
- 1 tsp. dried parsley flakes
- ½ tsp. dried thyme
- ½ tsp. dried tarragon
- ¼ tsp. pepper
- ¼ cup grated Parmesan cheese

In a large bowl, combine the first 8 ingredients; toss to coat. Transfer to an ungreased 15x10x1-in. baking pan. Bake at 425° until tender, 15-20 minutes, stirring occasionally. Sprinkle with cheese.

¾ cup: 107 cal., 7g fat (2g sat. fat), 4mg chol., 120mg sod., 9g carb. (4g sugars, 4g fiber), 5g pro. **Diabetic exchanges:** 2 vegetable, 1 fat.

Air-Fryer Sweet Potato Fries

I can never get enough of these sweet potato fries. Even though my grocery store sells them in the frozen foods section, I still prefer to pull sweet potatoes out of my garden and chop them up fresh.
—Amber Massey, Argyle, TX

- -

Takes: 20 min. • **Makes:** 4 servings

- 2 large sweet potatoes, cut into thin strips
- 2 Tbsp. canola oil
- 1 tsp. garlic powder
- 1 tsp. paprika
- 1 tsp. kosher salt
- ¼ tsp. cayenne pepper

Preheat air fryer to 400°. Combine all ingredients; toss to coat. Place on greased tray in air-fryer basket. Cook until lightly browned, 10-12 minutes, stirring once. Serve immediately.

1 serving: 243 cal., 7g fat (1g sat. fat), 0 chol., 498mg sod., 43g carb. (17g sugars, 5g fiber), 3g pro.

Balsamic Brussels Sprouts

These balsamic Brussels sprouts couldn't be easier to make—and you need only a few ingredients!
—Kallee Krong-Mccreery, Escondido, CA

- -

Takes: 15 min. • **Makes:** 4 servings

3	to 4 Tbsp. extra virgin olive oil
1	pkg. (16 oz.) frozen Brussels sprouts, thawed
2	Tbsp. balsamic vinegar
2	Tbsp. torn fresh basil leaves
½	to 1 tsp. flaky sea salt
½	tsp. coarsely ground pepper

In a large skillet, heat oil over medium-high heat. Add Brussels sprouts to skillet and cook until heated through, 5-7 minutes. Transfer to a serving bowl. Drizzle with vinegar; sprinkle with basil, salt and pepper.

⅔ cup: 145 cal., 11g fat (2g sat. fat), 0 chol., 252mg sod., 11g carb. (2g sugars, 4g fiber), 4g pro.
Diabetic exchanges: 2 fat, 1 vegetable.

Summer Orzo

I'm always looking for fun ways to use the fresh veggies that come in my Community Supported Agriculture box, and this tasty salad is one of my favorite creations. I like to improvise with whatever I have on hand, so feel free to do the same here!
—Shayna Marmar, Philadelphia, PA

- -

Prep: 30 min. + chilling
Makes: 16 servings

1	pkg. (16 oz.) orzo pasta
¼	cup water
1½	cups fresh or frozen corn
24	cherry tomatoes, halved
2	cups crumbled feta cheese
1	medium cucumber, seeded and chopped
1	small red onion, finely chopped
¼	cup minced fresh mint
2	Tbsp. capers, drained and chopped, optional
½	cup olive oil
¼	cup lemon juice
1	Tbsp. grated lemon zest
1½	tsp. salt
1	tsp. pepper
1	cup sliced almonds, toasted

1. Cook orzo according to package directions for al dente. Drain orzo; rinse with cold water and drain well. Transfer to a large bowl.
2. In a large nonstick skillet, heat water over medium heat. Add fresh corn; cook and stir until crisp-tender, 3-4 minutes. Add to orzo; stir in the tomatoes, feta cheese, cucumber, onion, mint and, if desired, capers. In a small bowl, whisk oil, lemon juice, lemon zest, salt and pepper until blended. Pour over orzo mixture; toss to coat. Refrigerate 30 minutes.
3. Just before serving, stir in the almonds.

¾ cup: 291 cal., 15g fat (4g sat. fat), 15mg chol., 501mg sod., 28g carb. (3g sugars, 3g fiber), 11g pro.

Sour Cream-Leek Biscuits

Try these savory biscuits with your favorite soup, stew or chili. I've made them with all-purpose white flour as well as whole wheat, and both yield delicious results.
—Bonnie Appleton, Canterbury, CT

- -

Takes: 30 min.
Makes: about 1 dozen

- ⅓ cup cold unsalted butter, divided
- 1½ cups finely chopped leeks (white portion only)
- 2 cups white whole wheat flour
- 2½ tsp. baking powder
- ½ tsp. salt
- ¼ tsp. baking soda
- ¾ cup reduced-fat sour cream
- ¼ cup water

1. Preheat the oven to 400°. In a small skillet over medium heat, melt 1 Tbsp. butter. Add leeks; cook until tender, 6-7 minutes. Cool.

2. Whisk together the flour, baking powder, salt and baking soda. Cut in the remaining butter until mixture resembles coarse crumbs. Stir in the leeks, sour cream and water just until moistened. Turn onto a lightly floured surface; knead 8-10 times.

3. Pat or roll out to ½-in. thickness; cut with a floured 2½-in. biscuit cutter. Place in a cast-iron or other ovenproof skillet. Bake until golden brown, 12-16 minutes. Serve warm.

1 biscuit: 166 cal., 7g fat (4g sat. fat), 20mg chol., 241mg sod., 20g carb. (2g sugars, 3g fiber), 4g pro.
Diabetic exchanges: 1½ fat, 1 starch.

Blackberry Balsamic Spinach Salad

This lightly dressed salad is packed with superfoods. When I have time, I make my vinaigrette from scratch.
—Mary Lou Timpson, Colorado City, AZ

- -

Takes: 15 min. • **Makes:** 6 servings

- 3 cups fresh baby spinach
- 2 cups fresh blackberries, halved
- 1½ cups cherry tomatoes, halved
- ⅓ cup crumbled feta cheese
- 2 green onions, thinly sliced
- ¼ cup chopped walnuts, toasted
- ⅓ cup balsamic vinaigrette

In a large bowl, combine the first 6 ingredients. Divide salad among 6 plates; drizzle with dressing.
1 cup: 106 cal., 7g fat (1g sat. fat), 3mg chol., 230mg sod., 9g carb. (4g sugars, 4g fiber), 3g pro.

> **TIMESAVING TIP**
>
> Not only are blackberries high in vitamin C, they are also rich in anthocyanins, which give them their dark purple-black color. This phytonutrient may help protect the brain from oxidative stress, dementia and Alzheimer's disease.

Pomegranate Splash Salad

The sparkling pomegranate gems make this salad irresistibly beautiful. My family loves it at holiday gatherings when pomegranates are in season. Even the children can't get enough of this antioxidant-rich delight.

—Emily Jamison, Champaign, IL

- -

Takes: 15 min. • **Makes:** 8 servings

- 4 cups fresh baby spinach
- 4 cups spring mix salad greens
- ¾ cup crumbled feta cheese
- ¾ cup pomegranate seeds
- ¾ cup fresh or frozen raspberries
- ⅓ cup pine nuts, toasted

CRANBERRY VINAIGRETTE

- ½ cup thawed cranberry juice concentrate
- 3 Tbsp. olive oil
- 2 Tbsp. rice vinegar
  Dash salt

In a large bowl, combine the first 6 ingredients. In a small bowl, whisk the vinaigrette ingredients. Serve with salad.

1 cup with about 4½ tsp. vinaigrette: 164 cal., 10g fat (2g sat. fat), 6mg chol., 140mg sod., 16g carb. (11g sugars, 2g fiber), 4g pro.
Diabetic exchanges: 2 fat, 1 starch.

Makeover Cheddar Biscuits

These biscuits have a cheesy richness that everyone will love. I like to serve them with steaming bowls of chili or a hearty beef soup.

—Alicia Rooker, Milwaukee, WI

- -

Takes: 30 min. • **Makes:** 15 biscuits

- 1 cup all-purpose flour
- 1 cup cake flour
- 1½ tsp. baking powder
- ¾ tsp. salt
- ½ tsp. garlic powder, divided
- ¼ tsp. baking soda
- 4 Tbsp. cold butter, divided
- ⅓ cup finely shredded cheddar cheese
- 1 cup buttermilk
- ½ tsp. dried parsley flakes

1. In a large bowl, combine flours, baking powder, salt, ¼ tsp. garlic powder and baking soda. Cut in 3 Tbsp. butter until mixture resembles coarse crumbs; add cheese. Stir in buttermilk just until moistened.
2. Drop by 2 tablespoonfuls 2 in. apart onto baking sheets coated with cooking spray. Bake at 425° until golden brown, 10-12 minutes. Melt remaining butter; stir in parsley and remaining garlic powder. Brush over biscuits. Serve warm.

1 biscuit: 106 cal., 4g fat (3g sat. fat), 11mg chol., 233mg sod., 14g carb. (1g sugars, 0 fiber), 3g pro.

READER REVIEW
"These biscuits are easy and delicious. I added Old Bay seasoning to my butter mixture as well as in the biscuit batter."

—LDBRELAND, TASTEOFHOME.COM

Socca

Socca is a traditional flatbread from Nice, France. A popular grilled street food, it's often chopped into pieces, sprinkled with salt, pepper and other toppings, and then scooped into a paper cone. This broiled version is easy to make at home. And because it's made with chickpea flour, it's naturally gluten-free.
—*Taste of Home* Test Kitchen

Prep: 5 min. + standing
Cook: 5 minutes • **Makes:** 6 servings

- 1 cup chickpea flour
- 1 cup water
- 2 Tbsp. extra virgin olive oil, divided
- ¾ tsp. salt
  Optional toppings: Za'atar seasoning, sea salt flakes, coarsely ground pepper and additional extra virgin olive oil

1. In a small bowl, whisk chickpea flour, water, 1 Tbsp. oil and salt until smooth. Let stand 30 minutes.
2. Meanwhile, preheat broiler. Place a 10-in. cast-iron skillet in oven until hot, about 5 minutes. Add remaining 1 Tbsp. oil to the pan; swirl to coat. Pour batter into the hot pan and tilt to coat evenly.
3. Broil 6 in. from heat until edges are crisp and browned and center just begins to brown, 5-7 minutes. Cut into wedges. If desired, top with optional ingredients.
1 wedge: 113 cal., 6g fat (1g sat. fat), 0 chol., 298mg sod., 12g carb. (2g sugars, 3g fiber), 4g pro.
Diabetic exchanges: 1 fat, ½ starch.
To make chickpea flour: Add dried chickpeas to a food processor. Cover and process until the chickpeas are powdery, 2-3 minutes. Sift through a fine sieve into a bowl. Add any larger pieces left in the sieve to a coffee or spice grinder; process until powdery.

TIMESAVING TIP

Socca is not only gluten-free, but also egg-free and dairy-free. Serve it as a side, snack or brunch offering, or add your favorite toppings.

Roasted Green Beans with Lemon & Walnuts

I first tasted roasted green beans at a restaurant and fell in love with the texture and flavor. This is my personal take, and it's always a big hit at our family table.
—Lily Julow, Lawrenceville, GA

- -

Takes: 25 min. • **Makes:** 8 servings

2	lbs. fresh green beans, trimmed
2	shallots, thinly sliced
6	garlic cloves, crushed
2	Tbsp. olive oil
¾	tsp. salt
¼	tsp. pepper
2	tsp. grated lemon zest
½	cup chopped walnuts, toasted

1. Preheat oven to 425°. In a large bowl, combine green beans, shallots and garlic; drizzle with oil and sprinkle with salt and pepper. Transfer to two 15x10x1-in. baking pans coated with cooking spray.
2. Roast 15-20 minutes or until tender and lightly browned, stirring occasionally. Remove from oven; stir in 1 tsp. lemon zest. Sprinkle with walnuts and remaining lemon zest.
Note: To toast nuts, bake in a shallow pan in a 350° oven for 5-10 minutes or cook in a skillet over low heat until lightly browned, stirring occasionally.
1 serving: 119 cal., 8g fat (1g sat. fat), 0 chol., 229mg sod., 11g carb. (3g sugars, 4g fiber), 3g pro.
Diabetic exchanges: 2 vegetable, 1½ fat.

Farmhouse Apple Coleslaw

A friend from church gave me this coleslaw recipe that her grandmother handed down to her. The flavors complement each other well, while the apple and raisins add a refreshing change of pace from typical coleslaw.
—Jan Myers, Atlantic, IA

- -

Prep: 20 min. + chilling
Makes: 12 servings

4	cups shredded cabbage
1	large apple, chopped
¾	cup raisins
½	cup chopped celery
¼	cup chopped onion
¼	cup mayonnaise
2	Tbsp. lemon juice
1	Tbsp. sugar
1	Tbsp. olive oil
½	tsp. salt
⅛	tsp. pepper

In a serving bowl, combine the cabbage, apple, raisins, celery and onion. In a small bowl, combine the remaining ingredients. Pour over cabbage mixture and toss to coat. Cover and refrigerate for at least 30 minutes.
⅔ cup: 87 cal., 5g fat (1g sat. fat), 0 chol., 131mg sod., 12g carb. (8g sugars, 1g fiber), 1g pro.
Diabetic exchanges: 1 vegetable, 1 fat, ½ starch.

Seasoned Oven Fries

Try these potato wedges for a speedy side dish or snack. They're just as tasty as the deep-fried version, but with less fat and less mess.
—Pat Fredericks, Oak Creek, WI

- -

Takes: 25 min. • **Makes:** 2 servings

2   medium baking potatoes
2   tsp. butter, melted
2   tsp. canola oil
¼   tsp. seasoned salt
    Minced fresh parsley, optional

1. Cut each potato lengthwise in half; cut each piece into 4 wedges. In a large shallow dish, combine butter, oil and seasoned salt. Add potatoes; turn to coat.
2. Place potatoes in a single layer on a baking sheet coated with cooking spray. Bake at 450° until tender, turning once, 20-25 minutes. If desired, sprinkle with parsley.
8 wedges: 263 cal., 9g fat (3g sat. fat), 10mg chol., 242mg sod., 44g carb. (3g sugars, 4g fiber), 4g pro.

Radish Asparagus Salad

Lemon zest and mustard in the homemade dressing add the perfect punch to crisp asparagus and spicy radishes in this fun spring salad. My family loves it!
—Nancy Latulippe, Simcoe, ON

- -

Takes: 25 min. • **Makes:** 6 servings

1   lb. fresh asparagus, trimmed and cut into 2-in. pieces
7   radishes, thinly sliced
2   Tbsp. sesame seeds
DRESSING
2   Tbsp. olive oil
2   Tbsp. thinly sliced green onion
1   Tbsp. white wine vinegar
1   Tbsp. lemon juice
2   tsp. honey
1   tsp. Dijon mustard
¼   tsp. garlic powder
¼   tsp. grated lemon zest
¼   tsp. pepper

1. In a large saucepan, bring 6 cups water to a boil. Add asparagus; cover and boil for 3 minutes. Drain and immediately place asparagus in ice water. Drain and pat dry.
2. Transfer to a large bowl; add radishes and sesame seeds. Place dressing ingredients in a jar with a tight-fitting lid; shake well. Pour over salad; toss to coat.
⅔ cup: 73 cal., 6g fat (1g sat. fat), 0 chol., 28mg sod., 5g carb. (3g sugars, 1g fiber), 2g pro.
Diabetic exchanges: 1 vegetable, 1 fat.

Whole Wheat Refrigerator Rolls

Here's an easy and versatile recipe for homemade rolls. I prepare the dough in advance and let it rise in the fridge. Everyone loves the aroma as it bakes.
—Sharon Mensing, Greenfield, IA

- -

Prep: 20 min. + rising • **Bake:** 10 min.
Makes: 2 dozen

2 pkg. (¼ oz. each) active dry yeast
2 cups warm water (110° to 115°)
½ cup sugar
1 large egg, room temperature
¼ cup canola oil
2 tsp. salt
4½ to 5 cups all-purpose flour
2 cups whole wheat flour

1. In a large bowl, dissolve yeast in warm water. Add the sugar, egg, oil, salt and 3 cups all-purpose flour. Beat on medium speed for 3 minutes. Stir in the whole wheat flour and enough remaining all-purpose flour to make a soft dough.

2. Turn out onto a lightly floured surface. Knead until smooth and elastic, 6 to 8 minutes. Place in a greased bowl, turning once to grease top. Cover and let rise until doubled or cover and refrigerate overnight.

3. Punch down dough; divide into 24 portions. Divide and shape each portion into 3 balls. Place 3 balls in each greased muffin cup. Cover and let rise until doubled, about 1 hour for roll dough prepared the same day or 1-2 hours for refrigerated dough.

4. Bake at 375° until light golden brown, 10-12 minutes. Serve warm. If desired, dough may be kept up to 4 days in the refrigerator. Punch down daily.

1 roll: 159 cal., 3g fat (0 sat. fat), 9mg chol., 200mg sod., 29g carb. (5g sugars, 2g fiber), 4g pro.

Sesame-Ginger Cucumber Salad

I love the marinated sides and salads that come with meals at Japanese restaurants and wanted to try them at home. After some research, I came up with this cool, crisp salad.
—Kimberly Ludvick, Newburgh, NY

- -

Takes: 15 min. • **Makes:** 6 servings

2 Tbsp. rice vinegar
4 tsp. soy sauce
1 Tbsp. olive oil
2 tsp. minced fresh gingerroot
2 tsp. sesame oil
1 tsp. honey
¼ tsp. Sriracha chili sauce
2 English cucumbers
1 tsp. sesame seeds, toasted
   Thinly sliced green onions

1. For dressing, mix the first 7 ingredients. Trim ends and cut cucumbers crosswise into 3-in. sections. Cut sections into julienne strips.

2. To serve, toss cucumbers with sesame seeds and dressing. Sprinkle with green onions.

¾ cup: 64 cal., 4g fat (1g sat. fat), 0 chol., 293mg sod., 7g carb. (4g sugars, 1g fiber), 1g pro.
Diabetic exchanges: 1 vegetable, 1 fat.

Broccoli Cauliflower Combo

Shallots, basil and broth rev up the taste of this nutritious vegetable medley. The bright color and fresh flavors will dress up your plate!
—Clara Coulson Minney, Washington Court House, OH

Takes: 25 min. • **Makes:** 6 servings

- 4   cups fresh broccoli florets
- 2   cups fresh cauliflowerets
- 3   shallots, chopped
- ½   cup reduced-sodium chicken broth or vegetable broth
- 1   tsp. dried basil
- ½   tsp. seasoned salt
- ⅛   tsp. pepper

In a large cast-iron or other heavy skillet, combine all ingredients. Cover and cook over medium heat until the vegetables are crisp-tender, 6-8 minutes, stirring occasionally.
¾ cup: 38 cal., 0 fat (0 sat. fat), 0 chol., 204mg sod., 8g carb. (2g sugars, 2g fiber), 3g pro.
Diabetic exchanges: 2 vegetable.

Black-Eyed Pea Tomato Salad

Spending time in the kitchen with my late aunt was so much fun because she was an amazing cook and teacher. This black-eyed pea salad was one of her specialties. It's easy to make and is a nice alternative to pasta or potato salad. Add cooked cubed chicken breast to make it a meal on its own.
—Patricia Ness, La Mesa, CA

Prep: 20 min. + chilling
Makes: 12 servings

- 4   cans (15½ oz. each) black-eyed peas, rinsed and drained
- 3   large tomatoes, chopped
- 1   large sweet red pepper, chopped
- 1   cup diced red onion
- 4   bacon strips, cooked and crumbled
- 1   jalapeno pepper, seeded and diced
- ½   cup canola oil
- ¼   cup sugar
- ¼   cup rice vinegar
- 2   Tbsp. minced fresh parsley
- 1½ tsp. salt
- ½   tsp. pepper
- ⅛   tsp. garlic powder

1. Combine the first 6 ingredients. In another bowl, whisk together the remaining ingredients. Add to bean mixture; toss to coat. Refrigerate, covered, for at least 6 hours or overnight. Stir just before serving.
Note: Wear disposable gloves when cutting hot peppers; the oils can burn skin. Avoid touching your face.
¾ cup: 242 cal., 11g fat (1g sat. fat), 3mg chol., 602mg sod., 29g carb. (9g sugars, 5g fiber), 9g pro.
Diabetic exchanges: 2 starch, 2 fat.

Yogurt Cornbread

My husband doesn't like traditional Texas cornbread, so I came up with this recipe using yogurt. Now it's the only kind he'll eat.

—Amanda Andrews, Mansfield, TX

Takes: 30 min. • **Makes:** 9 servings

- 1 cup yellow cornmeal
- ¼ cup all-purpose flour
- 2 tsp. baking powder
- ½ tsp. salt
- ¼ tsp. baking soda
- 1 large egg, lightly beaten, room temperature
- 1 cup fat-free plain yogurt
- ½ cup fat-free milk
- ¼ cup canola oil
- 1 Tbsp. honey

Preheat oven to 425°. Combine the first 5 ingredients. In another bowl, combine remaining ingredients. Stir into the dry ingredients just until moistened. Pour into an 8-in. square baking dish coated with cooking spray. Bake until a toothpick comes out clean, 16-20 minutes.

1 piece: 157 cal., 7g fat (1g sat. fat), 24mg chol., 349mg sod., 20g carb. (0 sugars, 1g fiber), 4g pro.
Diabetic exchanges: 1½ starch, 1 fat.

READER REVIEW
"I've been making this recipe for a long time— actually won't make any other. No alterations and it is perfect—moist and the right flavor that lets the cornmeal shine. I think the yogurt—thick Greek with fat—is the trick."

—MNBAKERANDMOM, TASTEOFHOME.COM

Marmalade Candied Carrots

My crisp-tender carrots have a sweet citrusy flavor that's perfect for special occasions. This is my favorite way to enjoy the bright vegetable.
—Heather Clemmons, Supply, NC

- -

Takes: 30 min. • **Makes:** 8 servings

- 2   lbs. fresh baby carrots
- ⅔   cup orange marmalade
- 3   Tbsp. brown sugar
- 2   Tbsp. butter
- ½   cup chopped pecans, toasted
- 1   tsp. rum extract

1. In a large saucepan, place steamer basket over 1 in. water. Place carrots in basket. Bring the water to a boil. Reduce heat to maintain a low boil; steam, covered, 12-15 minutes or until carrots are crisp-tender.
2. Meanwhile, in a small saucepan, combine marmalade, brown sugar and butter; cook and stir over medium heat until mixture is thickened and reduced to about ½ cup. Stir in pecans and extract.
3. Place carrots in a large bowl. Add marmalade mixture and toss gently to coat.
1 serving: 211 cal., 8g fat (2g sat. fat), 8mg chol., 115mg sod., 35g carb. (27g sugars, 4g fiber), 2g pro.

Edamame & Soba Noodle Bowl

Fans of Japanese cuisine will love this full-flavored dish. It includes soba noodles, which are made from buckwheat flour.
—Matthew Hass, Ellison Bay, WI

- -

Takes: 30 min. • **Makes:** 6 servings

- 1   pkg. (12 oz.) uncooked Japanese soba noodles or whole wheat spaghetti
- 2   Tbsp. sesame oil
- 2   cups fresh small broccoli florets
- 1   medium onion, halved and thinly sliced
- 3   cups frozen shelled edamame, thawed
- 2   large carrots, cut into ribbons
- 4   garlic cloves, minced
- 1   cup reduced-fat Asian toasted sesame salad dressing
- ¼   tsp. pepper
  Sesame seeds, toasted, optional

1. In a 6 qt. stockpot, cook noodles according to package directions; drain and return to pan.
2. Meanwhile, in a large skillet, heat oil over medium heat. Add broccoli and onion; cook and stir until crisp-tender, 4-6 minutes. Add edamame and carrots; cook and stir until tender, 6-8 minutes. Add garlic; cook 1 minute longer. Add vegetable mixture, dressing and pepper to noodles; toss to combine. Sprinkle with sesame seeds if desired.
1⅓ cups: 414 cal., 12g fat (1g sat. fat), 0 chol., 867mg sod., 64g carb. (12g sugars, 4g fiber), 18g pro.

Pressure-Cooker BBQ Baked Beans

I was under doctor's orders to reduce my sodium intake, but I just couldn't part with some of my favorite foods. After many experiments I came up with this potluck favorite—it has less sodium per serving than store-bought canned versions and tastes delicious!
—Sherrel Hendrix, Arkadelphia, AR

- -

Prep: 10 min. + soaking
Cook: 35 min. + releasing
Makes: 12 servings

- 1 pkg. (16 oz.) dried great northern beans
- 2 smoked ham hocks (about ½ lb. each)
- 2 cups water
- 1 medium onion, chopped
- 2 tsp. garlic powder, divided
- 2 tsp. onion powder, divided
- 1 cup barbecue sauce
- ¾ cup packed brown sugar
- ½ tsp. ground nutmeg
- ¼ tsp. ground cloves
- 2 tsp. hot pepper sauce, optional

1. Rinse and sort beans. Transfer to a 6-qt. electric pressure cooker. Add ham hocks, water, onion, 1 tsp. garlic powder and 1 tsp. onion powder. Lock lid; close pressure-release valve. Adjust to pressure-cook on high for 30 minutes. Let pressure release naturally for 10 minutes; quick-release any remaining pressure.
2. Remove ham hocks; cool slightly. Cut meat into small cubes, discarding bones; return the meat to pressure cooker. Stir in barbecue sauce, brown sugar, nutmeg, cloves, remaining garlic powder, remaining onion powder and, if desired, pepper sauce. Lock lid; close pressure-release valve. Adjust to pressure-cook on high for 3 minutes. Let the pressure release naturally for 5 minutes; quick-release any remaining pressure.
½ cup: 238 cal., 1g fat (0 sat. fat), 4mg chol., 347mg sod., 48g carb. (22g sugars, 8g fiber), 10g pro.

Cabbage & Rutabaga Slaw

This is a favorite crunchy slaw that's a perfect way to use cool-weather veggies. We love it as a side with any spicy main dish.
—Ann Sheehy, Lawrence, MA

- -

Prep: 10 min. + chilling
Makes: 4 servings

- 2 cups diced peeled rutabaga
- 2 cups finely chopped cabbage
- ½ cup finely chopped red onion
- ¼ cup minced fresh Italian parsley
- ½ cup reduced-fat apple cider vinaigrette

In a large bowl, toss together all ingredients. Refrigerate, covered, to allow flavors to blend, about 3 hours.
1 cup: 126 cal., 6g fat (1g sat. fat), 0 chol., 144mg sod., 19g carb. (11g sugars, 3g fiber), 2g pro.
Diabetic exchanges: 1 vegetable, 1 fat, ½ starch.

Miso-Buttered Succotash

The miso paste used in this simple recipe gives depth and a hint of sweetness to canned or fresh vegetables. To brighten the flavor profile even more, add a splash of your favorite white wine.
—William Milton III, Clemson, SC

- -

Takes: 20 min. • **Makes:** 6 servings

- 2 tsp. canola oil
- 1 small red onion, chopped
- 2 cans (15¼ oz. each) whole kernel corn, drained
- 1½ cups frozen shelled edamame, thawed
- ½ medium sweet red pepper, chopped (about ½ cup)
- 2 Tbsp. unsalted butter, softened
- 1 tsp. white miso paste
- 3 green onions, thinly sliced
    Coarsely ground pepper

1. In a large skillet, heat the oil over medium-high heat. Add red onion; cook and stir until crisp-tender, about 2-3 minutes. Add corn, edamame and red pepper. Cook until vegetables reach desired tenderness, about 4-6 minutes longer.

2. In a small bowl, mix butter and miso paste until combined; stir into pan until melted. Sprinkle with green onions and pepper before serving.

¾ cup: 193 cal., 9g fat (3g sat. fat), 10mg chol., 464mg sod., 20g carb. (11g sugars, 6g fiber), 8g pro.

READER REVIEW
"This vegetable dish is delicious and appealing to the eye with the mix of colors. It's a keeper, folks!"
—ANNRMS, TASTEOFHOME.COM

Best Ever Breadsticks

Present these long breadsticks in a tall clear glass alongside an Italian favorite like lasagna or spaghetti. They're an attractive and edible addition to the table setting!
—Carol Wolfer, Lebanon, OR

- -

Prep: 20 min. + rising
Bake: 10 min. + cooling
Makes: 2 dozen

- 3 to 3¼ cups all-purpose flour
- 1 pkg. (¼ oz.) quick-rise yeast
- 1 Tbsp. sugar
- 1 tsp. salt
- ¾ cup 2% milk
- ¼ cup plus 1 Tbsp. water, divided
- 1 Tbsp. butter
- 1 large egg white
    Coarse salt

1. Combine 1½ cups flour, yeast, sugar and salt. In a small saucepan, heat milk, ¼ cup water and butter to 120°-130°. Add to dry ingredients; beat on medium speed just until moistened. Stir in enough remaining flour to form a stiff dough.

2. Turn dough onto a lightly floured surface; knead until smooth and elastic, 6-8 minutes. Place dough in a greased bowl, turning once to grease the top. Cover and let rise in a warm place until doubled, 30 minutes.

3. Punch down dough. Pinch off golf ball-sized pieces. On a lightly floured surface, shape each piece into a 6-in. rope. Place on greased baking sheets 1 in. apart. Cover and let rise for 15 minutes.

4. Preheat oven to 400°. Beat egg white and remaining water; brush over breadsticks. Sprinkle with coarse salt. Bake until golden, about 10 minutes. Remove from pans to wire racks to cool.

1 breadstick: 69 cal., 1g fat (0 sat. fat), 2mg chol., 108mg sod., 13g carb. (1g sugars, 1g fiber), 2g pro.
Diabetic exchanges: 1 starch.

Air-Fryer Bacon Crescent Rolls

The aroma from these rolls will draw folks to the table. With only three ingredients, this recipe is incredibly simple to prepare. Using precooked bacon makes it even easier.
—Jane Nearing, Indianapolis, IN

- -

Prep: 10 min. • **Cook:** 10 min./batch
Makes: 8 servings

- 1 tube (8 oz.) refrigerated crescent rolls
- 6 bacon strips, cooked and crumbled
- 1 tsp. onion powder

1. Preheat air fryer to 300°. Unroll crescent dough and separate into 8 triangles. Set aside 1 Tbsp. of bacon. Sprinkle onion powder and remaining bacon over triangles. Roll up and sprinkle with remaining bacon, pressing lightly to adhere.
2. In batches, arrange rolls, point side down, in a single layer on an ungreased tray in air-fryer basket. Cook until rolls are golden brown, 8-10 minutes. Serve warm.
1 roll: 133 cal., 7g fat (1g sat. fat), 6mg chol., 322mg sod., 12g carb. (3g sugars, 0 fiber), 4g pro.

Creamed Garden Potatoes & Peas

New potatoes and tender peas are paired with a creamy sauce in this special side.
—Jane Uphoff, Cunningham, KS

- -

Takes: 25 min. • **Makes:** 12 servings

- 2 lbs. small red potatoes, quartered
- 3 cups fresh or frozen peas
- 2 Tbsp. chopped onion
- 2 Tbsp. butter
- 3 Tbsp. plus 1 tsp. all-purpose flour
- 1½ tsp. salt
- ¼ tsp. pepper
- 2 cups 2% milk
- 1 cup half-and-half cream

1. Place potatoes in a large saucepan and cover with water. Bring to a boil. Reduce heat; cover and simmer until tender, 8-12 minutes. Drain.
2. Meanwhile, place peas and 1 cup water in a small saucepan. Bring to a boil. Reduce heat; cover and simmer until tender, 3-5 minutes. Drain.
3. In a large saucepan, saute onion in butter until tender. Stir in flour, salt and pepper until blended; gradually add milk and cream. Bring to a boil; cook and stir until thickened, about 2 minutes. Stir in potatoes and peas; heat through.
⅔ cup: 156 cal., 5g fat (3g sat. fat), 18mg chol., 345mg sod., 22g carb. (6g sugars, 3g fiber), 6g pro.
Diabetic exchanges: 1½ starch, 1 fat.

Cool Beans Salad

This protein-filled dish could be served as a side dish or a meatless main entree. When you make it, double the recipe, because it will be gone in a flash! The basmati rice adds a unique flavor and the dressing gives it a bit of a tang.
—Janelle Lee, Appleton, WI

Takes: 20 min. • **Makes:** 6 servings

½ cup olive oil
¼ cup red wine vinegar
1 Tbsp. sugar
1 garlic clove, minced
1 tsp. salt
1 tsp. ground cumin
1 tsp. chili powder
¼ tsp. pepper
3 cups cooked basmati rice
1 can (16 oz.) kidney beans, rinsed and drained
1 can (15 oz.) black beans, rinsed and drained
1½ cups frozen corn, thawed
4 green onions, sliced
1 small sweet red pepper, chopped
¼ cup minced fresh cilantro

In a large bowl, whisk the first 8 ingredients. Add remaining ingredients; toss to coat. Chill until serving.

1⅓ cups: 440 cal., 19g fat (3g sat. fat), 0 chol., 659mg sod., 58g carb. (5g sugars, 8g fiber), 12g pro.

Soups & SANDWICHES

These perfect pairings are a breeze to put together, and they also offer lighter alternatives to their traditional counterparts.

Cranberry Turkey Wraps

Fruity and flavorful, these grab-and-go wraps are quick to assemble, easy to handle and low in calories.
—Bobbie Keefer, Byers, CO

- -

Takes: 15 min. • **Makes:** 8 servings

- 1 can (11 oz.) mandarin oranges, drained
- 1 medium tart apple, peeled and diced
- 3 Tbsp. dried cranberries
- ¾ cup fat-free plain yogurt
- 2 Tbsp. fat-free mayonnaise
- 8 flour tortillas (8 in.)
- 8 lettuce leaves
- 1½ lbs. thinly sliced deli turkey
- 8 slices (1 oz. each) part-skim mozzarella cheese
- 2 Tbsp. chopped pecans, toasted

In a small bowl, combine oranges, apple and cranberries. In another bowl, combine the yogurt and mayonnaise; spread over tortillas. Layer each tortilla with lettuce, turkey, cheese, fruit mixture and pecans. Roll up tightly.

1 wrap: 374 cal., 12g fat (4g sat. fat), 54mg chol., 1477mg sod., 40g carb. (9g sugars, 1g fiber), 27g pro.

Juicy Turkey Burgers

I'm always looking for heart-healthy, low-fat recipes. My husband enjoys these grilled turkey burgers with their herb flavor and garden-fresh garnish. They make an ideal summer sandwich or quick in-hand meal for when we're on the run.
—Trina Hopsecger, Elkhart, IN

- -

Takes: 25 min. • **Makes:** 6 servings

- 1 medium apple, peeled and finely shredded
- ½ cup cooked brown rice
- 2 Tbsp. grated onion
- 2 garlic cloves, minced
- 1½ tsp. rubbed sage
- 1 tsp. salt
- ½ tsp. pepper
- ½ tsp. dried thyme
- ¼ tsp. ground allspice
- ¼ tsp. cayenne pepper
- 1 lb. lean ground turkey
- 2 Tbsp. minced fresh parsley
- 6 whole wheat hamburger buns, split
- 6 lettuce leaves
- 6 tomato slices

1. In a large bowl, combine the first 10 ingredients. Crumble turkey over mixture and mix lightly but thoroughly. Shape into six ½-in.-thick patties.

2. Lightly grease grill rack. Prepare grill for indirect heat.

3. Grill burgers, covered, over indirect medium heat or broil 4 in. from the heat for 6-7 minutes on each side or until a thermometer reads 165° and juices run clear. Sprinkle with parsley. Serve on buns with lettuce and tomato.

1 serving: 265 cal., 9g fat (2g sat. fat), 60mg chol., 663mg sod., 28g carb. (0 sugars, 3g fiber), 18g pro.
Diabetic exchanges: 2 starch, 2 lean meat.

Lemony Mushroom-Orzo Soup for Two

Here's a versatile soup that works as a first course, appetizer or side for lunch. It's loaded with mushrooms and orzo pasta—and lemon livens up its mild flavor.
—Edrie O'Brien, Denver, CO

Takes: 30 min. • **Makes:** 2 servings

2½	cups sliced fresh mushrooms
2	green onions, chopped
1	Tbsp. olive oil
1	garlic clove, minced
1½	cups reduced-sodium chicken broth
1½	tsp. minced fresh parsley
¼	tsp. dried thyme
⅛	tsp. pepper
¼	cup uncooked orzo pasta
1½	tsp. lemon juice
⅛	tsp. grated lemon zest

1. In a small saucepan, saute the mushrooms and onions in oil until tender. Add garlic; cook 1 minute longer. Stir in the broth, parsley, thyme and pepper.

2. Bring to a boil. Stir in the orzo, lemon juice and zest. Cook until pasta is tender, 5-6 minutes.

1 cup: 191 cal., 8g fat (1g sat. fat), 0 chol., 437mg sod., 24g carb. (4g sugars, 2g fiber), 9g pro.
Diabetic exchanges: 1½ fat, 1 starch, 1 vegetable.

READER REVIEW
"We love orzo pasta and mushrooms, so how could we not enjoy this soup? The lemon zest and fresh lemon juice add a more delicate flavor. We will definitely make it again."
—RIVKAHFELDMAN, TASTEOFHOME.COM

Vegan Cream of Broccoli Soup

Pureed potatoes help give this vegan cream of broccoli soup a silky texture without the calorie-laden cream. This is a fantastic trick to make dairy-free soups super creamy.
—*Taste of Home* Test Kitchen

- -

Prep: 20 min. • **Cook:** 25 min.
Makes: 8 servings (2 qt.)

- 3 medium onions, chopped
- 2 celery ribs, chopped
- 2 Tbsp. canola oil
- 4 cups plus ½ cup vegetable broth
- 4 medium russet potatoes, peeled and cubed (about 4 cups)
- 6 cups chopped fresh broccoli (about 3 small heads)
- 1 tsp. salt
- ¼ tsp. pepper

1. In a large saucepan, saute onions and celery in oil until tender. Add 4 cups broth and potatoes; bring to a boil. Reduce heat; cover and simmer for 15-20 minutes or until potatoes are tender.
2. Cool slightly. In a blender, process soup in batches until smooth. Return to pan; add remaining broth and bring to a boil. Add broccoli, salt and pepper. Reduce heat; simmer, uncovered, 8-10 minutes or until broccoli is tender.

1 cup: 142 cal., 4g fat (0 sat. fat), 0 chol., 409mg sod., 24g carb. (5g sugars, 4g fiber), 4g pro.
Diabetic exchanges: 1½ starch, 1 vegetable, ½ fat.

Oven-Fried Green Tomato BLT

I have been broiling breaded eggplant slices in the oven for years. I recently tried the same method for green tomatoes. It worked! We now enjoy them in BLTs.
—Jolene Martinelli, Fremont, NH

- -

Takes: 25 min. • **Makes:** 4 servings

- 1 large green tomato (about 8 oz.)
- 1 large egg, beaten
- 1 cup panko bread crumbs
- ¼ tsp. salt
- ¼ cup reduced-fat mayonnaise
- 2 green onions, thinly sliced
- 1 tsp. snipped fresh dill or ¼ tsp. dill weed
- 8 slices whole wheat bread, toasted
- 8 cooked center-cut bacon strips
- 4 Bibb or Boston lettuce leaves

1. Preheat broiler. Cut tomato into 8 slices, each about ¼ in. thick. Place egg and bread crumbs in separate shallow bowls; mix salt into bread crumbs. Dip tomato slices in egg, then in bread crumb mixture, patting to help adhere.
2. Place tomato slices on a wire rack set in a 15x10x1-in. baking pan; broil 4-5 in. from heat until golden brown, about 30-45 seconds per side.
3. Mix mayonnaise, green onions and dill. Layer each of 4 slices of bread with 2 bacon strips, 1 lettuce leaf and 2 tomato slices. Spread mayonnaise mixture over the remaining slices of bread; place over top layer.

1 sandwich: 313 cal., 12g fat (2g sat. fat), 55mg chol., 744mg sod., 36g carb. (5g sugars, 4g fiber), 16g pro.
Diabetic exchanges: 2 starch, 2 high-fat meat, 1 fat.

TIMESAVING TIP

Bacon can be included in a healthy diet; just reach for the center-cut variety. It has much less fat and more lean meat.

Chicken Chili with Black Beans

Because this dish looks different than traditional chili, my family was a little hesitant to try it at first. Thanks to the full, hearty flavor, it's become one of our favorites.

—Jeanette Urbom, Louisburg, KS

- -

Prep: 10 min. • **Cook:** 25 min.
Makes: 10 servings (3 qt.)

- 1¾ lbs. boneless skinless chicken breasts, cubed
- 2 medium sweet red peppers, chopped
- 1 large onion, chopped
- 3 Tbsp. olive oil
- 1 can (4 oz.) chopped green chiles
- 4 garlic cloves, minced
- 2 Tbsp. chili powder
- 2 tsp. ground cumin
- 1 tsp. ground coriander
- 2 cans (15 oz. each) black beans, rinsed and drained
- 1 can (28 oz.) Italian stewed tomatoes, cut up
- 1 cup chicken broth or beer
- ½ to 1 cup water

In a Dutch oven, saute chicken, red peppers and onion in oil until chicken is no longer pink, about 5 minutes. Add green chiles, garlic, chili powder, cumin and coriander; cook 1 minute longer. Stir in the beans, tomatoes, broth and ½ cup water; bring to a boil. Reduce the heat and simmer, uncovered, for 15 minutes, stirring often and adding water as necessary.
1¼ cups: 236 cal., 6g fat (1g sat. fat), 44mg chol., 561mg sod., 21g carb. (5g sugars, 6g fiber), 22g pro.
Diabetic exchanges: 2 lean meat, 1½ starch, 1 fat.

Pear Waldorf Pitas

If you're looking for something new for a shower, luncheon or party, try this delicious twist on Waldorf salad. For an eye-catching presentation, I tuck each pita sandwich into a colorful folded napkin.

—Roxann Parker, Dover, DE

- -

Prep: 20 min. + chilling
Makes: 20 mini pitas halves

- 2 medium ripe pears, diced
- ½ cup thinly sliced celery
- ½ cup halved seedless red grapes
- 2 Tbsp. finely chopped walnuts
- 2 Tbsp. lemon yogurt
- 2 Tbsp. mayonnaise
- ⅛ tsp. poppy seeds
- 20 miniature pita pocket halves
  Lettuce leaves

1. In a large bowl, combine pears, celery, grapes and walnuts. In another bowl, whisk yogurt, mayonnaise and poppy seeds. Add to pear mixture; toss to coat. Refrigerate 1 hour or overnight.
2. Line pita halves with lettuce; fill each with 2 Tbsp. pear mixture.
1 pita half: 67 cal., 2g fat (0 sat. fat), 0 chol., 86mg sod., 12g carb. (3g sugars, 1g fiber), 2g pro.
Diabetic exchanges: 1 starch.

Pasta Fagioli Soup

My husband loves my version of this soup so much he stopped ordering it at restaurants. He'd rather savor it at home. It's so easy to make, yet hearty enough to be a full dinner.
—Brenda Thomas, Springfield, MO

- -

Takes: 30 min. • **Makes:** 5 servings

½ lb. Italian turkey sausage links, casings removed, crumbled
1 small onion, chopped
1½ tsp. canola oil
1 garlic clove, minced
2 cups water
1 can (15½ oz.) great northern beans, rinsed and drained
1 can (14½ oz.) diced tomatoes, undrained
1 can (14½ oz.) reduced-sodium chicken broth
¾ cup uncooked elbow macaroni
¼ tsp. pepper
1 cup fresh spinach leaves, cut as desired
5 tsp. shredded Parmesan cheese

1. In a large saucepan, cook sausage over medium heat until no longer pink; drain, remove from pan and set aside. In the same pan, saute onion in oil until tender. Add the garlic; saute 1 minute longer.
2. Add the water, beans, tomatoes, broth, macaroni and pepper; bring to a boil. Cook, uncovered, until macaroni is tender, 8-10 minutes.
3. Reduce heat to low; stir in sausage and spinach. Cook until spinach is wilted, 2-3 minutes. Garnish with cheese.
1⅓ cups: 228 cal., 7g fat (1g sat. fat), 29mg chol., 841mg sod., 27g carb. (4g sugars, 6g fiber), 16g pro. **Diabetic exchanges:** 1½ starch, 1 lean meat, 1 vegetable, ½ fat.

Sweet & Tangy Pulled Pork

The convenience of my slow cooker makes these sandwiches an ideal option for busy weeknights. The apricot preserves lend a sweet flavor to the pork.
—Megan Klimkewicz, Kaiser, MO

- -

Prep: 15 min. • **Cook:** 8 hours
Makes: 12 servings

- 1 jar (18 oz.) apricot preserves
- 1 large onion, chopped
- 2 Tbsp. reduced-sodium soy sauce
- 2 Tbsp. Dijon mustard
- 1 boneless pork shoulder butt roast (3 to 4 lbs.)
   Hamburger buns, split, optional

1. Mix first 4 ingredients. Place roast in a 4- or 5-qt. slow cooker; top with preserves mixture. Cook, covered, on low until meat is tender, 8-10 hours.
2. Remove pork from slow cooker. Skim fat from cooking juices. Shred pork with 2 forks; return to slow cooker and heat through. If desired, serve on buns.

½ cup pork mixture: 296 cal., 11g fat (4g sat. fat), 67mg chol., 243mg sod., 29g carb. (19g sugars, 0 fiber), 20g pro.

Chicken Corn Soup with Rivels

Traditional chicken soup gets a fun twist from a dumpling-like broth stretcher called rivels. It's light on fat and full of chicken, vegetables and herbs. You won't be able to resist it.
—Elissa Armbruster, Medford, NJ

- -

Takes: 25 min. • **Makes:** 7 servings

- 1 cup chopped carrots
- 1 celery rib, chopped
- 1 medium onion, chopped
- 2 tsp. canola oil
- 2 cans (14½ oz. each) reduced-sodium chicken broth
- 2 cups fresh or frozen corn
- 2 cups cubed cooked chicken breast
- ½ tsp. minced fresh parsley
- ¼ tsp. salt
- ¼ tsp. dried tarragon
- ¼ tsp. pepper
- ¾ cup all-purpose flour
- 1 large egg, beaten

1. In a large saucepan, saute carrots, celery and onion in oil until tender. Add broth, corn, chicken, parsley, salt, tarragon and pepper. Bring to a boil.
2. Meanwhile, for rivels, place the flour in a bowl; mix in egg with a fork just until blended. Drop dough by teaspoonfuls into the boiling soup, stirring constantly. Cook and stir until the rivels are cooked through, 1-2 minutes.

1 cup: 191 cal., 4g fat (1g sat. fat), 57mg chol., 482mg sod., 22g carb. (5g sugars, 2g fiber), 17g pro.
Diabetic exchanges: 1½ starch, 2 lean meat.

Shrimp Gazpacho

Here's a refreshing twist on the classic chilled tomato soup. Ours features shrimp, lime and plenty of avocado.
—*Taste of Home* Test Kitchen

Prep: 15 min. + chilling
Makes: 12 servings (3 qt.)

- 6 cups spicy hot V8 juice
- 2 cups cold water
- ½ cup lime juice
- ½ cup minced fresh cilantro
- ½ tsp. salt
- ¼ to ½ tsp. hot pepper sauce
- 1 lb. peeled and deveined cooked shrimp (31-40 per lb.), tails removed
- 1 medium cucumber, seeded and diced
- 2 medium tomatoes, seeded and chopped
- 2 medium ripe avocados, peeled and chopped

In a large nonreactive bowl, mix first 6 ingredients. Gently stir in remaining ingredients. Refrigerate, covered, 1 hour before serving.

Note: This recipe is best served the same day it's made.

1 cup: 112 cal., 4g fat (1g sat. fat), 57mg chol., 399mg sod., 9g carb. (5g sugars, 3g fiber), 10g pro.

Diabetic exchanges: 1 lean meat, 2 vegetable, 1 fat.

> **TIMESAVING TIP**
>
> Not all soups are served hot. One of the most famous cold soups is gazpacho, a raw, blended vegetable soup popular throughout Spain and Portugal. Common ingredients include tomato, cucumber, bell peppers, garlic, stale bread, olive oil and wine vinegar.

Dilly Chickpea Salad Sandwiches

This chickpea salad is super flavorful and contains less fat and cholesterol than chicken salad. These make delightful picnic sandwiches.
—Deanna Wolfe, Muskegon, MI

Takes: 15 min. • **Makes:** 6 servings

- 1 can (15 oz.) chickpeas or garbanzo beans, rinsed and drained
- ½ cup finely chopped onion
- ½ cup finely chopped celery
- ½ cup reduced-fat mayonnaise or vegan mayonnaise
- 3 Tbsp. honey mustard or Dijon mustard
- 2 Tbsp. snipped fresh dill
- 1 Tbsp. red wine vinegar
- ¼ tsp. salt
- ¼ tsp. paprika
- ¼ tsp. pepper
- 12 slices multigrain bread
  Optional: Romaine leaves, tomato slices, dill pickle slices and sweet red pepper rings

Place chickpeas in a large bowl; mash to desired consistency. Stir in onion, celery, mayonnaise, mustard, dill, vinegar, salt, paprika and pepper. Spread over each of 6 bread slices; layer with toppings of your choice and remaining bread.

1 sandwich: 295 cal., 11g fat (2g sat. fat), 7mg chol., 586mg sod., 41g carb. (9g sugars, 7g fiber), 10g pro.

Beefy Mushroom Soup

Here's a tasty way to use leftover roast or steak and get a delicious meal on the table in about a half hour. The warm, rich taste of this mushroom soup is sure to please.
—Ginger Ellsworth, Caldwell, ID

- -

Takes: 30 min. • **Makes:** 3 cups

- 1 medium onion, chopped
- ½ cup sliced fresh mushrooms
- 2 Tbsp. butter
- 2 Tbsp. all-purpose flour
- 2 cups reduced-sodium beef broth
- ⅔ cup cubed cooked roast beef
- ½ tsp. garlic powder
- ¼ tsp. paprika
- ¼ tsp. pepper
- ⅛ tsp. salt
  Dash hot pepper sauce

Shredded part-skim mozzarella cheese, optional

1. In a large saucepan, saute onion and mushrooms in butter until onion is tender; remove with a slotted spoon and set aside. In a small bowl, whisk flour and broth until smooth; gradually add to the pan. Bring to a boil; cook and stir until thickened, 1-2 minutes.

2. Add the roast beef, garlic powder, paprika, pepper, salt, pepper sauce and onion mixture; cook and stir until heated through. Garnish with cheese if desired.

1 cup: 180 cal., 9g fat (5g sat. fat), 52mg chol., 470mg sod., 9g carb. (3g sugars, 1g fiber), 14g pro.
Diabetic exchanges: 2 lean meat, 2 fat, 1 vegetable.

Tender Turkey Burgers

Juicy, tender patties on whole wheat buns make wholesome, satisfying sandwiches. We especially enjoy grilling them for get-togethers.
—Sherry Hulsman, Louisville, KY

- -

Takes: 30 min. • **Makes:** 6 servings

- ⅔ cup soft whole wheat bread crumbs
- ½ cup finely chopped celery
- ¼ cup finely chopped onion
- 1 large egg, lightly beaten
- 1 Tbsp. minced fresh parsley
- 1 tsp. Worcestershire sauce
- 1 tsp. dried oregano
- ½ tsp. salt
- ¼ tsp. pepper
- 1¼ lbs. lean ground turkey
  Whole wheat hamburger buns, split, optional

1. In a large bowl, combine the first 9 ingredients. Crumble the turkey over mixture and mix lightly but thoroughly. Shape into 6 patties.

2. Pan-fry, grill or broil burgers until a thermometer reads 165° and juices run clear. Serve on buns if desired.

1 burger: 177 cal., 8g fat (2g sat. fat), 96mg chol., 317mg sod., 5g carb. (1g sugars, 1g fiber), 21g pro.
Diabetic exchanges: 3 lean meat, 3 very lean meat, 1 vegetable, ½ starch.

Salsa Black Bean Burgers

Meatless meals are tasty when these hearty bean burgers are on the menu. Guacamole and sour cream make them seem decadent.

—Jill Reichardt, St. Louis, MO

- -

Takes: 20 min. • **Makes:** 4 servings

- 1 can (15 oz.) black beans, rinsed and drained
- ⅔ cup dry bread crumbs
- 1 small tomato, seeded and finely chopped
- 1 jalapeno pepper, seeded and finely chopped
- 1 large egg
- 1 tsp. minced fresh cilantro
- 1 garlic clove, minced
- 1 Tbsp. olive oil
- 4 whole wheat hamburger buns, split
  Optional: Reduced-fat sour cream, guacamole, spicy ranch salad dressing, lettuce, sliced tomato and sliced red onions

1. Place beans in a food processor; cover and process until blended. Transfer to a large bowl. Add the bread crumbs, tomato, jalapeno, egg, cilantro and garlic. Mix until combined. Shape into 4 patties.
2. In a large nonstick skillet, cook patties in oil over medium heat until lightly browned, 4-6 minutes on each side. Serve on buns; add toppings as desired.
Note: Wear disposable gloves when cutting hot peppers; the oils can burn skin. Avoid touching your face.
1 burger: 323 cal., 8g fat (1g sat. fat), 53mg chol., 557mg sod., 51g carb. (6g sugars, 9g fiber), 13g pro.

Dill Chicken Soup

I could eat soup for every meal of the day, all year long. I particularly like dill and spinach—they add a brightness to this light and healthy soup.

—Robin Haas, Hyde Park, MA

- -

Takes: 30 min.
Makes: 6 servings (2 qt.)

- 1 Tbsp. canola oil
- 2 medium carrots, chopped
- 1 small onion, coarsely chopped
- 2 garlic cloves, minced
- ½ cup uncooked whole wheat orzo pasta
- 1½ cups coarsely shredded rotisserie chicken
- 6 cups reduced-sodium chicken broth
- 1½ cups frozen peas (about 6 oz.)
- 8 oz. fresh baby spinach (about 10 cups)
- 2 Tbsp. chopped fresh dill or 1 Tbsp. dill weed
- 2 Tbsp. lemon juice
  Coarsely ground pepper, optional

1. In a 6-qt. stockpot, heat oil over medium heat. Add carrots, onion and garlic; saute until carrots are tender, 4-5 minutes.
2. Stir in orzo, chicken and broth; bring to a boil. Reduce heat; simmer, uncovered, 5 minutes. Stir in peas, spinach and dill; return to a boil. Reduce heat; simmer, uncovered, until orzo is tender, 3-4 minutes. Stir in lemon juice. If desired, top each serving with coarsely ground pepper.
1⅓ cups: 198 cal., 6g fat (1g sat. fat), 31mg chol., 681mg sod., 20g carb. (4g sugars, 5g fiber), 18g pro.
Diabetic exchanges: 2 lean meat, 1 starch, 1 vegetable, ½ fat.

Arborio Rice & White Bean Soup

Soup is the ultimate comfort food. This hearty, satisfying soup with arborio rice is low in fat and comes together in less than 30 minutes.
—Deanna Wolfe, Muskegon, MI

Takes: 30 min. • **Makes:** 4 servings

- 1 Tbsp. olive oil
- 3 garlic cloves, minced
- ¾ cup uncooked arborio rice
- 1 carton (32 oz.) vegetable broth
- ¾ tsp. dried basil
- ½ tsp. dried thyme
- ¼ tsp. dried oregano
- 1 pkg. (16 oz.) frozen broccoli-cauliflower blend
- 1 can (15 oz.) cannellini beans, rinsed and drained
- 2 cups fresh baby spinach
  Lemon wedges, optional

1. In a large saucepan, heat oil over medium heat; saute garlic 1 minute. Add rice; cook and stir 2 minutes. Stir in broth and herbs; bring to a boil. Reduce heat; simmer, covered, until rice is al dente, about 10 minutes.

2. Stir in frozen vegetables and beans; cook, covered, over medium heat until heated through and rice is tender, 8-10 minutes, stirring occasionally. Stir in baby spinach until wilted. If desired, serve with lemon wedges.

1¾ cups: 303 cal., 4g fat (1g sat. fat), 0 chol., 861mg sod., 52g carb. (2g sugars, 6g fiber), 9g pro.

Neutral flavor and tender skin make white beans a versatile addition to any soup or stew. They add almost 4 grams of fiber per serving in this recipe.

Spicy Buffalo Chicken Wraps

These wraps have a real kick, and are one of my husband's favorite meals. They're ready in a flash, are easily doubled and the closest thing to restaurant Buffalo wings I've ever tasted in a sandwich version.
—Jennifer Beck, Meridian, ID

Takes: 25 min. • **Makes:** 2 servings

- ½ **lb. boneless skinless chicken breast, cubed**
- ½ **tsp. canola oil**
- 2 **Tbsp. Louisiana-style hot sauce**
- 1 **cup shredded lettuce**
- 2 **flour tortillas (6 in.), warmed**
- 2 **tsp. reduced-fat ranch salad dressing**
- 2 **Tbsp. crumbled blue cheese**

1. In a large nonstick skillet, cook chicken in oil over medium heat for 6 minutes; drain. Stir in hot sauce. Bring to a boil. Reduce heat; simmer, uncovered, until sauce is thickened and the chicken is no longer pink, 3-5 minutes.

2. Place lettuce on tortillas; drizzle with ranch dressing. Top with chicken mixture and blue cheese; roll up.

1 wrap: 273 cal., 11g fat (3g sat. fat), 70mg chol., 453mg sod., 15g carb. (1g sugars, 1g fiber), 28g pro.
Diabetic exchanges: 3 lean meat, 1½ fat, 1 starch.

Colorful Three-Bean Soup

When I was growing up, my mother prepared many different soups, each seasoned just right. She often made this colorful combination that's full of harvest-fresh goodness. It showcases an appealing assortment of beans, potatoes, carrots and spinach.
—Valerie Lee, Snellville, GA

- -

Prep: 20 min. • **Cook:** 15 min.
Makes: 12 servings (about 3 qt.)

- 1 medium onion, chopped
- 1 Tbsp. canola oil
- 3 small potatoes, peeled and cubed
- 2 medium carrots, sliced
- 3 cans (14½ oz. each) chicken or vegetable broth
- 3 cups water
- 2 Tbsp. dried parsley flakes
- 2 tsp. dried basil
- 1 tsp. dried oregano
- 1 garlic clove, minced
- ½ tsp. pepper
- 1 can (15½ oz.) great northern beans, rinsed and drained
- 1 can (15 oz.) pinto beans, rinsed and drained
- 1 can (15 oz.) garbanzo beans or chickpeas, rinsed and drained
- 3 cups chopped fresh spinach

In a Dutch oven, saute onion in oil. Add the next 9 ingredients. Simmer, uncovered, until the vegetables are tender. Add the beans and spinach; heat through.

1 cup: 158 cal., 2g fat (0 sat. fat), 2mg chol., 604mg sod., 28g carb. (3g sugars, 6g fiber), 7g pro.
Diabetic exchanges: 2 starch, 1½ meat.

Greek Beef Pitas

A local restaurant that's famous for pitas inspired me to make my own Greek-style sandwiches at home. Feel free to add olives if you like.
—Nancy Sousley, Lafayette, IN

- -

Takes: 25 min. • **Makes:** 4 servings

- 1 lb. lean ground beef (90% lean)
- 1 small onion, chopped
- 3 garlic cloves, minced
- 1 tsp. dried oregano
- ¾ tsp. salt, divided
- 1 cup reduced-fat plain Greek yogurt
- 1 medium tomato, chopped
- ½ cup chopped peeled cucumber
- 1 tsp. dill weed
- 4 whole pita breads, warmed
   Optional: Additional chopped tomatoes and cucumber

1. In a large skillet, cook beef, onion and garlic over medium heat until beef is no longer pink and vegetables are tender, 8-10 minutes; crumble beef; drain. Stir in dried oregano and ½ tsp. salt.
2. In a small bowl, mix Greek yogurt, tomato, cucumber, dill and remaining ¼ tsp. salt. Spoon ¾ cup beef mixture over each pita bread; top with 3 Tbsp. yogurt sauce. If desired, top with additional tomatoes and cucumbers. Serve with remaining yogurt sauce.
1 serving: 407 cal., 11g fat (4g sat. fat), 74mg chol., 851mg sod., 40g carb. (5g sugars, 2g fiber), 34g pro.

Golden Beet & Peach Soup with Tarragon

One summer we had a bumper crop of peaches from our two trees, so I had fun experimenting with different recipes. After seeing a beet soup recipe in a cookbook, I changed it a bit to include our homegrown golden beets and sweet peaches.
—Sue Gronholz, Beaver Dam, WI

- -

Prep: 20 min.
Bake: 40 min. + chilling
Makes: 6 servings

- 2 **lbs. fresh golden beets, peeled and cut into 1-in. cubes**
- 1 **Tbsp. olive oil**
- 2 **cups white grape-peach juice**
- 2 **Tbsp. cider vinegar**
- ¼ **cup plain Greek yogurt**
- ¼ **tsp. finely chopped fresh tarragon**
- 2 **medium fresh peaches, peeled and diced**
  Fresh tarragon sprigs

1. Preheat oven to 400°. Place beets in a 15x10x1-in. baking pan. Drizzle with oil; toss to coat. Roast until tender, 40-45 minutes. Cool slightly.
2. Transfer beets to a blender or food processor. Add the juice and vinegar; process until smooth. Refrigerate at least 1 hour. In a small bowl, combine Greek yogurt and chopped fresh tarragon; refrigerate.
3. To serve, divide beet mixture among individual bowls; place a spoonful of yogurt mixture in each bowl. Top with diced peaches and tarragon sprigs.
⅔ cup: 159 cal., 4g fat (1g sat. fat), 3mg chol., 129mg sod., 31g carb. (26g sugars, 4g fiber), 3g pro.
Diabetic exchanges: 2 vegetable, 1 fruit, ½ fat.

TIMESAVING TIP

For a different taste, use ½ tsp. chopped fresh basil, thyme or chives instead of tarragon. If you like, blend the herb of your choice with the beets instead of mixing it with the yogurt.

Turkey Sandwich with Raspberry-Mustard Spread

My hearty sandwich has unique yet complementary flavors and textures. It's filled with delicious flavor and healthy nutrients, without the fats, sodium and added sugar many other sandwiches have.

—Sarah Savage, Buena Vista, VA

Takes: 25 min. • **Makes:** 2 servings

- 1 Tbsp. honey
- 1 Tbsp. spicy brown mustard
- 1 tsp. red raspberry preserves
- ¼ tsp. mustard seed
- 1 Tbsp. olive oil
- 4 oz. fresh mushrooms, thinly sliced
- 1 cup fresh baby spinach, coarsely chopped
- 1 garlic clove, minced
- ½ tsp. chili powder
- 4 slices multigrain bread, toasted
- 6 oz. sliced cooked turkey breast
- ½ medium ripe avocado, sliced

1. Combine honey, spicy mustard, preserves and mustard seed; set aside. In a large skillet, heat oil over medium-high heat. Add mushrooms; cook and stir until tender, about 4-5 minutes. Add spinach, garlic and chili powder; cook and stir until spinach is wilted, 3-4 minutes.

2. Spread half of mustard mixture over 2 slices of toast. Layer with turkey, mushroom mixture and avocado. Spread remaining mustard mixture over remaining toast; place over top.

1 sandwich: 449 cal., 16g fat (3g sat. fat), 68mg chol., 392mg sod., 40g carb. (14g sugars, 7g fiber), 35g pro.

Hazelnut Asparagus Soup

My heart is happy when bundles of tender local asparagus start to appear at my grocery store in spring. No one would ever guess this restaurant-quality vegetarian soup can be prepared in about 30 minutes.
—Cindy Beberman, Orland Park, IL

Prep: 20 min. • **Cook:** 15 min.
Makes: 4 servings (3 cups)

- 1 **Tbsp. olive oil**
- ½ **cup chopped sweet onion**
- 3 **garlic cloves, sliced**
  Dash crushed red pepper flakes
- 2½ **cups cut fresh asparagus (about 1½ lbs.), trimmed**
- 2 **cups vegetable broth**
- ⅓ **cup whole hazelnuts, toasted**
- 2 **Tbsp. chopped fresh basil**
- 2 **Tbsp. lemon juice**
- ½ **cup unsweetened almond milk**
- 2 **tsp. reduced-sodium tamari soy sauce**
- ¼ **tsp. salt**
  Shaved asparagus, optional

1. In a large saucepan, heat oil over medium heat. Add onion, garlic and pepper flakes; cook and stir until onion is softened, 4-5 minutes. Add asparagus and broth; bring to a boil. Reduce heat; simmer, covered, until asparagus is tender, 6-8 minutes. Remove from heat; cool slightly.

2. Place nuts, basil and lemon juice in a blender. Add asparagus mixture. Process until smooth and creamy. Return to saucepan. Stir in almond milk, tamari sauce and salt. Heat through, taking care not to boil soup. If desired, top with shaved asparagus.

Note: To toast nuts, bake in a shallow pan in a 350° oven for 5-10 minutes or cook in a skillet over low heat until lightly browned, stirring occasionally.

¾ cup: 164 cal., 13g fat (1g sat. fat), 0 chol., 623mg sod., 11g carb. (4g sugars, 4g fiber), 5g pro.
Diabetic exchanges: 2½ fat, ½ starch.

Grilled Watermelon Gazpacho

This is the perfect starter for a warm-weather lunch or dinner. It's cool and tangy with lots of grilled flavor. If you like a little spice, add more jalapenos.
—George Levinthal, Goleta, CA

- -

Prep: 10 min. + chilling
Grill: 10 min. + cooling
Makes: 4 servings

2 Tbsp. olive oil, divided
¼ seedless watermelon, cut into three 1½-in.-thick slices
1 large beefsteak tomato, halved
½ English cucumber, peeled and halved lengthwise
1 jalapeno pepper, seeded and halved lengthwise
¼ cup plus 2 Tbsp. diced red onion, divided
2 Tbsp. sherry vinegar
1 Tbsp. lime juice
½ tsp. kosher or sea salt
¼ tsp. pepper
1 small ripe avocado, peeled, pitted and diced

1. Brush 1 Tbsp. oil over watermelon, tomato, cucumber and jalapeno; grill, covered, on a greased grill rack over medium-high direct heat until seared, 5-6 minutes on each side. Remove from the heat, reserving 1 slice of watermelon.

2. When cool enough to handle, remove the rind from remaining watermelon slices; cut flesh into chunks. Remove skin and seeds from tomato and jalapeno; chop. Coarsely chop cucumber. Combine grilled vegetables; add ¼ cup onion, vinegar, lime juice and seasonings. Process in batches in a blender until smooth, adding remaining olive oil during final minute. If desired, strain through a fine-mesh strainer; adjust seasonings as needed. Refrigerate gazpacho, covered, until chilled.

3. To serve, pour gazpacho into bowls or glasses. Top with diced avocado and remaining onion. Cut the reserved watermelon slice into wedges. Garnish bowls or glasses with wedges.

1 cup: 181 cal., 12g fat (2g sat. fat), 0 chol., 248mg sod., 19g carb. (13g sugars, 4g fiber), 2g pro.
Diabetic exchanges: 2 fat, 1 vegetable, 1 fruit.

Herbed Tuna Sandwiches

A delightful combination of herbs and reduced-fat cheese makes this simple tuna sandwich a standout.

—Marie Connor, Virginia Beach, VA

- -

Takes: 20 min. • **Makes:** 4 servings

- 1 can (12 oz.) light tuna in water, drained and flaked
- 2 hard-boiled large eggs, chopped
- ⅓ cup reduced-fat mayonnaise
- ¼ cup minced chives
- 2 tsp. minced fresh parsley
- ½ tsp. dried basil
- ¼ tsp. onion powder
- 8 slices whole wheat bread, toasted
- ½ cup shredded reduced-fat cheddar cheese

1. Preheat broiler. Combine the first 7 ingredients. Place 4 slices of toast on an ungreased baking sheet; top with the tuna mixture and sprinkle with cheese.

2. Broil 3-4 in. from the heat until cheese is melted, 1-2 minutes. Top with remaining toast.

1 sandwich: 367 cal., 15g fat (4g sat. fat), 141mg chol., 718mg sod., 27g carb. (4g sugars, 4g fiber), 31g pro.
Diabetic exchanges: 4 lean meat, 2 starch, 2 fat.

White Turkey Chili

Cut the fat and calories while savoring all the comfort, heartiness and flavor you love. This recipe makes it easy!

—Tina Barrett, Houston, TX

- -

Prep: 10 min. • **Cook:** 35 min.
Makes: 6 servings (1½ qt.)

- 2 cans (15 oz. each) cannellini beans, rinsed and drained
- 1 can (10¾ oz.) reduced-fat reduced-sodium condensed cream of chicken soup, undiluted
- 2 cups cubed cooked turkey breast
- 1⅓ cups fat-free milk
- 1 can (4 oz.) chopped green chiles, drained
- 1 Tbsp. minced fresh cilantro
- 1 Tbsp. dried minced onion
- 1 tsp. garlic powder
- 1 tsp. ground cumin
- 1 tsp. dried oregano
- 6 Tbsp. fat-free sour cream

In a large saucepan, combine the first 10 ingredients; bring to a boil, stirring occasionally. Reduce heat; simmer, covered, 25-30 minutes or until heated through. Top servings with sour cream.

1 cup with 1 Tbsp. sour cream: 250 cal., 2g fat (1g sat. fat), 47mg chol., 510mg sod., 31g carb. (0 sugars, 6g fiber), 23g pro.
Diabetic exchanges: 3 lean meat, 2 starch.

Creamy Cauliflower Pakora Soup

My husband and I enjoy pakoras, crispy deep-fried fritters from India. I wanted to get the same flavors but use a healthier cooking technique, so I made soup using all the classic spices and our favorite veggie—cauliflower!
—Melody Johnson, Pulaski, WI

- -

Prep: 20 min. • **Cook:** 20 min.
Makes: 8 servings (3 qt.)

- 1   large head cauliflower, cut into small florets
- 5   medium potatoes, peeled and diced
- 1   large onion, diced
- 4   medium carrots, peeled and diced
- 2   celery ribs, diced
- 1   carton (32 oz.) vegetable stock
- 1   tsp. garam masala
- 1   tsp. garlic powder
- 1   tsp. ground coriander
- 1   tsp. ground turmeric
- 1   tsp. ground cumin
- 1   tsp. pepper
- 1   tsp. salt
- ½   tsp. crushed red pepper flakes

Water or additional vegetable stock
Fresh cilantro leaves
Lime wedges, optional

In a Dutch oven over medium-high heat, bring first 14 ingredients to a boil. Cook and stir until vegetables are tender, about 20 minutes. Remove from heat; cool slightly. Process in batches in a blender or food processor until smooth. Adjust consistency as desired with water or additional stock. Sprinkle with fresh cilantro. Serve hot, with lime wedges if desired.

Freeze option: Before adding the cilantro, freeze cooled soup in freezer containers. To use, partially thaw in refrigerator overnight. Heat through in a saucepan, stirring occasionally; add water if necessary. Sprinkle with cilantro. If desired, serve with lime wedges.

Note: Look for garam masala in the spice aisle.

1½ cups: 135 cal., 1g fat (0 sat. fat), 0 chol., 645mg sod., 30g carb. (6g sugars, 5g fiber), 4g pro.
Diabetic exchanges: 1½ starch, 1 vegetable.

Feta Mushroom Burgers

My son-in-law gave me this recipe and I tweaked it to make it healthier. The burgers are so quick to whip up on the grill.
—Dolores Block, Frankenmuth, MI

- -

Takes: 25 min. • **Makes:** 6 servings

- 1 lb. lean ground beef (90% lean)
- 3 Italian turkey sausage links (4 oz. each), casings removed
- 2 tsp. Worcestershire sauce
- ½ tsp. garlic powder
- 2 Tbsp. balsamic vinegar
- 1 Tbsp. olive oil
- 6 large portobello mushrooms, stems removed
- 1 large onion, cut into ½-in. slices
- 6 Tbsp. crumbled feta or blue cheese
- 6 whole wheat hamburger buns or sourdough rolls, split
- 10 fresh basil leaves, thinly sliced

1. Combine first 4 ingredients; mix lightly but thoroughly. Shape into six ½-in.-thick patties. Mix vinegar and oil; brush over mushrooms.
2. Place burgers, mushrooms and onion on an oiled grill rack over medium heat. Grill, covered, until a thermometer inserted in burgers reads 160° and mushrooms and onion are tender, 4-6 minutes per side.
3. Fill mushroom caps with cheese; grill, covered, until cheese is melted, 1-2 minutes. Grill buns, cut side down, until toasted, 30-60 seconds. Serve burgers on buns; top with mushrooms, basil and onion.
1 burger: 371 cal., 15g fat (5g sat. fat), 72mg chol., 590mg sod., 31g carb. (8g sugars, 5g fiber), 28g pro.

California Roll Wraps

I love the California rolls I order at sushi restaurants and wanted to capture those flavors in a sandwich I could take to work. I started with the standard ingredients, added a few others and came up with a hit.
—Mary Pax-Shipley, Bend, OR

Takes: 20 min. • **Makes:** 6 wraps

½   cup wasabi mayonnaise
6   whole wheat tortillas (8 in.)
2   pkg. (8 oz. each) imitation crabmeat
1   medium ripe avocado, peeled and thinly sliced
1½ cups julienned peeled jicama
1   medium sweet red pepper, julienned
1   small cucumber, seeded and julienned
¾   cup bean sprouts

Divide wasabi mayonnaise evenly among 6 tortillas and spread to within ½ in. of edges. Layer tortillas with crabmeat, avocado, jicama, red pepper, cucumber and bean sprouts. Roll up tightly.
1 wrap: 365 cal., 18g fat (3g sat. fat), 10mg chol., 647mg sod., 39g carb. (2g sugars, 7g fiber), 13g pro.
Diabetic exchanges: 2 starch, 2 fat, 1 vegetable, 1 lean meat.

TIMESAVING TIP

Making this ahead of time? Toss avocado slices with a splash of rice wine vinegar or lemon juice to keep them from turning brown.

Chickpea Tortilla Soup

Looking for soup that's healthy, flavorful and filling? Try this vegan tortilla soup. My family loves it, and we have fun playing around with the different toppings each time we eat it.
—Julie Peterson, Crofton, MD

- -

Takes: 30 min.
Makes: 8 servings (3 qt.)

- 1 Tbsp. olive oil
- 1 medium red onion, chopped
- 4 garlic cloves, minced
- 1 to 2 jalapeno peppers, seeded and chopped, optional
- ¼ tsp. pepper
- 8 cups vegetable broth
- 1 cup red quinoa, rinsed
- 2 cans (15 oz. each) no-salt-added chickpeas or garbanzo beans, rinsed and drained
- 1 can (15 oz.) no-salt-added black beans, rinsed and drained
- 3 medium tomatoes, chopped
- 1 cup fresh or frozen corn
- ⅓ cup minced fresh cilantro
  Optional ingredients: Crushed tortilla chips, cubed avocado, lime wedges and additional chopped cilantro

Heat the oil in a Dutch oven over medium-high heat. Add the red onion, garlic, jalapeno if desired, and pepper; cook and stir until tender, 3-5 minutes. Add broth and quinoa. Bring to a boil; reduce heat. Simmer, uncovered, until quinoa is tender, about 10 minutes. Add the chickpeas, beans, tomatoes, corn and cilantro; heat through. If desired, serve with optional ingredients.

Note: Wear disposable gloves when cutting hot peppers; the oils can burn skin. Avoid touching your face.

1½ cups: 289 cal., 5g fat (0 sat. fat), 0 chol., 702mg sod., 48g carb. (5g sugars, 9g fiber), 13g pro.

Snappy Tuna Melts

I lightened up a tuna melt by switching mayo to creamy balsamic vinaigrette. Both kids and adults enjoy this hot and tasty open-faced sandwich.
—Christine Schenher, Exeter, CA

- -

Takes: 15 min. • **Makes:** 4 servings

- 1 pouch (11 oz.) light tuna in water
- 1 hard-boiled large egg, coarsely chopped
- 2 Tbsp. reduced-fat creamy balsamic vinaigrette
- 1 Tbsp. stone-ground mustard, optional
- 4 whole wheat hamburger buns, split
- 8 slices tomato
- 8 slices reduced-fat Swiss cheese

1. In a small bowl, mix tuna, egg, vinaigrette and, if desired, mustard. Place buns on an ungreased baking sheet, cut side up. Broil 4-6 in. from the heat until golden brown, roughly 1-2 minutes.

2. Spread tuna mixture over buns; top with tomato and cheese. Broil 2-3 minutes longer or until cheese is melted.

2 open-faced sandwiches: 341 cal., 13g fat (5g sat. fat), 105mg chol., 557mg sod., 27g carb. (6g sugars, 4g fiber), 35g pro.
Diabetic exchanges: 4 lean meat, 2 starch, 1 fat.

30-Minute CLASSICS

Short on time doesn't mean short on flavor! These meals are perfect for busy nights—each one is ready in 30 minutes or less.

Pressure-Cooker Beef & Beans

This deliciously spicy steak and beans over rice will have friends asking for more. It's a favorite in my recipe collection, and the pressure cooker makes it easy.
—Marie Leamon, Bethesda, MD

- -

Prep: 10 min. • **Cook:** 15 min.
Makes: 8 servings

1½ lbs. boneless round steak
1 Tbsp. prepared mustard
1 Tbsp. chili powder
½ tsp. salt
¼ tsp. pepper
1 garlic clove, minced
2 cans (14½ oz. each) diced tomatoes, undrained
1 medium onion, chopped
½ cup water
1 tsp. beef bouillon granules
1 can (16 oz.) kidney beans, rinsed and drained
Hot cooked rice

1. Cut steak into thin strips. Combine mustard, chili powder, salt, pepper and garlic in a bowl; add steak and toss to coat. Transfer to a 6-qt. electric pressure cooker; add the tomatoes, onion, water and bouillon.
2. Lock lid; close pressure-release valve. Adjust to pressure-cook on high for 15 minutes. Quick-release pressure. Stir in beans; heat through. Serve with rice.

1 cup: 185 cal., 3g fat (1g sat. fat), 48mg chol., 574mg sod., 16g carb. (5g sugars, 5g fiber), 24g pro.
Diabetic exchanges: 3 lean meat, 1 starch.

Almond-Topped Fish

A co-worker gave me this recipe, but I didn't try it until recently. What a mistake to wait! It's easier than dipping, coating and frying—and the flavor is outstanding. Once you've tried this tender fish, you'll never go back to fried.
—Heidi Kirsch, Waterloo, IA

Takes: 30 min. • **Makes:** 4 servings

- 1 Tbsp. butter
- 1 small onion, thinly sliced
- 4 cod or haddock fillets (6 oz. each)
- 1 tsp. seasoned salt
- ½ tsp. dill weed
- ¼ tsp. pepper
- ¼ cup grated Parmesan cheese
- ¼ cup reduced-fat mayonnaise
- 1 Tbsp. minced fresh parsley
- 1 Tbsp. lemon juice
- 2 Tbsp. sliced almonds, toasted

1. Place butter in a 13x9-in. baking dish; heat in a 400° oven until melted. Spread butter over bottom of dish; cover with onion.

2. Arrange fish over onion; sprinkle with salt, dill and pepper. Combine Parmesan cheese, mayonnaise, parsley and lemon juice; spread over fish.

3. Bake, uncovered, at 400° for 18-20 minutes or until fish flakes easily with a fork. Sprinkle with almonds.

1 fillet: 220 cal., 9g fat (2g sat. fat), 74mg chol., 658mg sod., 5g carb. (2g sugars, 1g fiber), 29g pro.
Diabetic exchanges: 4 lean meat, 2 fat.

Chicken Nuggets

I like to make these golden chicken nuggets because they're quick and easy and the whole family loves them. The seasoning can also be used on chicken breast halves for sandwiches.
—Annette Ellyson, Carolina, WV

- -

Takes: 30 min. • **Makes:** 8 servings

- 1 cup all-purpose flour
- 4 tsp. seasoned salt
- 1 tsp. poultry seasoning
- 1 tsp. ground mustard
- 1 tsp. paprika
- ½ tsp. pepper
- 2 lbs. boneless skinless chicken breasts
- ¼ cup canola oil

1. In a large shallow dish, combine first 6 ingredients. Flatten chicken to ½-in. thickness, then cut into 1½-in. pieces. Add chicken, a few pieces at a time, to dish and turn to coat.

2. In a large skillet, cook chicken in oil in batches until meat is no longer pink, 6-8 minutes.

3 oz. cooked chicken: 212 cal., 10g fat (2g sat. fat), 63mg chol., 435mg sod., 6g carb. (0 sugars, 0 fiber), 24g pro.

Diabetic exchanges: 3 lean meat, 1½ fat, ½ starch.

Easy Beef Stroganoff

I took my mother-in-law's wonderful stroganoff and lightened it to come up with this spinoff. We call it "special noodles" in our house.
—Jennifer Riordan, St. Louis, MO

- -

Takes: 30 min. • **Makes:** 6 servings

- 4½ cups uncooked yolk-free noodles
- 1 lb. lean ground beef (90% lean)
- ½ lb. sliced fresh mushrooms
- 1 large onion, halved and sliced
- 3 garlic cloves, minced
- 1 Tbsp. reduced-fat butter
- 2 Tbsp. all-purpose flour
- 1 can (14½ oz.) reduced-sodium beef broth
- 2 Tbsp. tomato paste
- 1 cup reduced-fat sour cream
- ¼ tsp. salt
- ¼ tsp. pepper
  Chopped fresh parsley, optional

1. Cook noodles according to the package directions. Meanwhile, in a large saucepan, cook ground beef, mushrooms and onion over medium heat until meat is no longer pink. Add garlic; cook 1 minute longer. Drain. Remove and keep warm.

2. In the same pan, melt butter. Stir in flour until smooth; gradually add broth and tomato paste. Bring to a boil; cook and stir until thickened, about 2 minutes.

3. Carefully return beef mixture to pan. Add the sour cream, salt and pepper; cook and stir until heated through (do not boil). Drain noodles; serve with beef mixture. If desired, top with chopped parsley.

Note: This recipe was tested with Land O'Lakes light stick butter.

⅔ cup beef mixture with ¾ cup noodles: 333 cal., 11g fat (5g sat. fat), 58mg chol., 329mg sod., 33g carb. (7g sugars, 3g fiber), 25g pro.

Diabetic exchanges: 2 starch, 2 lean meat, 1 vegetable, 1 fat.

Turkey Biscuit Skillet

My mother made this comforting meal while I was growing up. Now I make it for my family. I cut the biscuits into smaller pieces so they will brown nicely on top. If you're watching your salt consumption, use reduced-sodium broth.
—Keri Boffeli, Monticello, IA

- -

Takes: 30 min. • **Makes:** 6 servings

1 Tbsp. butter
⅓ cup chopped onion
¼ cup all-purpose flour
1 can (10½ oz.) condensed chicken broth, undiluted
¼ cup fat-free milk
⅛ tsp. pepper
2 cups cubed cooked turkey breast
2 cups frozen peas and carrots (about 10 oz.), thawed
1 tube (12 oz.) refrigerated buttermilk biscuits, quartered

1. Preheat oven to 400°. Melt the butter in a 10-in. cast-iron or other ovenproof skillet over medium-high heat. Add onion; cook and stir until tender, 2-3 minutes.
2. In a small bowl, mix flour, broth, milk and pepper until smooth; stir into pan. Bring to a boil, stirring constantly; cook and stir mixture until thickened, 1-2 minutes. Add turkey and frozen vegetables; heat through. Arrange biscuits over stew. Bake until biscuits are golden brown, 15-20 minutes.

1 serving: 319 cal., 10g fat (4g sat. fat), 43mg chol., 878mg sod., 36g carb. (4g sugars, 2g fiber), 22g pro.

Pork Paprika

A nicely spiced sauce with diced tomatoes seasons cubes of pork in this hearty entree. I often scramble to put a meal on the table, but this comes together so quickly. My family oohs and aahs the whole time they're eating it.
—Monette Johnson, San Antonio, TX

- -

Takes: 30 min. • **Makes:** 4 servings

1 lb. pork tenderloin, cut into cubes
1 Tbsp. canola oil
1 large onion, chopped
1 medium green pepper, chopped
2 garlic cloves, minced
1 can (14½ oz.) diced tomatoes, undrained
½ cup white wine or chicken broth
4 tsp. paprika
1 tsp. sugar
1 tsp. grated lemon zest, optional
½ tsp. caraway seeds
½ tsp. dried marjoram
¼ tsp. salt
¼ tsp. pepper
Hot cooked noodles, optional
¼ cup reduced-fat sour cream

In a large nonstick skillet, cook pork in oil until no longer pink; remove and keep warm. Add the onion, green pepper and garlic to pan; cook and stir until crisp-tender. Add the next 9 ingredients; bring to a boil. Reduce heat; cover and simmer for 10-15 minutes or until slightly thickened. Stir in pork. Serve over noodles if desired. Dollop with sour cream.

1 cup: 258 cal., 9g fat (2g sat. fat), 65mg chol., 372mg sod., 15g carb. (8g sugars, 4g fiber), 26g pro.
Diabetic exchanges: 3 lean meat, 2 vegetable, 1 fat.

Fettuccine with Black Bean Sauce

When my husband had to go on a heart-smart diet, I decided to come up with new and delicious ways to incorporate more vegetables into our daily menus. This meatless spaghetti sauce is a winner. It's especially good with spinach fettuccine.
—Marianne Neuman, East Troy, WI

- -

Takes: 30 min. • **Makes:** 5 servings

6	oz. uncooked fettuccine
1	small green pepper, chopped
1	small onion, chopped
1	Tbsp. olive oil
2	cups garden-style pasta sauce
1	can (15 oz.) black beans, rinsed and drained
2	Tbsp. minced fresh basil or 2 tsp. dried basil
1	tsp. dried oregano
½	tsp. fennel seed
¼	tsp. garlic salt
1	cup shredded part-skim mozzarella cheese Additional chopped fresh basil, optional

1. Cook fettuccine according to the package directions. Meanwhile, in a large saucepan, saute pepper and onion in oil until tender. Stir in pasta sauce, black beans and seasonings.
2. Bring to a boil. Reduce heat; simmer, uncovered, for 5 minutes. Drain fettuccine. Top with sauce and sprinkle with cheese. If desired, top with chopped fresh basil.
¾ cup sauce with ¾ cup pasta: 350 cal., 10g fat (3g sat. fat), 17mg chol., 761mg sod., 51g carb. (12g sugars, 8g fiber), 16g pro.
Diabetic exchanges: 2½ starch, 2 vegetable, 1 lean meat, 1 fat.

Simple Grilled Steak Fajitas

After moving to a new state with two toddlers, I needed effortless dinners. These fajitas came to the rescue! They make a quick meal cooked on the grill or in a cast-iron skillet.
—Shannen Mahoney, Yelm, WA

- -

Takes: 30 min. • **Makes:** 4 servings

1	beef top sirloin steak (¾-in. thick and 1 lb.)
2	Tbsp. fajita seasoning mix
1	large sweet onion, cut crosswise into ½-in. slices
1	medium sweet red pepper, halved
1	medium green pepper, halved
1	Tbsp. olive oil
4	whole wheat tortillas (8 in.), warmed Optional: Sliced avocado, minced fresh cilantro and lime wedges

1. Rub steak with fajita seasoning mix. Brush onion and peppers with oil.
2. Grill steak and vegetables, covered, on a greased rack over medium direct heat 4-6 minutes on each side or until meat reaches desired doneness (for medium-rare, a thermometer should read 135°; medium, 140°; and medium-well, 145°) and vegetables are tender. Remove from grill. Let steak stand, covered, for 5 minutes before slicing.
3. Cut the vegetables and steak into strips; serve in tortillas. If desired, top with avocado and cilantro and serve with lime wedges.
1 serving: 363 cal., 13g fat (4g sat. fat), 54mg chol., 686mg sod., 34g carb. (6g sugars, 5g fiber), 27g pro.
Diabetic exchanges: 3 lean meat, 2 starch, 1 vegetable, ½ fat.

TIMESAVING TIP

As long as you're eating a healthy, nutrient-rich dinner, switch up your noodle game, too. Instead of fettuccine, try this with whole wheat, buckwheat, quinoa, multigrain or chickpea pasta.

Lemon-Caper
Pork Medallions

Looking for an elegant but easy dinner you can put together in a flash for guests or unexpected visitors? These lightly breaded medallions are truly special!
—*Taste of Home* Test Kitchen

Takes: 30 min. • **Makes:** 4 servings

- 1 pork tenderloin (1 lb.), cut into 12 slices
- ½ cup all-purpose flour
- ½ tsp. salt
- ¼ tsp. pepper
- 1 Tbsp. butter
- 1 Tbsp. olive oil
- 1 cup reduced-sodium chicken broth
- ¼ cup white wine or additional reduced-sodium chicken broth
- 1 garlic clove, minced
- 1 Tbsp. capers, drained
- 1 Tbsp. lemon juice
- ½ tsp. dried rosemary, crushed

1. Flatten pork slices to ¼-in. thickness. In a large shallow dish, combine the flour, salt and pepper. Add pork, a few pieces at a time, and turn to coat.

2. In a large nonstick skillet over medium heat, cook pork in butter and oil in batches until juices run clear. Remove and keep warm.

3. Add broth, wine and garlic to the pan, stirring to loosen browned bits. Bring to a boil; cook until liquid is reduced by half. Stir in the capers, lemon juice and rosemary; heat through. Serve with pork.

3 medallions: 232 cal., 10g fat (4g sat. fat), 71mg chol., 589mg sod., 7g carb. (1g sugars, 0 fiber), 24g pro. **Diabetic exchanges:** 3 lean meat, 1½ fat, ½ starch.

Summertime Orzo & Chicken

This easy-as-can-be main dish is likely to become a summer staple at your house. It's that good! If you prefer, grill the chicken breasts instead of cooking them in a skillet.
—Fran MacMillan,
West Melbourne, FL

- -

Takes: 30 min. • **Makes:** 4 servings

- ¾ **cup uncooked orzo pasta**
- 1 **lb. boneless skinless chicken breasts, cut into 1-in. pieces**
- 1 **medium cucumber, chopped**
- 1 **small red onion, chopped**
- ¼ **cup minced fresh parsley**
- 2 **Tbsp. lemon juice**
- 1 **Tbsp. olive oil**
- 1 **tsp. salt**
- ¼ **tsp. pepper**
- ¼ **cup crumbled reduced-fat feta cheese**

1. Cook pasta according to package directions; drain.
2. Meanwhile, in a large skillet coated with cooking spray, cook and stir chicken over medium heat until no longer pink, 6-8 minutes. Transfer to a large bowl.
3. Add cucumber, onion, parsley and pasta. In a small bowl, mix lemon juice, oil, salt and pepper; toss with chicken mixture. Serve immediately or refrigerate and serve cold. Top with cheese before serving.
1¼ cups: 320 cal., 7g fat (2g sat. fat), 65mg chol., 742mg sod., 32g carb. (3g sugars, 2g fiber), 30g pro.
Diabetic exchanges: 3 lean meat, 2 starch, 1 fat.

Garlic-Mushroom Turkey Slices

My daughter is a picky eater, and even she likes this turkey dish, so I know it's a winner. It has minimal fat, and it's delicious and affordable for easy weeknight dining.
—Rick Fleishman, Beverly Hills, CA

- -

Takes: 30 min. • **Makes:** 4 servings

- ½ cup all-purpose flour
- ½ tsp. dried oregano
- ½ tsp. paprika
- ¾ tsp. salt, divided
- ¼ tsp. pepper, divided
- 1 Tbsp. olive oil
- 1 pkg. (17.6 oz.) turkey breast cutlets
- ½ lb. sliced fresh mushrooms
- ¾ cup reduced-sodium chicken broth
- ¼ cup dry white wine or additional broth
- 2 garlic cloves, minced

1. In a large shallow dish, mix flour, oregano, paprika, ½ tsp. salt and ⅛ tsp. pepper. Dip cutlets in flour mixture to coat both sides; shake off excess flour.

2. In a large nonstick skillet, heat oil over medium heat. In batches, add turkey and cook 1-2 minutes on each side or until no longer pink; remove from pan.

3. Add the remaining ingredients to the skillet; stir in the remaining salt and pepper. Cook, uncovered, 4-6 minutes or until the mushrooms are tender, stirring occasionally. Return turkey to pan; heat through, turning to coat.

1 serving: 218 cal., 4g fat (1g sat. fat), 77mg chol., 440mg sod., 8g carb. (1g sugars, 1g fiber), 34g pro.
Diabetic exchanges: 4 lean meat, ½ starch, ½ fat.

Grilled Halibut with Blueberry Salsa

Give halibut a new summery spin. The salsa may seem sophisticated, but it's a cinch to prepare.
—Donna Goutermont, Sequim, WA

- -

Takes: 30 min. • **Makes:** 6 servings

- 2 cups fresh blueberries, divided
- 1 small red onion, chopped
- ¼ cup minced fresh cilantro
- 1 jalapeno pepper, seeded and chopped
- 2 Tbsp. orange juice
- 1 Tbsp. balsamic vinegar
- 1 tsp. plus 2 Tbsp. olive oil, divided
- ⅛ tsp. plus 1 tsp. salt, divided
- ⅛ tsp. pepper
- 6 halibut fillets (5 oz. each)

1. In a bowl, coarsely mash 1 cup blueberries. Stir in onion, cilantro, jalapeno, orange juice, balsamic vinegar, 1 tsp. oil, ⅛ tsp. salt, pepper and remaining blueberries. Cover and chill until serving.

2. Meanwhile, drizzle halibut fillets with the remaining oil; sprinkle with remaining salt. Grill halibut, covered, over medium heat for 4-5 minutes on each side or until the fish flakes easily with a fork. Serve with salsa.

Note: Wear disposable gloves when cutting hot peppers; the oils can burn skin. Avoid touching your face.

1 fillet with ⅓ cup salsa: 239 cal., 9g fat (1g sat. fat), 45mg chol., 521mg sod., 9g carb. (6g sugars, 1g fiber), 30g pro.
Diabetic exchanges: 4 lean meat, 1 fat, ½ starch.

Using chicken tenders instead of chicken breast halves speeds along the bake time to make this a quick dinner.

Baked Chicken with Bacon-Tomato Relish

We eat a lot of poultry for dinner, so I'm always trying to do something a little different with it. My children love the crispness of this chicken and my husband and I love the relish—you can't go wrong with bacon!
—Elisabeth Larsen, Pleasant Grove, UT

- -

Takes: 30 min. • **Makes:** 4 servings

- 1   cup panko bread crumbs
- 2   Tbsp. plus 1 tsp. minced fresh thyme, divided
- ½   tsp. salt, divided
- ½   tsp. pepper, divided
- ⅓   cup all-purpose flour
- 1   large egg, beaten
- 1   lb. chicken tenderloins
- 4   bacon strips, cut into ½-in. pieces
- 1½   cups grape tomatoes, halved
- 1   Tbsp. red wine vinegar
- 1   Tbsp. brown sugar

1. Preheat oven to 425°. In a shallow bowl, mix bread crumbs, 2 Tbsp. thyme, and ¼ tsp. each salt and pepper. Place the flour and egg in separate shallow bowls. Dip chicken in flour; shake off excess. Dip in egg, then in crumb mixture, patting to help coating adhere. Place chicken on a greased rack in a 15x10x1-in. baking pan. Bake until a thermometer reads 165°, about 15 minutes.

2. Meanwhile, in a large skillet, cook bacon over medium heat until crisp, stirring occasionally, about 5 minutes. Remove with a slotted spoon; drain on paper towels. Reserve 2 Tbsp. drippings in pan; discard remaining drippings.

3. Add tomatoes, vinegar, sugar and remaining salt and pepper to the drippings; cook and stir until tomatoes are tender, 2-3 minutes. Stir in bacon and remaining thyme. Serve with chicken.

2 chicken tenders with ¼ cup relish: 326 cal., 13g fat (4g sat. fat), 95mg chol., 602mg sod., 19g carb. (6g sugars, 2g fiber), 34g pro. **Diabetic exchanges:** 4 lean meat, 2 fat, 1 starch.

Deviled Chicken Thighs

I make this dish when I invite my next-door neighbor over for supper. It's just enough for the two of us. The tasty chicken is tender and moist with a bit of crunch from the cashews.
—Bernice Morris, Marshfield, MO

- -

Takes: 30 min. • **Makes:** 2 servings

- 1   tsp. butter, softened
- 1   tsp. cider vinegar
- 1   tsp. prepared mustard
- 1   tsp. paprika
      Dash pepper
- 2   boneless skinless chicken thighs (about ½ lb.)
- 3   Tbsp. soft bread crumbs
- 2   Tbsp. chopped cashews

1. In a large bowl, combine butter, vinegar, mustard, paprika and pepper. Spread over chicken thighs. Place in a greased 11x7-in. baking dish. Sprinkle with bread crumbs.

2. Bake, uncovered, at 400° for 15 minutes. Sprinkle with cashews. Bake until juices run clear and the topping is golden brown, 7-12 minutes longer.

Note: To make soft bread crumbs, tear bread into pieces and place in a food processor or blender. Cover and pulse until crumbs form. One slice of bread yields ½ to ¾ cup crumbs.

1 chicken thigh: 246 cal., 14g fat (4g sat. fat), 81mg chol., 189mg sod., 6g carb. (1g sugars, 1g fiber), 23g pro. **Diabetic exchanges:** 3 lean meat, 1 fat, ½ starch.

Tuscan Fish Packets

My husband does a lot of fishing, so I'm always looking for new ways to cook what he catches. A professional chef shared this recipe with me, and I played around with some different veggie combinations until I found the one my family liked best.
—Kathy Morrow, Hubbard, OH

- -

Takes: 30 min. • **Makes:** 4 servings

- 1   **can (15 oz.) great northern beans, rinsed and drained**
- 4   **plum tomatoes, chopped**
- 1   **small zucchini, chopped**
- 1   **medium onion, chopped**
- 1   **garlic clove, minced**
- ¼   **cup white wine**
- ¾   **tsp. salt, divided**
- ¼   **tsp. pepper, divided**
- 4   **tilapia fillets (6 oz. each)**
- 1   **medium lemon, cut into 8 thin slices**

1. Preheat oven to 400°. In a bowl, combine beans, tomatoes, zucchini, onion, garlic, wine, ½ tsp. salt and ⅛ tsp. pepper.

2. Rinse fish and pat dry. Place each tilapia fillet on an 18x12-in. piece of heavy-duty foil; season fish with the remaining salt and pepper. Spoon the bean mixture over fish; top with lemon slices. Fold foil around fish and crimp edges to seal. Transfer packets to a baking sheet.

3. Bake until fish just begins to flake easily with a fork and vegetables are tender, 15-20 minutes. Be careful to avoid escaping steam when opening the foil packets.

1 serving: 270 cal., 2g fat (1g sat. fat), 83mg chol., 658mg sod., 23g carb. (4g sugars, 7g fiber), 38g pro. **Diabetic exchanges:** 5 lean meat, 1 starch, 1 vegetable.

Apple & Onion Topped Chops

Now that my husband and I are trying to lose weight, I look for healthy dishes that are flavorful, quick and appealing to us and our daughter. This one fits the bill on all counts.
—Beverly McLain, Endicott, NY

- -

Takes: 30 min. • **Makes:** 4 servings

- 4 tsp. canola oil, divided
- 4 boneless pork loin chops (5 oz. each)
- 3 cups sweet onion slices
- 2 medium Granny Smith apples, peeled and sliced
- ½ cup water
- 2 Tbsp. brown sugar
- 1 Tbsp. cider vinegar
- 1 tsp. garlic powder
- ½ tsp. salt
- ¼ to ½ tsp. pepper
- ¼ tsp. dried rosemary, crushed

1. In a large nonstick skillet heat 2 tsp. canola oil over medium-high heat; cook chops until browned, about 3 minutes on each side. Remove meat; set aside and keep warm.

2. In the same skillet, cook and stir onion in remaining 2 tsp. canola oil until golden brown, about 7 minutes. Add the apple slices; cook and stir 3 minutes longer.

3. Combine the water, brown sugar, vinegar, garlic powder, salt, pepper and rosemary. Stir into skillet. Bring to a boil. Return meat to pan. Reduce heat; cover and cook until the apples are crisp-tender and a thermometer inserted in the center of the pork reads 145°, 6-8 minutes. Let stand 5 minutes before serving.

1 serving: 326 cal., 13g fat (3g sat. fat), 68mg chol., 340mg sod., 24g carb. (17g sugars, 3g fiber), 28g pro. **Diabetic exchanges:** 4 lean meat, 1 vegetable, 1 fat, ½ starch, ½ fruit.

Tequila Lime Shrimp Zoodles

This tangy shrimp and zucchini dish is a smart way to cut carbohydrates without sacrificing flavor. If you don't have a spiralizer, use thinly julienned zucchini to get the same effect.
—Brigette Schroeder, Yorkville, IL

- -

Takes: 30 min. • **Makes:** 4 servings

    3   Tbsp. butter, divided
    1   shallot, minced
    2   garlic cloves, minced
    ¼   cup tequila
    1½ tsp. grated lime zest
    2   Tbsp. lime juice
    1   Tbsp. olive oil
    1   lb. uncooked shrimp (31-40
        per lb.), peeled and deveined
    2   medium zucchini, spiralized
        (about 6 cups)
    ½   tsp. salt
    ¼   tsp. pepper
    ¼   cup minced fresh parsley
        Additional grated lime zest

1. In a large cast-iron or other heavy skillet, heat 2 Tbsp. butter over medium heat. Add shallot and garlic; cook 1-2 minutes. Remove from heat; stir in tequila, lime zest and lime juice. Cook over medium heat until liquid is almost evaporated, 2-3 minutes.
2. Add olive oil and remaining butter; stir in shrimp and zucchini. Sprinkle with salt and pepper. Cook and stir until shrimp begin to turn pink and zucchini is crisp-tender, 4-5 minutes. Sprinkle with parsley and additional lime zest.
1¼ cups: 246 cal., 14g fat (6g sat. fat), 161mg chol., 510mg sod., 7g carb. (3g sugars, 1g fiber), 20g pro.
Diabetic exchanges: 3 lean meat, 3 fat, 1 vegetable.

Glazed Rosemary Pork

This honey-glazed pork tenderloin feels elegant, but it's super easy, too. It's ideal for weekend dinner parties and weeknight suppers alike.
—Barbara Sistrunk, Fultondale, AL

- -

Takes: 30 min. • **Makes:** 6 servings

    ¼   cup reduced-sodium chicken
        broth
    3   Tbsp. honey
    1   Tbsp. minced fresh rosemary
        or 1 tsp. dried rosemary,
        crushed
    1   Tbsp. Dijon mustard
    1   tsp. balsamic vinegar
    ⅛   tsp. salt
    ⅛   tsp. pepper
    2   pork tenderloins (1 lb. each)
    2   Tbsp. olive oil, divided
    4   garlic cloves, minced

1. Whisk together first 7 ingredients. Cut tenderloins crosswise into 1-in. slices; pound each with a meat mallet to ½-in. thickness.
2. In a large nonstick skillet, heat 1 Tbsp. oil over medium-high heat. In batches, cook pork tenderloins until a thermometer reads 145°, 3-4 minutes per side. Remove from pan.
3. In same skillet, heat remaining oil over medium heat; saute garlic until tender, about 1 minute. Stir in broth mixture; bring to a boil, stirring to loosen browned bits from pan. Add pork, turning to coat; heat through.
4 oz. cooked pork: 255 cal., 10g fat (2g sat. fat), 85mg chol., 194mg sod., 10g carb. (9g sugars, 0 fiber), 31g pro.
Diabetic exchanges: 4 lean meat, 1 fat, ½ starch.

Spinach & Feta Stuffed Chicken

My baked chicken bundles are simple to put together. Serve them with couscous and roasted green beans for a comforting meal.
—Jim Knepper,
Mount Holly Springs, PA

- -

Takes: 30 min. • **Makes:** 2 servings

8	oz. fresh spinach (about 10 cups)
1½	tsp. cider vinegar
½	tsp. sugar
⅛	tsp. pepper
2	boneless skinless chicken thighs
½	tsp. chicken seasoning
3	Tbsp. crumbled feta cheese
1	tsp. olive oil
¾	cup reduced-sodium chicken broth
1	tsp. butter

1. Preheat oven to 375°. In a large skillet, cook and stir spinach over medium-high heat until wilted. Stir in vinegar, sugar and pepper; cool mixture slightly.

2. Pound chicken thighs with a meat mallet to flatten slightly; sprinkle with chicken seasoning. Top chicken with spinach mixture and cheese. Roll up chicken from a long side; tie securely with kitchen string.

3. In an ovenproof skillet, heat oil over medium-high heat; add chicken and brown on all sides. Transfer to the oven; roast until a thermometer inserted in center of chicken reads 170°, 13-15 minutes.

4. Remove chicken from pan; keep warm. On stovetop, add broth and butter to skillet; bring to a boil, stirring to loosen browned bits from pan. Cook until slightly thickened, 3-5 minutes. Serve with chicken.

Note: This recipe was tested with McCormick's Montreal Chicken Seasoning. Look for it in the spice aisle.

1 chicken roll-up with 2 Tbsp. sauce: 253 cal., 14g fat (5g sat. fat), 86mg chol., 601mg sod., 5g carb. (2g sugars, 2g fiber), 26g pro.
Diabetic exchanges: 3 lean meat, 2 vegetable, 1½ fat.

Grilled Garden Veggie Pizza

Pile on the veggies—this crisp, grilled crust can take it! The colorful, healthy pizza looks as fresh as it tastes.
—Diane Halferty, Corpus Christi, TX

Takes: 30 min. • **Makes:** 6 servings

- 1 **medium red onion, cut crosswise into ½-in. slices**
- 1 **large sweet red pepper, halved, stemmed and seeded**
- 1 **small zucchini, cut lengthwise into ½-in. slices**
- 1 **yellow summer squash, cut lengthwise into ½-in. slices**
- 2 **Tbsp. olive oil**
- ½ **tsp. salt**
- ¼ **tsp. pepper**
- 1 **prebaked 12-in. thin whole wheat pizza crust**
- 3 **Tbsp. jarred roasted minced garlic**
- 2 **cups shredded part-skim mozzarella cheese, divided**
- ⅓ **cup torn fresh basil**

1. Brush the vegetables with oil; sprinkle with salt and pepper. Grill, covered, over medium heat until tender, 4-5 minutes per side for onion and pepper, 3-4 minutes per side for zucchini and squash.

2. Separate onion into rings; cut pepper into strips. Spread pizza crust with garlic; sprinkle with 1 cup cheese. Top with grilled vegetables, then remaining cheese.

3. Grill pizza, covered, over medium heat until bottom is golden brown and cheese is melted, 5-7 minutes. Top with basil.

1 piece: 324 cal., 15g fat (6g sat. fat), 24mg chol., 704mg sod., 30g carb. (5g sugars, 5g fiber), 16g pro.
Diabetic exchanges: 2 starch, 2 medium-fat meat, 1 fat.

Cacciatore Chicken Breasts

Here's my easy version of traditional chicken cacciatore. The tasty sauce and chicken can be served over rice or noodles. To lower the sodium, use garlic powder instead of garlic salt.
—JoAnn McCauley, Dubuque, IA

- -

Takes: 30 min. • **Makes:** 2 servings

- ½   medium onion, sliced and separated into rings
- ½   medium green pepper, sliced
- 1   Tbsp. olive oil
- 2   boneless skinless chicken breast halves (5 oz. each)
- ¾   cup canned stewed tomatoes
- 2   Tbsp. white wine or chicken broth
- ¼   tsp. garlic salt
- ¼   tsp. dried rosemary, crushed
- ⅛   tsp. pepper

1. In a large skillet, saute onion and green pepper in oil until crisp-tender. Remove and keep warm. Cook the chicken over medium-high heat until juices run clear, 4-5 minutes on each side. Remove and set aside.

2. Add tomatoes, wine, garlic salt, rosemary and pepper to the skillet. Stir in the onion mixture and heat through. Serve with chicken.

1 chicken breast half with ¾ cup sauce: 272 cal., 10g fat (2g sat. fat), 78mg chol., 462mg sod., 12g carb. (7g sugars, 2g fiber), 30g pro. **Diabetic exchanges:** 4 lean meat, 2 vegetable, 1½ fat.

Salmon with Horseradish Pistachio Crust

Impress everyone at your table with this elegant but easy salmon. Feel free to switch up the ingredients to suit your tastes. You can use scallions in place of the shallot or try almonds or pecans instead of pistachios. The nutty coating also plays well with chicken and pork.

—Linda Press Wolfe, Cross River, NY

Takes: 30 min. • **Makes:** 6 servings

- 6   salmon fillets (4 oz. each)
- ⅓   cup sour cream
- ⅔   cup dry bread crumbs
- ⅔   cup chopped pistachios
- ½   cup minced shallots
- 2   Tbsp. olive oil
- 1   to 2 Tbsp. prepared horseradish
- 1   Tbsp. snipped fresh dill or 1 tsp. dill weed
- ½   tsp. grated lemon or orange zest
- ¼   tsp. crushed red pepper flakes
- 1   garlic clove, minced

Preheat oven to 350°. Place salmon, skin side down, in an ungreased 15x10x1-in. baking pan. Spread sour cream over each fillet. Combine the remaining ingredients. Pat crumb-nut mixture onto tops of salmon fillets, pressing to help coating adhere. Bake until fish just begins to flake easily with a fork, 12-15 minutes.

1 salmon fillet: 376 cal., 25g fat (5g sat. fat), 60mg chol., 219mg sod., 15g carb. (3g sugars, 2g fiber), 24g pro. **Diabetic exchanges:** 3 lean meat, 2 fat.

TIMESAVING TIP

Make sure to use plain prepared horseradish, not horseradish sauce or creamed horseradish. For a nice mild flavor, add 1 Tbsp. of horseradish, but feel free to increase to 2 or 3 Tbsp. if you like a little more bite.

Braised Pork Loin Chops

An easy herb rub gives sensational flavor to these pork chops. The meat turns out tender and delicious.
—Marilyn Larsen, Port Orange, FL

Takes: 30 min. • **Makes:** 4 servings

- 1 garlic clove, minced
- 1 tsp. rubbed sage
- 1 tsp. dried rosemary, crushed
- ½ tsp. salt
- ⅛ tsp. pepper
- 4 boneless pork loin chops (½ in. thick and 4 oz. each)
- 1 Tbsp. butter
- 1 Tbsp. olive oil
- ¾ cup dry white wine or apple juice
- 1 Tbsp. minced fresh parsley

1. Mix first 5 ingredients; rub over both sides of pork chops. In a large nonstick skillet, heat butter and oil over medium-high heat; brown chops on both sides. Remove from pan.
2. In same pan, bring wine to a boil, stirring to loosen browned bits from pan. Cook, uncovered, until liquid is reduced to ½ cup. Add chops; return to a boil. Reduce the heat; simmer, covered, until the pork is tender, 6-8 minutes. Sprinkle with parsley.
1 pork chop with 2 Tbsp. sauce: 218 cal., 13g fat (5g sat. fat), 62mg chol., 351mg sod., 3g carb. (2g sugars, 0 fiber), 22g pro.
Diabetic exchanges: 3 lean meat, 1½ fat.

One-Pot Sausage & Basil Pasta

Nothing is better than coming home and being able to have dinner on the table in about 30 minutes. Feel free to top the cooked pasta dish with sauteed mushrooms, zucchini, yellow squash or peppers to get a few extra veggies in your meal. Or add different kinds of sausage or seasonings to create your own version.

—Erin Raatjes, New Lenox, IL

- -

Takes: 30 min. • **Makes:** 8 servings

- 1 pkg. (16 oz.) spaghetti
- 1 pkg. (13 to 14 oz.) smoked turkey sausage, thinly sliced
- 3 cups grape tomatoes, halved
- 2 cups fresh basil leaves, loosely packed
- 1 large onion, thinly sliced
- 4 garlic cloves, thinly sliced
- 4½ cups water
- 1 cup grated Parmesan cheese
- ¾ tsp. salt
- ½ tsp. pepper
- ¾ tsp. crushed red pepper flakes, optional

In a Dutch oven, combine the first 7 ingredients. Bring to a boil; reduce heat and simmer, uncovered, until the pasta is al dente, 8-10 minutes, stirring occasionally. Add Parmesan, salt, and pepper; stir until cheese is melted. If desired, mix in crushed red pepper flakes and top with additional Parmesan cheese.

1 cup: 332 cal., 6g fat (3g sat. fat), 37mg chol., 862mg sod., 49g carb. (5g sugars, 3g fiber), 19g pro.

TIMESAVING TIP

A diet high in sodium can lead to high blood pressure and raise your chances of developing heart disease. To reduce the sodium in this pasta dish, opt for a low-sodium sausage or replace the sausage with cooked shrimp or grilled chicken. To make it even healthier, use whole-wheat spaghetti noodles.

Cajun Grilled Shrimp

The kicked-up marinade on these shrimp makes this a flavor-packed dish. Serve over rice, and make sure to squeeze those charred lemons over the shrimp—that makes them taste extra bright and delicious.
—Sharon Delaney-Chronis, South Milwaukee, WI

Takes: 30 min. • **Makes:** 6 servings

- 3 green onions, finely chopped
- 2 Tbsp. lemon juice
- 1 Tbsp. olive oil
- 3 garlic cloves, minced
- 2 tsp. paprika
- 1 tsp. salt
- ¼ tsp. pepper
- ¼ tsp. cayenne pepper
- 2 lbs. uncooked medium shrimp, peeled and deveined with tails on
- 4 medium lemons, each cut into 8 wedges

1. In a large shallow dish, combine the first 8 ingredients. Add shrimp and turn to coat. Cover; refrigerate for 15 minutes.

2. Drain shrimp, discarding marinade. On 12 metal or soaked wooden skewers, thread the shrimp and lemon wedges.

3. Grill, covered, over medium heat or broil 4 in. from heat until shrimp turn pink, turning once, 6-8 minutes.

2 skewers: 168 cal., 5g fat (1g sat. fat), 184mg chol., 575mg sod., 7g carb. (1g sugars, 2g fiber), 25g pro. **Diabetic exchanges:** 3 lean meat, ½ fruit, ½ fat.

Weeknight Chicken Chop Suey

If you'd like a little extra crunch, serve with chow mein noodles.
—George Utley, South Hill, VA

Takes: 30 min. • **Makes:** 6 servings

- 4 tsp. olive oil
- 1 lb. boneless skinless chicken breasts, cut into 1-in. cubes
- ½ tsp. dried tarragon
- ½ tsp. dried basil
- ½ tsp. dried marjoram
- ½ tsp. grated lemon zest
- 1½ cups chopped carrots
- 1 cup unsweetened pineapple tidbits, drained (reserve juice)
- 1 can (8 oz.) sliced water chestnuts, drained
- 1 medium tart apple, chopped
- ½ cup chopped onion
- 1 cup cold water, divided
- 3 Tbsp. unsweetened pineapple juice
- 3 Tbsp. reduced-sodium teriyaki sauce
- 2 Tbsp. cornstarch
- 3 cups hot cooked brown rice

1. In a large cast-iron or other heavy skillet, heat oil over medium heat. Add chicken, herbs and lemon zest; saute until lightly browned. Add next 5 ingredients. Stir in ¾ cup water, pineapple juice and teriyaki sauce; bring to a boil. Reduce heat; simmer, covered, until chicken is no longer pink and the carrots are tender, 10-15 minutes.

2. Combine the cornstarch and remaining water. Gradually stir into the chicken mixture. Bring to a boil; cook and stir until thickened, about 2 minutes. Serve with rice.

1 cup: 302 cal., 7g fat (1g sat. fat), 63mg chol., 237mg sod., 34g carb. (20g sugars, 5g fiber), 25g pro. **Diabetic exchanges:** 3 lean meat, 3 vegetable, 1 fruit, 1 fat.

Chicken with Peach-Avocado Salsa

This super-fresh dinner is pure summer—juicy peaches, creamy avocado, grilled chicken and a kick of hot sauce and lime. To get it on the table even quicker, make the salsa ahead of time.
—Shannon Norris, Cudahy, WI

Takes: 30 min. • **Makes:** 4 servings

1	medium peach, peeled and chopped
1	medium ripe avocado, peeled and cubed
½	cup chopped sweet red pepper
3	Tbsp. finely chopped red onion
1	Tbsp. minced fresh basil
1	Tbsp. lime juice
1	tsp. hot pepper sauce
½	tsp. grated lime zest
¾	tsp. salt, divided
½	tsp. pepper, divided
4	boneless skinless chicken breast halves (6 oz. each)

1. For salsa, in a small bowl, combine peaches, avocado, red pepper, onion, basil, lime juice, hot sauce, lime zest, ¼ tsp. salt and ¼ tsp. pepper.

2. Sprinkle chicken with remaining salt and pepper. On a lightly greased grill rack, grill chicken, covered, over medium heat for 5 minutes. Turn; grill until a thermometer inserted in chicken reads 165°, 7-9 minutes longer. Serve the chicken with salsa.

1 chicken breast half with ½ cup salsa: 265 cal., 9g fat (2g sat. fat), 94mg chol., 536mg sod., 9g carb. (4g sugars, 3g fiber), 36g pro.
Diabetic exchanges: 5 lean meat, 1 fat, ½ starch.

Walnut & Oat-Crusted Salmon

This tasty salmon is loaded with heart-healthy omega-3 fatty acids. The oat and walnut crust gives it a delicious crunch.
—Cristen Dutcher, Marietta, GA

- -

Takes: 30 min. • **Makes:** 2 servings

2	salmon fillets (6 oz. each), skin removed
¼	tsp. salt
¼	tsp. pepper
3	Tbsp. quick-cooking oats, crushed
3	Tbsp. finely chopped walnuts
2	Tbsp. olive oil

Preheat oven to 400°. Place salmon on a baking sheet; sprinkle with salt and pepper. Combine remaining ingredients; press onto salmon. Bake until fish just begins to flake easily with a fork, 12-15 minutes.

1 fillet: 484 cal., 37g fat (6g sat. fat), 85mg chol., 381mg sod., 7g carb. (0 sugars, 2g fiber), 32g pro. **Diabetic exchanges:** 5 lean meat, 3 fat, ½ starch.

TIMESAVING TIP

Salmon is a terrific source of omega-3 fatty acids, which can help reduce risk of cardiovascular disease and other chronic illnesses.

Air-Fryer Chicken Thighs

Get ready for chicken that is crispy on the outside and juicy on the inside. The paprika and garlic seasoning blend comes through beautifully.
—*Taste of Home* Test Kitchen

- -

Takes: 20 min. • **Makes:** 4 servings

4	**bone-in chicken thighs (about 1½ lbs.)**
1	**Tbsp. olive oil**
¾	**tsp. salt**
½	**tsp. paprika**
¼	**tsp. garlic powder**
¼	**tsp. pepper**

Preheat air fryer to 375°. Brush the chicken with oil. Combine the remaining ingredients; sprinkle over chicken. Place chicken, skin side up, in a single layer on tray in air-fryer basket. Cook 15-17 minutes, or until a thermometer inserted in chicken reads 170°-175°.

1 chicken thigh: 255 cal., 18g fat (4g sat. fat), 81mg chol., 511mg sod., 0 carb. (0 sugars, 0 fiber), 23g pro.

Sheet-Pan
SUPPERS

Grab a sheet pan and a handful of ingredients and serve up a
tasty one-dish meal that will become a new weeknight favorite!

Pepperoni Pizza Baked Potatoes

These taters became a spur-of-the-moment recipe born of leftovers. It's a true mashup meal that combines two dinnertime favorites into one super fun dish.
—Dawn Lowenstein, Huntingdon Valley, PA

- -

Takes: 30 min. • **Makes:** 4 servings

4	medium russet potatoes (about 8 oz. each)
1	Tbsp. olive oil
1	cup sliced fresh mushrooms
1	small green pepper, chopped
1	small onion, chopped
1	garlic clove, minced
1	can (8 oz.) pizza sauce
⅓	cup mini sliced turkey pepperoni
½	cup shredded Italian cheese blend
	Optional: Fresh oregano leaves or dried oregano

1. Preheat oven to 400°. Scrub the potatoes; place on a microwave-safe plate. Pierce several times with a fork. Microwave, uncovered, on high until tender, 12-15 minutes.

2. In a skillet, heat oil over medium-high heat; saute the mushrooms, pepper and onion until tender, 6-8 minutes. Add garlic; cook and stir 1 minute. Stir in pizza sauce and pepperoni; heat through.

3. Place potatoes on a baking sheet; cut an X in the top of each. Fluff pulp with a fork. Top with the vegetable mixture; sprinkle with cheese. Bake until cheese is melted, 5-7 minutes. If desired, sprinkle with oregano.

1 baked potato with toppings: 311 cal., 9g fat (3g sat. fat), 23mg chol., 515mg sod., 46g carb. (5g sugars, 6g fiber), 13g pro. **Diabetic exchanges:** 3 starch, 1 medium-fat meat, ½ fat.

Cod & Asparagus Bake

The lemon pulls this flavorful and healthy dish together. You can also use grated Parmesan cheese instead of Romano.
—Thomas Faglon, Somerset, NJ

Takes: 30 min. • **Makes:** 4 servings

- 4 cod fillets (4 oz. each)
- 1 lb. fresh thin asparagus, trimmed
- 1 pint cherry tomatoes, halved
- 2 Tbsp. lemon juice
- 1½ tsp. grated lemon zest
- ¼ cup grated Romano cheese

1. Preheat oven to 375°. Place cod and asparagus in a 15x10x1-in. baking pan brushed with oil. Add tomatoes, cut sides down. Brush the fish with lemon juice; sprinkle with lemon zest. Sprinkle fish and vegetables with Romano cheese. Bake until fish just begins to flake easily with a fork, about 12 minutes.

2. Remove pan from oven; preheat broiler. Broil cod mixture 3-4 in. from the heat until vegetables are lightly browned, 2-3 minutes.

1 serving: 141 cal., 3g fat (2g sat. fat), 45mg chol., 184mg sod., 6g carb. (3g sugars, 2g fiber), 23g pro.
Diabetic exchanges: 3 lean meat, 1 vegetable.

TIMESAVING TIP

We tested this recipe with cod fillets that were about ¾ in. thick. You'll need to adjust the bake time up or down if your fillets are thicker or thinner.

Lemon-Dijon Pork Sheet-Pan Supper

This sheet-pan dish is an all-time favorite, not only because of its bright flavors, but also because cleanup is super speedy!
—Elisabeth Larsen,
Pleasant Grove, UT

- - - - - - - - - - - - - - - - - -

Prep: 20 min. • **Bake:** 20 min.
Makes: 4 servings

- 4 tsp. Dijon mustard
- 2 tsp. grated lemon zest
- 1 garlic clove, minced
- ½ tsp. salt
- 2 Tbsp. canola oil
- 1½ lbs. sweet potatoes (about 3 medium), cut into ½-in. cubes
- 1 lb. fresh Brussels sprouts (about 4 cups), quartered
- 4 boneless pork loin chops (6 oz. each)
  Coarsely ground pepper, optional

1. Preheat oven to 425°. In a large bowl, mix first 4 ingredients; gradually whisk in oil. Reserve 1 Tbsp. mixture. Add vegetables to remaining mixture; toss to coat.

2. Place pork chops and vegetables in a 15x10x1-in. pan coated with cooking spray. Brush chops with reserved mustard mixture. Roast for 10 minutes.

3. Turn chops and stir vegetables; roast until a thermometer inserted in the pork reads 145° and vegetables are tender, 10-15 minutes longer. If desired, sprinkle with pepper. Let stand 5 minutes before serving.

1 pork chop with 1¼ cups vegetables: 516 cal., 17g fat (4g sat. fat), 82mg chol., 505mg sod., 51g carb. (19g sugars, 9g fiber), 39g pro.

TIMESAVING TIP

Cutting the Brussels sprouts and potatoes fairly small means they'll be perfectly tender by the time the pork is cooked.

Sneaky Turkey Meatballs

Like most kids, mine refuse to eat certain veggies. In order to get healthy foods into their diets, I have to be sneaky sometimes. The recipe's veggies give the meatballs a pleasing texture while providing valuable nutrients—and I'm happy to say that my kids love 'em.
—Courtney Stultz, Weir, KS

- -

Prep: 15 min. • **Bake:** 20 min.
Makes: 6 servings

- ¼ head cauliflower, broken into florets
- ½ cup finely shredded cabbage
- 1 Tbsp. potato starch or cornstarch
- 1 Tbsp. balsamic vinegar
- 1 tsp. sea salt
- 1 tsp. dried basil
- ½ tsp. pepper
- 1 lb. ground turkey
  Optional: Barbecue sauce and fresh basil leaves

1. Preheat oven to 400°. Place the cauliflower in a food processor; pulse until finely chopped. Transfer to a large bowl. Add the cabbage, potato starch, vinegar, salt, basil and pepper.
2. Add ground turkey; mix lightly but thoroughly. With an ice cream scoop or wet hands, shape into 1½-in. balls. Place meatballs on a greased rack in a 15x10x1-in. baking pan. Bake for 20-24 minutes or until cooked through. If desired, toss with the barbecue sauce and top with basil.
2 meatballs: 125 cal., 6g fat (1g sat. fat), 50mg chol., 370mg sod., 4g carb. (1g sugars, 1g fiber), 15g pro.
Diabetic exchanges: 2 medium-fat meat.

Cashew Chicken Sheet-Pan Supper

Enjoy a chicken sheet-pan meal that is tender, flavorful and tangy. The veggies brown up nicely, and the cashews add something extra.
—Jennifer Gilbert, Brighton, MI

- -

Prep: 20 min. • **Bake:** 15 min.
Makes: 4 servings

- ½ cup reduced-sodium soy sauce
- 2 shallots, minced
- 2 Tbsp. brown sugar
- 2 Tbsp. chili sauce
- 1 Tbsp. cider vinegar
- 1 Tbsp. sesame oil
- 2 tsp. rice vinegar
- ½ tsp. ground ginger
- ¼ tsp. garlic powder
- ¼ tsp. pepper
- 1 lb. chicken tenderloins, cubed
- 1 large sweet yellow pepper, cut into strips
- 1 large sweet red pepper, cut into strips
- 4 cups fresh broccoli florets
- 1 cup fresh sugar snap peas
- 1 cup salted cashews

Preheat oven to 400°. Whisk the first 10 ingredients until combined. Place chicken, peppers, broccoli and peas in a foil-lined 15x10x1-in. baking pan. Drizzle with the soy sauce mixture; toss to coat. Sprinkle with cashews. Bake until chicken is no longer pink and vegetables are crisp-tender, 15-20 minutes.
1 serving: 492 cal., 22g fat (4g sat. fat), 56mg chol., 1553mg sod., 38g carb. (17g sugars, 6g fiber), 39g pro.

One-Pan Sweet Chili Shrimp & Veggies

This recipe has everything I'm looking for in a weeknight family dinner: quick, flavorful, nutritious and all three of my kids will eat it. My oldest son loves shrimp, and I thought it could work really well as a sheet-pan supper. I was right!
—Elisabeth Larsen, Pleasant Grove, UT

- -

Takes: 30 min. • **Makes:** 4 servings

- 1   lb. uncooked shrimp (16-20 per lb.), peeled and deveined
- 2   medium zucchini, halved and sliced
- ½   lb. sliced fresh mushrooms
- 1   medium sweet orange pepper, julienned
- 3   Tbsp. sweet chili sauce
- 1   Tbsp. canola oil
- 1   Tbsp. lime juice
- 1   Tbsp. reduced-sodium soy sauce
- 3   green onions, chopped
- ¼   cup minced fresh cilantro

1. Preheat oven to 400°. Place shrimp, zucchini, mushrooms and pepper in a greased 15x10x1-in. baking pan. Combine chili sauce, oil, lime juice and soy sauce. Pour over shrimp mixture and toss to coat.
2. Bake 12-15 minutes or until the shrimp turn pink and vegetables are tender. Sprinkle with green onions and cilantro.
1 serving: 199 cal., 6g fat (1g sat. fat), 138mg chol., 483mg sod., 15g carb. (11g sugars, 3g fiber), 22g pro.

Chicken Provolone

Chicken provolone, though one of my simplest dishes, is one of my husband's favorites. It is easy to prepare and looks fancy served on a dark plate with a garnish of fresh parsley or basil. Add some buttered noodles for an easy side.
—Dawn Bryant, Thedford, NE

- -

Takes: 25 min. • **Makes:** 4 servings

- 4   boneless skinless chicken breast halves (4 oz. each)
- ¼   tsp. pepper
     Butter-flavored cooking spray
- 8   fresh basil leaves
- 4   thin slices prosciutto or deli ham
- 4   slices provolone cheese

1. Sprinkle the chicken with pepper. In a large skillet coated with cooking spray, cook chicken over medium heat until a thermometer reads 165°, 4-5 minutes on each side.

2. Transfer chicken to an ungreased baking sheet; top with the basil, prosciutto and cheese. Broil 6-8 in. from the heat until cheese is melted, 1-2 minutes.
1 serving: 236 cal., 11g fat (6g sat. fat), 89mg chol., 435mg sod., 1g carb. (0 sugars, 0 fiber), 33g pro.
Diabetic exchanges: 4 lean meat.

TIMESAVING TIP

If you're watching your calorie intake, try these easy tips. When you fill your plate, start with smaller portions and don't go back for seconds. If the plate looks too sparse, add some leafy greens. Or use a salad/luncheon plate rather than a dinner plate. Your plate will look full and you can clean it without guilt.

Sheet-Pan Jambalaya with Cauliflower Rice

Sheet-pan dinners are a busy cook's dream with easy prep and cleanup. This Cajun-inspired recipe is a healthy twist on a classic that uses cauliflower rice for a lower-carb supper.
—Julie Peterson, Crofton, MD

- -

Prep: 20 min. • **Bake:** 15 min.
Makes: 4 servings

- 1 medium onion, chopped
- 1 medium green pepper, chopped
- 2 celery ribs, chopped
- 4 oz. boneless skinless chicken breasts, cut into 1-in. pieces
- 2 fully cooked andouille sausage links, sliced
- 4 garlic cloves, minced
- 3 Tbsp. olive oil
- 4 tsp. reduced-sodium Creole seasoning, divided
- 1 pkg. (10 oz.) frozen riced cauliflower
- ½ lb. uncooked shrimp (26-30 per lb.), peeled and deveined
- 2 cups cherry tomatoes, halved

1. Preheat oven to 425°. Place the first 6 ingredients in a 15x10x1-in. baking pan. Drizzle with the oil and sprinkle with 2 tsp. Creole seasoning; toss to coat. Bake 8 minutes.
2. Meanwhile, cook the cauliflower according to package directions. Toss shrimp with remaining 2 tsp. Creole seasoning. Add shrimp, tomatoes and cauliflower to pan; stir to combine. Bake until the shrimp turn pink, 5-7 minutes longer.

1½ cups: 366 cal., 23g fat (6g sat. fat), 158mg chol., 1301mg sod., 14g carb. (6g sugars, 4g fiber), 29g pro.

Baked Teriyaki Pork & Veggies

Minimal preparation makes this dish easy. I use precut broccoli and boneless, trimmed pork chops to save time. Sometimes I throw in multicolored carrots for extra prettiness. Try it served over rice or noodles.
—Billie Davis, Spring Creek, NV

Prep: 15 min. • **Bake:** 30 min.
Makes: 4 servings

- 2 cups fresh broccoli florets
- 1 lb. fresh baby carrots, halved lengthwise
- 1 Tbsp. olive oil
- 1 tsp. minced fresh gingerroot
- ½ tsp. pepper
- ¼ tsp. salt
- 4 boneless pork loin chops (6 oz. each)
- 4 Tbsp. reduced-sodium teriyaki sauce
  Toasted sesame seeds, optional

1. Preheat oven to 375°. Line a 15x10x1-in. pan with foil; add the broccoli and carrots. Toss with olive oil, ginger, pepper and salt; spread out into a single layer.
2. Place the pork chops on top of vegetables; drizzle with teriyaki sauce. Bake until a thermometer inserted in pork reads 145°, about 30 minutes. If desired, preheat broiler; broil chops and vegetables 2-4 in. from heat until browned, 1-2 minutes. Top with the sesame seeds if desired.

1 pork chop with 1 cup vegetables: 322 cal., 13g fat (4g sat. fat), 82mg chol., 613mg sod., 14g carb. (9g sugars, 3g fiber), 35g pro.
Diabetic exchanges: 5 lean meat, 2 vegetable, ½ fat.

Walnut-Crusted Salmon

Whenever I can get salmon for a good price, I always turn to this simple and delicious recipe. It's good served with mashed potatoes and green beans.
—Edie DeSpain, Logan, UT

Takes: 25 min. • **Makes:** 4 servings

- 4 salmon fillets (4 oz. each)
- 4 tsp. Dijon mustard
- 4 tsp. honey
- 2 slices whole wheat bread, torn into pieces
- 3 Tbsp. finely chopped walnuts
- 2 tsp. canola oil
- ½ tsp. dried thyme

1. Preheat oven to 400°. Place salmon on a baking sheet coated with cooking spray. Mix mustard and honey; brush over salmon. Place bread in a food processor; pulse until coarse crumbs form. Transfer to a small bowl. Stir in walnuts, oil and dried thyme; press onto salmon.
2. Bake for 12-15 minutes or until topping is lightly browned and fish just begins to flake easily with a fork.

1 fillet: 295 cal., 17g fat (3g sat. fat), 57mg chol., 243mg sod., 13g carb. (7g sugars, 1g fiber), 22g pro.
Diabetic exchanges: 3 lean meat, 1 starch, ½ fat.

Ham & Pineapple Kabobs

For a twist on the usual fare, my family turns ham and pineapple into juicy sheet-pan kabobs. The marinade gets its unique zip from hoisin, teriyaki and soy sauces.
—Chandra Lane Sirois, Kansas City, MO

- -

Prep: 30 min. + marinating
Bake: 15 min. • **Makes:** 12 servings

¼   cup hoisin sauce
¼   cup unsweetened pineapple juice
¼   cup teriyaki sauce
1   Tbsp. honey
1½ tsp. rice vinegar
1½ tsp. reduced-sodium soy sauce
KABOBS
2   lbs. fully cooked boneless ham, cut into 1-in. pieces
1   large fresh pineapple, peeled, cored and cut into 1-in. cubes (about 4 cups)

1. In a large shallow dish, combine the first 6 ingredients. Add ham; turn to coat. Refrigerate, covered, overnight.
2. Preheat oven to 350°. Drain ham, reserving marinade. For the glaze, pour marinade into a small saucepan; bring to a boil. Reduce the heat; simmer, uncovered, 5-7 minutes or until slightly thickened, stirring occasionally. Remove from heat.
3. Meanwhile, on 12 metal or soaked wooden skewers, alternately thread the ham and pineapple; place in a foil-lined 15x10x1-in. baking pan. Brush kabobs with the glaze. Bake, uncovered, for 15-20 minutes or until lightly browned.
1 kabob: 144 cal., 3g fat (1g sat. fat), 39mg chol., 1109mg sod., 15g carb. (12g sugars, 1g fiber), 15g pro.

Chicken Quinoa Bowls with Balsamic Dressing

I love this recipe because its simplicity allows me to spend time with my family while not sacrificing taste or nutrition. Plus the fresh flavors really shine through!
—Allyson Meyler, Greensboro, NC

- -

Prep: 30 min. + cooling
Broil: 10 min. • **Makes:** 2 servings

¼   cup balsamic vinegar
⅔   cup water
⅓   cup quinoa, rinsed
2   boneless skinless chicken breast halves (6 oz. each)
3   tsp. olive or coconut oil, divided
¼   tsp. garlic powder
½   tsp. salt, divided
¼   tsp. pepper, divided
½   lb. fresh asparagus, trimmed
¼   cup plain Greek yogurt
½   tsp. spicy brown mustard
½   medium ripe avocado, peeled and sliced
6   cherry tomatoes, halved

1. Place vinegar in a small saucepan; bring to a boil. Cook until slightly thickened, 2-3 minutes. Transfer to a bowl; cool completely.
2. In a small saucepan, bring water to a boil. Add quinoa. Reduce the heat; simmer, covered, until the liquid is absorbed, 10-12 minutes. Keep warm.
3. Preheat broiler. Toss chicken with 2 tsp. oil, garlic powder, ¼ tsp. salt and ⅛ tsp. pepper. Place on 1 half of a 15x10x1-in. pan coated with cooking spray. Broil 4 in. from heat 5 minutes. Meanwhile, toss asparagus with the remaining oil, salt and pepper.
4. Remove the pan from oven; turn chicken over. Add asparagus. Broil until a thermometer inserted in the chicken reads 165° and asparagus is tender, 3-5 minutes. Let chicken stand 5 minutes before slicing.
5. For the dressing, stir yogurt and mustard into balsamic reduction. To serve, spoon quinoa into bowls; top with chicken, asparagus, avocado and tomatoes. Serve with dressing.
1 serving: 491 cal., 21g fat (5g sat. fat), 101mg chol., 715mg sod., 35g carb. (12g sugars, 6g fiber), 42g pro.

Sheet-Pan Pineapple Chicken Fajitas

For our fajitas, I combine chicken and pineapple for a different flavor. These fajitas are more on the sweet side, but my family loves them!
—Nancy Heishman, Las Vegas, NV

- -

Prep: 20 min. • **Cook:** 20 min.
Makes: 6 servings

- 2 Tbsp. coconut oil, melted
- 3 tsp. chili powder
- 2 tsp. ground cumin
- 1 tsp. garlic powder
- ¾ tsp. kosher salt
- 1½ lbs. chicken tenderloins, halved lengthwise
- 1 large red or sweet onion, halved and sliced (about 2 cups)
- 1 large sweet red pepper, cut into ½-in. strips
- 1 large green pepper, cut into ½-in. strips
- 1 Tbsp. minced seeded jalapeno pepper
- 2 cans (8 oz. each) unsweetened pineapple tidbits, drained
- 2 Tbsp. honey
- 2 Tbsp. lime juice
- 12 corn tortillas (6 in.), warmed
  Optional: Pico de gallo, sour cream, shredded Mexican cheese blend, sliced avocado and lime wedges

1. Preheat oven to 425°. In a large bowl, mix first 5 ingredients; stir in the chicken. Add onion, peppers, pineapple, honey and lime juice; toss to combine. Spread evenly in 2 greased 15x10x1-in. baking pans.
2. Roast 10 minutes, rotating pans halfway through cooking. Remove pans from oven; preheat broiler.
3. Broil, 1 pan at a time, 3-4 in. from the heat until vegetables are lightly browned and chicken is no longer pink, 3-5 minutes. Serve in tortillas, with optional toppings and lime wedges as desired.
2 fajitas: 359 cal., 8g fat (4g sat. fat), 56mg chol., 372mg sod., 45g carb. (19g sugars, 6g fiber), 31g pro.
Diabetic exchanges: 3 starch, 3 lean meat, 1 fat.

TIMESAVING TIP

If you love pineapple, add even more as a topping or serve with a fruit salsa like peach or pineapple salsa.

Sliced Ham with Roasted Vegetables

To prepare this colorful, zesty oven meal, I shop in my backyard for the fresh garden vegetables and oranges (we have our own tree) that liven up the ham's hearty flavor. It's my family's favorite main dish.
—Margaret Pache, Mesa, AZ

Prep: 10 min. • **Bake:** 35 min.
Makes: 6 servings

Cooking spray
6 medium potatoes, peeled and cubed
5 medium carrots, sliced
1 medium turnip, peeled and cubed
1 large onion, cut into thin wedges
6 slices (4 to 6 oz. each) fully cooked ham, halved
¼ cup thawed orange juice concentrate
2 Tbsp. brown sugar
1 tsp. prepared horseradish
1 tsp. grated orange zest
Coarsely ground pepper

1. Grease two 15x10x1-in. baking pans with cooking spray. Add the potatoes, carrots, turnip and onion; generously coat with cooking spray. Bake, uncovered, at 425° for 25-30 minutes or until tender.
2. Arrange cooked ham slices over vegetables. In a bowl, combine orange juice concentrate, brown sugar, horseradish and orange zest. Spoon over ham and vegetables. Bake until ham is heated through, about 10 minutes longer. Sprinkle with pepper.
1 serving: 375 cal., 5g fat (1g sat. fat), 71mg chol., 1179mg sod., 55g carb. (15g sugars, 7g fiber), 31g pro.

TIMESAVING TIP

Keep an eye on the salmon. If the skillet gets too hot, the outside of the salmon will get too dark before it's cooked through.

Pan-Seared Salmon with Dill Sauce

This is one of my husband's favorite recipes. Salmon is a go-to for busy nights because it cooks so quickly and goes with so many different flavors. The creamy dill sauce with cucumber tastes light and fresh.
—Angela Spengler, Niceville, FL

Takes: 25 min. • **Makes:** 4 servings

1 Tbsp. canola oil
4 salmon fillets (6 oz. each)
1 tsp. Italian seasoning
¼ tsp. salt
½ cup reduced-fat plain yogurt
¼ cup reduced-fat mayonnaise
¼ cup finely chopped cucumber
1 tsp. snipped fresh dill

1. In a large skillet, heat the oil over medium-high heat. Sprinkle salmon with Italian seasoning and salt. Place in skillet, skin side down. Reduce heat to medium. Cook until the fish just begins to flake easily with a fork, about 5 minutes on each side.
2. Meanwhile, combine yogurt, mayonnaise, cucumber and dill. Serve with salmon.
1 salmon fillet with ¼ cup sauce: 366 cal., 25g fat (4g sat. fat), 92mg chol., 349mg sod., 4g carb. (3g sugars, 0 fiber), 31g pro.
Diabetic exchanges: 4 lean meat, 2½ fat.

Chicken Veggie Fajitas

Our family loves the spicy flavor of these fajitas. I also appreciate that they're fast to fix.
—Eleanor Martens, Rosenort, MB

Takes: 20 min. • **Makes:** 4 servings

- 3 Tbsp. lemon juice
- 1 Tbsp. soy sauce
- 1 Tbsp. Worcestershire sauce
- 2 tsp. canola oil
- 1 garlic clove, minced
- ½ tsp. ground cumin
- ½ tsp. dried oregano
- ¾ lb. boneless skinless chicken breasts, cut into ½-in. strips
- 1 small onion, sliced and separated into rings
- ½ each medium green, sweet red and yellow pepper, julienned
- 4 flour tortillas (6 in.), warmed Shredded cheddar cheese, optional

1. In a small bowl, combine the first 7 ingredients. Place the chicken and vegetables in a single layer in a greased 15x10x1-in. baking pan; drizzle with ¼ cup of lemon juice mixture. Broil 4-6 in. from the heat for 4 minutes.

2. Turn chicken and vegetables; drizzle with remaining lemon juice mixture. Broil 4 minutes longer or until chicken juices run clear. Serve on tortillas, with cheese if desired.

1 fajita: 231 cal., 7g fat (1g sat. fat), 47mg chol., 460mg sod., 20g carb. (3g sugars, 1g fiber), 21g pro.
Diabetic exchanges: 2½ lean meat, 1 starch, 1 vegetable.

Rosemary Salmon & Veggies

My husband and I eat a lot of salmon. One night while in a rush to get dinner on the table, I created this meal. It's a keeper! You can also include sliced zucchini, small cauliflower florets or fresh green beans.
—Elizabeth Bramkamp, Gig Harbor, WA

Takes: 30 min. • **Makes:** 4 servings

- 1½ lbs. salmon fillets, cut into 4 portions
- 2 Tbsp. melted coconut oil or olive oil
- 2 Tbsp. balsamic vinegar
- 2 tsp. minced fresh rosemary or ¾ tsp. dried rosemary, crushed
- 1 garlic clove, minced
- ½ tsp. salt
- 1 lb. fresh asparagus, trimmed
- 1 medium sweet red pepper, cut into 1-in. pieces
- ¼ tsp. pepper Lemon wedges, optional

1. Preheat oven to 400°. Place salmon in a greased 15x10x1-in. baking pan. Combine oil, vinegar, rosemary, garlic and salt. Pour half over salmon. Place asparagus and red pepper in a large bowl; drizzle with remaining oil mixture and toss to coat. Arrange around salmon in pan; sprinkle with pepper.

2. Bake until the salmon flakes easily with a fork and vegetables are tender, 12-15 minutes. Serve with lemon wedges if desired.

1 serving: 357 cal., 23g fat (9g sat. fat), 85mg chol., 388mg sod., 7g carb. (4g sugars, 2g fiber), 31g pro.
Diabetic exchanges: 4 lean meat, 1½ fat, 1 vegetable.

Baked Chicken Chimichangas

I developed this quick and easy recipe through trial and error. I used to garnish it with sour cream, too, but I eliminated it in order to lighten the recipe. My friends all love it when I cook these chimichangas, and they're much healthier than deep-fried.
—Rickey Madden, Clinton, SC

- -

Prep: 20 min. • **Bake:** 20 min.
Makes: 6 servings

- 1½ cups cubed cooked chicken breast
- 1½ cups picante sauce, divided
- ½ cup shredded reduced-fat cheddar cheese
- ⅔ cup chopped green onions, divided
- 1 tsp. ground cumin
- 1 tsp. dried oregano
- 6 flour tortillas (8 in.), warmed
- 1 Tbsp. butter, melted
  Sour cream, optional

1. Preheat oven to 375°. In a small bowl, combine chicken, ¾ cup picante sauce, cheese, ¼ cup onions, cumin and oregano. Spoon ½ cup mixture down the center of each tortilla. Fold sides and ends over filling and roll up. Place seam side down in a 15x10x1-in. baking pan coated with cooking spray. Brush with butter.

2. Bake, uncovered, until heated through, 20-25 minutes. If desired, broil until browned, 1 minute. Top with the remaining picante sauce and onions. If desired, serve with sour cream.

Freeze option: Cool the baked chimichangas; wrap and freeze for up to 3 months. Place chimichangas on a baking sheet coated with cooking spray. Preheat oven to 400°. Bake until heated through, 10-15 minutes.

1 chimichanga: 269 cal., 8g fat (3g sat. fat), 39mg chol., 613mg sod., 31g carb. (3g sugars, 1g fiber), 17g pro. **Diabetic exchanges:** 2 lean meat, 1½ starch, 1 vegetable, ½ fat.

Salmon with Balsamic-Honey Glaze

Look no further—you've just found the first, last and only way you'll ever want to fix salmon again. The sweet and tangy flavors blend beautifully in this easy-to-remember recipe.
—Mary Lou Timpson, CO City, AZ

- -

Takes: 30 min. • **Makes:** 8 servings

- ½ cup balsamic vinegar
- 2 Tbsp. white wine or chicken broth
- 2 Tbsp. Dijon mustard
- 2 Tbsp. honey
- 5 garlic cloves, minced
- 1 Tbsp. olive oil
- 8 salmon fillets (6 oz. each)
- ½ tsp. salt
- ½ tsp. pepper
- 1 Tbsp. minced fresh oregano

1. Combine the first 6 ingredients in a small saucepan. Bring to a boil; cook and stir for 4-5 minutes or until thickened.

2. Place salmon skin side down on a greased 15x10x1-in. baking pan. Sprinkle with salt and pepper. Spoon glaze over salmon; top with oregano.

3. Bake, uncovered, at 400° for 12-15 minutes or until fish flakes easily with a fork.

1 fillet: 319 cal., 17g fat (3g sat. fat), 85mg chol., 323mg sod., 9g carb. (8g sugars, 0 fiber), 29g pro. **Diabetic exchanges:** 4 lean meat, ½ starch, ½ fat.

Sweet & Tangy Salmon with Green Beans

I'm always up for new ways to cook salmon. In this dish, a sweet sauce gives the fish and green beans some down-home barbecue tang. Even my kids love it.
—Aliesha Caldwell, Robersonville, NC

- -

Prep: 20 min. • **Bake:** 15 min.
Makes: 4 servings

- 4   salmon fillets (6 oz. each)
- 1   Tbsp. butter
- 2   Tbsp. brown sugar
- 2   Tbsp. reduced-sodium soy sauce
- 2   Tbsp. Dijon mustard
- 1   Tbsp. olive oil
- ½   tsp. pepper
- ⅛   tsp. salt
- 1   lb. fresh green beans, trimmed

1. Preheat oven to 425°. Place fillets in a 15x10x1-in. baking pan coated with cooking spray. In a small skillet, melt butter; stir in brown sugar, soy sauce, mustard, oil, pepper and salt. Brush half of mixture over salmon.
2. Place green beans in a large bowl; drizzle with remaining brown sugar mixture and toss to coat. Arrange green beans around fillets. Roast until fish just begins to flake easily with a fork and green beans are crisp-tender, 14-16 minutes.

1 fillet with ¾ cup green beans: 394 cal., 22g fat (5g sat. fat), 93mg chol., 661mg sod., 17g carb. (10g sugars, 4g fiber), 31g pro.
Diabetic exchanges: 5 lean meat, 1½ fat, 1 vegetable, ½ starch.

Sheet-Pan Tandoori Chicken

This tandoori chicken is easy for busy nights since it uses just one pan, but it's also special enough for company.
—Anwar Khan, Irving, TX

- -

Prep: 20 min. + marinating
Bake: 25 min. • **Makes:** 4 servings

- 1   cup plain Greek yogurt
- 3   Tbsp. tandoori masala seasoning
- ⅛   to ¼ tsp. crushed red pepper flakes, optional
- 8   bone-in chicken thighs (about 3 lbs.), skin removed
- 2   medium sweet potatoes, peeled and cut into ½-in. wedges
- 1   Tbsp. olive oil
- 16 cherry tomatoes
     Lemon slices
     Optional: Minced fresh cilantro and naan flatbreads

1. In a large bowl, whisk the yogurt, seasoning and, if desired, red pepper flakes until blended. Add chicken; turn to coat. Cover and refrigerate 6-8 hours, turning occasionally.
2. Preheat oven to 450°. Drain the chicken, discarding marinade in bowl. Place the chicken in a greased 15x10x1-in. baking pan. Add sweet potatoes; drizzle with oil. Bake for 15 minutes. Add tomatoes and lemon. Bake until a thermometer inserted into the chicken reads 170°-175°, 10-15 minutes longer. Broil 4-5 in. from the heat until browned, 4-5 minutes. If desired, serve with cilantro and naan.

2 chicken thighs with 1 cup sweet potatoes and 4 tomatoes: 589 cal., 27g fat (9g sat. fat), 186mg chol., 187mg sod., 29g carb. (13g sugars, 6g fiber), 52g pro.

Parmesan Chicken with Artichoke Hearts

With all the praise it gets, this dinner is so much fun to serve.
—Carly Giles, Ephraim, UT

- -

Prep: 20 min. • **Bake:** 20 min.
Makes: 4 servings

- 4   boneless skinless chicken breast halves (6 oz. each)
- 3   tsp. olive oil, divided
- 1   tsp. dried rosemary, crushed
- ½   tsp. dried thyme
- ½   tsp. pepper
- 2   cans (14 oz. each) water-packed artichoke hearts, drained and quartered
- 1   medium onion, coarsely chopped
- ½   cup white wine or reduced-sodium chicken broth
- 2   garlic cloves, chopped
- ¼   cup shredded Parmesan cheese
- 1   lemon, cut into 8 slices
- 2   green onions, thinly sliced

1. Preheat oven to 375°. Place the chicken in a 15x10x1-in. baking pan coated with cooking spray; drizzle with 1½ tsp. oil. In a small bowl, mix the rosemary, thyme and pepper; sprinkle half over chicken.
2. In a large bowl, combine artichoke hearts, onion, wine, garlic, remaining oil and remaining herb mixture; toss to coat. Arrange around the chicken. Sprinkle with cheese; top with lemon.
3. Roast for 20-25 minutes or until a thermometer inserted in the chicken reads 165°. Sprinkle with green onions.

1 chicken breast half with ¾ cup artichoke mixture: 339 cal., 9g fat (3g sat. fat), 98mg chol., 667mg sod., 18g carb. (2g sugars, 1g fiber), 42g pro.
Diabetic exchanges: 5 lean meat, 1 vegetable, 1 fat, ½ starch.

Pork & Asparagus Sheet-Pan Dinner

When time is of the essence, it's nice to have this easy recipe on hand.
—Joan Hallford,
North Richland Hills, TX

- -

Prep: 20 min. • **Bake:** 20 min.
Makes: 4 servings

- ¼   cup olive oil, divided
- 3   cups diced new potatoes
- 3   cups cut fresh asparagus (1-in. pieces)
- ¼   tsp. salt
- ¼   tsp. pepper
- 1   large gala or Honeycrisp apple, peeled and cut into 1-in. wedges
- 2   tsp. brown sugar
- 1   tsp. ground cinnamon
- ¼   tsp. ground ginger
- 4   boneless pork loin chops (1 in. thick and about 6 oz. each)
- 2   tsp. Southwest seasoning

1. Preheat oven to 425°. Line a 15x10x1-in. baking pan with foil; brush with 2 tsp. olive oil.
2. In a large bowl, toss potatoes with 1 Tbsp. olive oil. Place in 1 section of prepared baking pan. In same bowl, toss asparagus with 1 Tbsp. olive oil; place in another section of the pan. Sprinkle salt and pepper over the potatoes and asparagus.
3. In same bowl, toss apple with 1 tsp. olive oil. In a small bowl, mix brown sugar, cinnamon and ginger; sprinkle over apples and toss to coat. Transfer to a different section of pan.
4. Brush pork chops with remaining 1 Tbsp. olive oil; sprinkle both sides with Southwest seasoning. Place chops in remaining section of pan. Bake until a thermometer inserted in pork reads 145° and potatoes and apples are tender, 20-25 minutes. Let stand 5 minutes before serving.
1 serving: 486 cal., 23g fat (5g sat. fat), 82mg chol., 447mg sod., 32g carb. (10g sugars, 5g fiber), 37g pro.

Easy Weeknight BOWLS

Leave the plates in the cupboard tonight. These light and simple dinner ideas taste best when scooped from a bowl.

Asian Chicken Rice Bowl

This super flavorful, nutrient-packed dish makes use of supermarket conveniences like coleslaw mix and rotisserie chicken. This recipe is easily doubled or tripled for large families.
—Christianna Gozzi, Astoria, NY

- -

Takes: 20 min. • **Makes:** 4 servings

¼   cup rice vinegar
1   green onion, minced
2   Tbsp. reduced-sodium soy sauce
1   Tbsp. toasted sesame seeds
1   Tbsp. sesame oil
1   Tbsp. honey
1   tsp. minced fresh gingerroot
1   pkg. (8.8 oz.) ready-to-serve brown rice
4   cups coleslaw mix (about 9 oz.)
2   cups shredded rotisserie chicken, chilled
2   cups frozen shelled edamame, thawed

1. For dressing, whisk together first 7 ingredients. Cook rice according to package directions. Divide among 4 bowls.

2. In a large bowl, toss coleslaw mix and chicken with half of the dressing. Serve edamame and slaw mixture over rice; drizzle with remaining dressing.

1 serving: 429 cal., 15g fat (2g sat. fat), 62mg chol., 616mg sod., 38g carb. (13g sugars, 5g fiber), 32g pro. **Diabetic exchanges:** 3 lean meat, 2 starch, 1 vegetable, 1 fat.

Chicken & Bows

I first made this when I was working as a professional nanny. It comes together quickly at dinnertime when the kids are hungry.
—Danette Forbes, Overland Park, KS

- -

Takes: 25 min. • **Makes:** 8 servings

- 1 pkg. (16 oz.) bow tie pasta
- 2 lbs. boneless skinless chicken breasts, cut into strips
- 1 cup chopped sweet red pepper
- ¼ cup butter, cubed
- 2 cans (10¾ oz. each) condensed cream of chicken soup, undiluted
- 2 cups frozen peas
- 1½ cups 2% milk
- 1 tsp. garlic powder
- ¼ to ½ tsp. salt
- ¼ tsp. pepper
- ⅔ cup grated Parmesan cheese
  Crushed red pepper flakes, optional

1. Cook pasta according to package directions. Meanwhile, in a Dutch oven, cook the chicken and red pepper in butter over medium heat until chicken is no longer pink, 5-6 minutes.

2. Stir in soup, peas, milk, garlic powder, salt and pepper; heat through. Stir in Parmesan cheese. Drain pasta; add to chicken mixture and toss to coat. If desired, sprinkle with crushed red pepper flakes.

1¼ cups: 536 cal., 18g fat (8g sat. fat), 94mg chol., 908mg sod., 57g carb. (7g sugars, 5g fiber), 37g pro.
Diabetic exchanges: 3 lean meat, 3 very lean meat, 2 starch, 2 fat.

Stir-Fry Rice Bowl

My meatless version of Korean bibimbap is tasty, pretty and easy to tweak for different spice levels.
—Devon Delaney, Westport, CT

- -

Takes: 30 min. • **Makes:** 4 servings

- 1 Tbsp. canola oil
- 2 medium carrots, julienned
- 1 medium zucchini, julienned
- ½ cup sliced baby portobello mushrooms
- 1 cup bean sprouts
- 1 cup fresh baby spinach
- 1 Tbsp. water
- 1 Tbsp. reduced-sodium soy sauce
- 1 Tbsp. chili garlic sauce
- 4 large eggs
- 3 cups hot cooked brown rice
- 1 tsp. sesame oil

1. In a large skillet, heat canola oil over medium-high heat. Add carrots, zucchini and mushrooms; cook and stir 3-5 minutes or until carrots are crisp-tender. Add bean sprouts, spinach, water, soy sauce and chili sauce; cook and stir just until the spinach is wilted. Remove from heat; keep warm.

2. Place 2-3 in. of water in a large skillet with high sides. Bring to a boil; adjust the heat to maintain a gentle simmer. Break cold eggs, 1 at a time, into a small bowl; holding bowl close to surface of water, gently slip each egg into water.

3. Cook, uncovered, 3-5 minutes or until whites are completely set and yolks begin to thicken but are not hard. Using a slotted spoon, lift eggs out of water.

4. Serve rice in bowls; top with vegetables. Drizzle with sesame oil. Top each serving with a poached egg.

1 serving: 305 cal., 11g fat (2g sat. fat), 186mg chol., 364mg sod., 40g carb. (4g sugars, 4g fiber), 12g pro.
Diabetic exchanges: 2 starch, 1 vegetable, 1 medium-fat meat, 1 fat.

Israeli Couscous & Chicken Sausage Skillet

Craving a plate full of comfort? With sausage, onion, celery, a touch of heat and a sprinkle of feta, this is hearty, satisfying and a little bit different. My family loves it.

—Angela Spengler, Niceville, FL

- -

Takes: 30 min. • **Makes:** 4 servings

2 tsp. olive oil
1 pkg. (12 oz.) fully cooked spinach and feta chicken sausage links or flavor of your choice, sliced
1 small onion, finely chopped
1 celery rib, finely chopped
1 garlic clove, minced
1 cup reduced-sodium chicken broth
1 cup water
¼ tsp. crushed red pepper flakes
1¼ cups uncooked pearl (Israeli) couscous
2 Tbsp. minced fresh parsley
¼ cup crumbled feta cheese, optional

1. In a large nonstick skillet, heat oil over medium-high heat. Add sausage, onion and celery; cook and stir until sausage is browned, 6-8 minutes. Add garlic; cook 1 minute longer.
2. Stir in broth, water and pepper flakes; bring to a boil. Stir in the couscous. Reduce heat; simmer, covered, until liquid is absorbed, 10-12 minutes. Remove from heat; let stand, covered, 5 minutes. Stir in parsley. If desired, sprinkle with cheese.
1 cup: 343 cal., 10g fat (3g sat. fat), 65mg chol., 694mg sod., 41g carb. (1g sugars, 1g fiber), 22g pro.
Diabetic exchanges: 3 starch, 3 lean meat, ½ fat.

Groundnut Stew

My Aunt Linda was a missionary in Africa for more than 40 years and gave me the recipe for this cozy stew with a hint of peanut butter.

—Heather Ewald, Bothell, WA

- -

Takes: 30 min. • **Makes:** 7 servings

6 oz. lamb stew meat, cut into ½-in. pieces
6 oz. pork stew meat, cut into ½-in. pieces
2 Tbsp. peanut oil
1 large onion, cut into wedges
1 large green pepper, cut into wedges
1 cup chopped tomatoes
4 cups cubed eggplant
2 cups water
½ cup fresh or frozen sliced okra
½ cup creamy peanut butter
1 tsp. salt
½ tsp. pepper
   Hot cooked rice
   Chopped green onions, optional

1. In a large skillet, brown meat in oil; set aside. In a food processor, combine the onion, green pepper and tomatoes; cover and process until blended.
2. In a large saucepan, combine eggplant, water, okra and onion mixture. Bring to a boil. Reduce heat; cook, uncovered, until the vegetables are tender, 7-9 minutes.
3. Stir in the peanut butter, salt, pepper and browned meat. Cook, uncovered, until heated through, about 10 minutes. Serve with hot cooked rice. If desired, top with chopped green onions.
Freeze option: Freeze cooled stew in freezer containers. To use, partially thaw in refrigerator overnight. Heat through in a saucepan, stirring occasionally; add a little broth or water if necessary.
1 cup: 230 cal., 13g fat (3g sat. fat), 31mg chol., 470mg sod., 14g carb. (7g sugars, 4g fiber), 16g pro.
Diabetic exchanges: 2 lean meat, 1 starch, 1 fat.

Sesame Beef & Asparagus Salad

Cooking is one of my all-time favorite hobbies—especially when it involves experimenting with fresh ingredients. This meaty salad is wonderful at the start of asparagus season.
—Tamara Steeb, Issaquah, WA

- -

Takes: 30 min. • **Makes:** 6 servings

- 1 beef top round steak (1 lb.)
- 4 cups cut fresh asparagus (2-in. pieces)
- 3 Tbsp. reduced-sodium soy sauce
- 2 Tbsp. sesame oil
- 1 Tbsp. rice vinegar
- ½ tsp. grated gingerroot
  Sesame seeds
  Optional: Lettuce leaves, julienned carrot and radishes, cilantro leaves and lime wedges

1. Preheat broiler. Place steak on a broiler pan. Broil 2-3 in. from heat until meat reaches desired doneness (for medium-rare, a thermometer should read 135°), 6-7 minutes per side. Let steak stand 5 minutes before slicing.

2. In a large saucepan, bring ½ in. water to a boil. Add asparagus; cook, uncovered, just until crisp-tender, 3-5 minutes. Drain and cool.

3. Mix soy sauce, sesame oil, vinegar and ginger; toss with the beef and asparagus. Sprinkle with sesame seeds. If desired, serve over lettuce with carrot, radishes, cilantro and lime wedges.

1 cup: 160 cal., 7g fat (1g sat. fat), 42mg chol., 350mg sod., 5g carb. (2g sugars, 2g fiber), 19g pro.
Diabetic exchanges: 2 lean meat, 1 vegetable, 1 fat.

Egg Roll Noodle Bowl

We love Asian egg rolls, but they can be challenging to make. Simplify everything with this deconstructed egg roll made on the stovetop and served in a bowl.
—Courtney Stultz, Weir, KS

- -

Takes: 30 min. • **Makes:** 4 servings

- 1 Tbsp. sesame oil
- ½ lb. ground pork
- 1 Tbsp. soy sauce
- 1 garlic clove, minced
- 1 tsp. ground ginger
- ½ tsp. salt
- ¼ tsp. ground turmeric
- ¼ tsp. pepper
- 6 cups shredded cabbage (about 1 small head)
- 2 large carrots, shredded (about 2 cups)
- 4 oz. rice noodles
- 3 green onions, thinly sliced
  Additional soy sauce, optional

1. In a large cast-iron or other heavy skillet, heat oil over medium-high heat; cook and crumble pork until browned, 4-6 minutes. Stir in soy sauce, garlic and seasonings. Add cabbage and carrots; cook until vegetables are tender, stirring occasionally, 4-6 minutes longer.

2. Cook rice noodles according to the package directions; drain and immediately add to pork mixture, tossing to combine. Sprinkle with green onions. If desired, serve with additional soy sauce.

1½ cups: 302 cal., 12g fat (4g sat. fat), 38mg chol., 652mg sod., 33g carb. (2g sugars, 4g fiber), 14g pro.
Diabetic exchanges: 2 vegetable, 2 medium-fat meat, 1½ starch, ½ fat.

Pressure-Cooker Spicy Lime Chicken

This tender chicken with light lime flavor is a natural filling for tacos, but my son Austin also loves it spooned over cooked rice and sprinkled with his favorite taco toppings.
—Christine Hair, Odessa, FL

- -

Prep: 10 min. • **Cook:** 10 min.
Makes: 6 servings

- 4 boneless skinless chicken breast halves (6 oz. each)
- 2 cups chicken broth
- 3 Tbsp. lime juice
- 1 Tbsp. chili powder
- 1 tsp. grated lime zest
   Fresh cilantro leaves, optional

1. Place chicken in a 6-qt. electric pressure cooker. Combine broth, lime juice and chili powder; pour over chicken. Lock lid; close the pressure-release valve. Adjust to pressure-cook on high for 6 minutes.

2. Quick-release pressure. Insert a thermometer in the thickest part of chicken. Thermometer should read at least 165°.

3. Remove the chicken. When cool enough to handle, shred meat with 2 forks; return to pressure cooker. Stir in lime zest. If desired, serve with cilantro.

Freeze option: Freeze cooled meat mixture in freezer containers. To use, partially thaw in the refrigerator overnight. Microwave, covered, on high in a microwave-safe dish until heated through, stirring occasionally; add a little broth if necessary.

1 serving: 132 cal., 3g fat (1g sat. fat), 64mg chol., 420mg sod., 2g carb. (1g sugars, 1g fiber), 23g pro.
Diabetic exchanges: 3 lean meat.

Pressure-Cooker Red Beans & Rice

My family loves New Orleans-style cooking, so I make this dish often. I appreciate how simple it is, and the smoky ham flavor is scrumptious.
—Celinda Dahlgren, Napa, CA

- -

Prep: 20 min.
Cook: 45 min. + releasing
Makes: 6 servings

- 3 cups water
- 2 smoked ham hocks (about 1 lb.)
- 1 cup dried red beans
- 1 medium onion, chopped
- 1½ tsp. minced garlic
- 1 tsp. ground cumin
- 1 medium tomato, chopped
- 1 medium green pepper, chopped
- 1 tsp. salt
- 4 cups hot cooked rice

1. Place the first 6 ingredients in a 6-qt. electric pressure cooker. Lock lid; close pressure-release valve. Adjust to pressure-cook on high for 35 minutes. Let pressure release naturally.

2. Remove ham hocks; cool slightly. Remove meat from bones. Finely chop meat and return to pressure cooker; discard bones. Stir in tomato, green pepper and salt. Select saute setting and adjust for low heat. Simmer, stirring constantly, until the pepper is tender, 8-10 minutes. Serve with rice.

Freeze option: Freeze cooled bean mixture in freezer containers. To use, partially thaw in the refrigerator overnight. Microwave, covered, on high in a microwave-safe dish until heated through, gently stirring and adding a little water if necessary.

⅓ cup bean mixture with ⅔ cup rice: 216 cal., 2g fat (0 sat. fat), 9mg chol., 671mg sod., 49g carb. (3g sugars, 12g fiber), 12g pro.

For maximum juiciness, look for bright, smooth limes at the supermarket and steer away from any with dry skin.

Sausage, Spinach & Gnocchi

I get creative in the kitchen when I'm too busy to go to the grocery store. My daughter loves this dish, and it's easy for her little fingers to pick up while she's still learning to use utensils.

—Carla Andrews, Lorton, VA

- -

Takes: 30 min. • **Makes:** 4 servings

- 1 **pkg. (16 oz.) potato gnocchi**
- 1 **Tbsp. olive oil**
- 3 **Italian turkey sausage links (4 oz. each), casings removed**
- 1 **garlic clove, minced**
- 1 **pkg. (6 oz.) fresh baby spinach**
- 2 **medium tomatoes, coarsely chopped**
- 1½ **cups spaghetti sauce**

1. Cook gnocchi according to the package directions; drain. Meanwhile, in a large skillet, heat oil over medium heat; cook sausage 5-7 minutes or until no longer pink, breaking up the sausage into crumbles. Add garlic; cook 1 minute longer. Drain. Add the spinach and tomatoes; cook and stir just until spinach is wilted.
2. Stir in gnocchi and spaghetti sauce; heat through.

Freeze option: Freeze cooled gnocchi mixture in freezer containers. To use, partially thaw in refrigerator overnight. Heat through in a skillet, stirring occasionally and adding a little water if necessary.

Note: Look for potato gnocchi in the pasta or frozen foods section.

1¼ cups: 442 cal., 14g fat (3g sat. fat), 42mg chol., 1341mg sod., 60g carb. (15g sugars, 6g fiber), 20g pro.

Quickpea Curry

This colorful curry is a nice change of pace for a busy night. I substitute fresh peas for frozen when they're in season.

—Beth Fleming, Downers Grove, IL

- -

Prep: 15 min. • **Cook:** 35 min.
Makes: 6 servings

- 1 **Tbsp. canola oil**
- 1 **medium onion, finely chopped**
- 2 **garlic cloves, minced**
- 1 **Tbsp. curry powder**
- 2 **cans (14½ oz. each) diced tomatoes, undrained**
- 2 **cans (15 oz. each) chickpeas or garbanzo beans, rinsed and drained**
- 2 **cups cubed peeled sweet potato (about 1 medium)**
- 1 **cup light coconut milk**
- 2 **tsp. sugar**
- ¼ **tsp. crushed red pepper flakes**
- 1 **cup uncooked whole wheat pearl (Israeli) couscous**
- 1½ **cups frozen peas (about 6 oz.)**
- ¼ **tsp. salt**
  Chopped fresh parsley
  Plain yogurt, optional

1. In a large skillet, heat oil over medium heat; saute onion and garlic with curry powder until tender, 3-4 minutes. Stir in the tomatoes, chickpeas, sweet potato, coconut milk, sugar and pepper flakes; bring to a boil. Reduce heat; simmer, uncovered, until mixture is thickened and potatoes are tender, 25-30 minutes, stirring occasionally.
2. Meanwhile, prepare couscous and peas separately according to package directions. Stir salt into peas.
3. To serve, divide couscous among 6 bowls. Top with chickpea mixture, peas, parsley and, if desired, yogurt.

1 serving: 390 cal., 8g fat (2g sat. fat), 0 chol., 561mg sod., 68g carb. (14g sugars, 13g fiber), 13g pro.

Slow-Cooker Honey Teriyaki Chicken

This recipe is a snap to whip up on a workday, and tastes just like Chinese takeout! My kids love it, and they don't even know it's healthy.
—Rachel Ruiz, Fort Walton Beach, FL

Prep: 20 min. • **Cook:** 3¾ hours
Makes: 8 servings

- 2 lbs. boneless skinless chicken thighs
- 1 medium onion, thinly sliced
- 4 garlic cloves, minced
- 1 Tbsp. minced fresh gingerroot
- 1 cup chicken broth
- ¼ cup soy sauce
- ¼ cup honey
- ½ to 1 tsp. crushed red pepper flakes
- ¼ tsp. pepper
- 3 Tbsp. cornstarch
- 3 Tbsp. cold water
  Hot cooked rice
  Optional: Minced fresh cilantro and sesame seeds

1. Place chicken in a 3- or 4-qt. slow cooker. Top with onion, garlic and ginger. Combine broth, soy sauce, honey, pepper flakes and pepper; pour over chicken. Cook, covered, on low until chicken is no longer pink, 3½-4 hours.

2. In a small bowl, mix cornstarch and water until smooth; gradually stir into slow cooker. Cook, covered, on high until the sauce is thickened, 15-30 minutes. When chicken is cool enough to handle, shred with 2 forks; return to slow cooker. Serve with rice. If desired, garnish with cilantro and sesame seeds.

⅔ cup: 223 cal., 8g fat (2g sat. fat), 76mg chol., 647mg sod., 14g carb. (9g sugars, 0 fiber), 22g pro.
Diabetic exchanges: 3 lean meat, 1 starch.

Vermicelli Beef Stew

I love to try new recipes, whether I'm making something new for guests while entertaining or whipping up a small meal for just for my husband and me. This stew is different from most because of the vermicelli.
—Sharon Delaney-Chronis, South Milwaukee, WI

- -

Prep: 20 min. • **Cook:** 8½ hours
Makes: 8 servings (2 qt.)

- 1½ lbs. beef stew meat, cut into 1-in. cubes
- 1 medium onion, chopped
- 2 Tbsp. canola oil
- 3 cups water
- 1 can (14½ oz.) diced tomatoes
- 1 pkg. (16 oz.) frozen mixed vegetables, thawed
- 1 Tbsp. dried basil
- 1 tsp. salt
- 1 tsp. dried oregano
- 6 oz. uncooked vermicelli, broken into 2-in. pieces
- ¼ cup grated Parmesan cheese

1. In a large skillet, brown meat and onion in oil; drain. Transfer to a 5-qt. slow cooker. Stir in water, tomatoes, vegetables, basil, salt and oregano. Cover and cook on low 8-10 hours or until meat and vegetables are tender.
2. Stir in vermicelli. Cover and cook for 30 minutes or until pasta is tender. Sprinkle with cheese.
1 cup: 294 cal., 10g fat (3g sat. fat), 55mg chol., 455mg sod., 28g carb. (5g sugars, 5g fiber), 22g pro.
Diabetic exchanges: 2 vegetable, 2 lean meat, 1 starch, 1 fat.

Shrimp & Spinach Salad with Hot Bacon Dressing

When I meet former co-workers for lunch at our favorite restaurant, we always order this salad. I wanted to share it with my husband, so I made it my challenge to re-create it at home. Mission accomplished!
—Lisa Bynum, Brandon, MS

- -

Takes: 30 min. • **Makes:** 6 servings

1½ **lbs. uncooked shrimp (31-40 per lb.), peeled and deveined**
1 **tsp. Montreal steak seasoning**
4 **bacon strips, chopped**
1 **shallot, finely chopped**
⅓ **cup cider vinegar**
1 **Tbsp. olive oil**
1 **tsp. Dijon mustard**
½ **tsp. sugar**
½ **tsp. salt**
¼ **tsp. pepper**
1 **pkg. (10 oz.) fresh spinach**
¾ **cup julienned roasted sweet red peppers**
¼ **cup sliced almonds**

1. Sprinkle the shrimp with steak seasoning. On 4 metal or soaked wooden skewers, thread shrimp. Grill, covered, over medium heat or broil 4 in. from heat until shrimp turn pink, 2-3 minutes on each side.

2. Meanwhile, in a large skillet, cook bacon over medium heat until crisp, stirring occasionally. Remove with a slotted spoon; drain on paper towels. Discard all but 1 Tbsp. drippings. Add shallot; cook and stir over medium heat until tender, 1-2 minutes. Stir in next 6 ingredients; bring to a boil. Remove from heat.

3. In a large serving bowl, combine spinach and dressing; toss to coat. Layer with shrimp and pepper slices; top with cooked bacon and almonds.

1½ cups: 212 cal., 10g fat (2g sat. fat), 145mg chol., 739mg sod., 6g carb. (2g sugars, 1g fiber), 22g pro. **Diabetic exchanges:** 3 lean meat, 2 vegetable, 2 fat.

Chicken Orzo Skillet

As a busy mom with a home-based business, I try to make quick dinners that are healthy for my husband, myself and our two young children. I combined two recipes to come up with this family favorite.
—Kathleen Farrell, Rochester, NY

- -

Takes: 30 min. • **Makes:** 6 servings

- 1 **cup uncooked orzo pasta**
- 1 **lb. boneless skinless chicken breasts, cubed**
- 3 **tsp. olive oil, divided**
- 3 **garlic cloves, minced**
- 2 **cans (14½ oz. each) stewed tomatoes, cut up**
- 1 **can (15 oz.) cannellini beans, rinsed and drained**
- 1½ **tsp. Italian seasoning**
- ½ **tsp. salt**
- 1 **pkg. (16 oz.) frozen broccoli florets, thawed**

1. Cook orzo according to package directions. Meanwhile, in a large nonstick skillet, cook chicken in 2 tsp. oil for 6-7 minutes or until no longer pink. Remove and keep warm.

2. In the same skillet, cook garlic in remaining oil for 1 minute or until tender. Stir in the tomatoes, beans, Italian seasoning and salt. Bring to a boil. Stir in broccoli and chicken; heat through. Drain orzo; stir into chicken mixture.

1½ cups: 342 cal., 5g fat (1g sat. fat), 42mg chol., 589mg sod., 49g carb. (9g sugars, 7g fiber), 25g pro.
Diabetic exchanges: 3 vegetable, 2 starch, 2 lean meat, ½ fat.

Chili Mac

This recipe has regularly appeared on my family menus for more than 40 years, and it's never failed to please at potlucks and other bring-a-dish gatherings. Sometimes I turn it into soup by adding a can of beef broth.
—Marie Posavec, Berwyn, IL

- -

Prep: 15 min. • **Cook:** 6 hours
Makes: 6 servings

- 1 lb. lean ground beef (90% lean), cooked and drained
- 2 cans (16 oz. each) hot chili beans, undrained
- 2 large green peppers, chopped
- 1 large onion, chopped
- 4 celery ribs, chopped
- 1 can (8 oz.) no-salt-added tomato sauce
- 2 Tbsp. chili seasoning mix
- 2 garlic cloves, minced
- 1 pkg. (7 oz.) elbow macaroni, cooked and drained
  Salt and pepper to taste
  Optional: Shredded pepper jack cheese and sliced jalapeno pepper

In a 5-qt. slow cooker, combine the first 8 ingredients. Cover and cook on low for 6 hours or until heated through. Stir in macaroni. Season with salt and pepper. If desired, top the servings with cheese and sliced jalapenos.

1 serving: 348 cal., 8g fat (3g sat. fat), 47mg chol., 713mg sod., 49g carb. (8g sugars, 12g fiber), 27g pro.
Diabetic exchanges: 3 starch, 3 lean meat.

Weeknight Pasta Squiggles

This zesty pasta dish is ideal for busy weeknights. It calls for only a few basic ingredients and is easy to prep. Your family will love the warm, comforting flavor when the weather turns cool. A salad on the side makes it a meal.
—Stacey Brown, Spring, TX

- -

Takes: 30 min. • **Makes:** 8 servings

1	pkg. (19½ oz.) Italian turkey sausage links, casings removed
1	can (28 oz.) whole plum tomatoes with basil
1	can (14½ oz.) no-salt-added whole tomatoes
4	cups uncooked spiral pasta (about 12 oz.)
1	can (14½ oz.) reduced-sodium chicken broth
¼	cup water
½	cup crumbled goat or feta cheese

1. In a Dutch oven, cook and crumble turkey sausage over medium-high heat for 5-7 minutes or until no longer pink. Meanwhile, coarsely chop tomatoes, reserving juices.
2. Add tomatoes and reserved juices to sausage; stir in pasta, broth and water. Bring to a boil. Reduce heat to medium; cook, uncovered, until pasta is al dente, 15-18 minutes, stirring occasionally. Top with cheese.
1½ cups: 278 cal., 7g fat (2g sat. fat), 34mg chol., 622mg sod., 38g carb. (5g sugars, 4g fiber), 16g pro.
Diabetic exchanges: 2½ starch, 2 medium-fat meat.

Shredded Barbecue Chicken over Grits

There's nothing like juicy barbecue-flavored meat sitting atop a scoop of hot grits. The ancho chile pepper and pepper jack cheese give it a nice Southwestern zip, but it's easy to adjust if you don't like it too spicy.
—Erin Mylroie, Santa Clara, UT

- -

Prep: 20 min. • **Cook:** 25 min.
Makes: 6 servings

1	lb. boneless skinless chicken breasts
¼	tsp. pepper
1	can (14½ oz.) reduced-sodium chicken broth, divided
1	cup hickory smoke-flavored barbecue sauce
¼	cup molasses
1	Tbsp. ground ancho chile pepper
½	tsp. ground cinnamon
2¼	cups water
1	cup quick-cooking grits
1	cup canned pumpkin
¾	cup shredded pepper jack cheese
1	medium tomato, seeded and chopped
6	Tbsp. reduced-fat sour cream
2	green onions, chopped
2	Tbsp. minced fresh cilantro

1. Sprinkle chicken with pepper; place in a large nonstick skillet.
2. In a large bowl, combine 1 cup broth, barbecue sauce, molasses, chile pepper and cinnamon; pour over the chicken. Bring to a boil. Reduce heat; cover and simmer until a thermometer inserted in chicken reads 165°, 20-25 minutes. Shred meat with 2 forks and return to the skillet.
3. Meanwhile, in a large saucepan, bring water and remaining broth to a boil. Slowly stir in grits and pumpkin. Reduce heat; cook and stir until thickened, 5-7 minutes. Stir in cheese until melted.
4. Divide grits among 6 serving bowls; top each with ½ cup chicken mixture. Serve with tomato, sour cream, green onions and cilantro.
1 serving: 345 cal., 9g fat (4g sat. fat), 62mg chol., 718mg sod., 42g carb. (17g sugars, 4g fiber), 25g pro.
Diabetic exchanges: 3 lean meat, 2½ starch, 1 fat.

Korean Beef & Rice

A friend raved about Korean bulgogi—beef cooked in soy sauce and ginger—so I tried it. It's delicious! Dazzle the table with this tasty version of beef and rice.
—Elizabeth King, Duluth, MN

Takes: 15 min. • **Makes:** 4 servings

- 1 lb. lean ground beef (90% lean)
- 3 garlic cloves, minced
- ¼ cup packed brown sugar
- ¼ cup reduced-sodium soy sauce
- 2 tsp. sesame oil
- ¼ tsp. ground ginger
- ¼ tsp. crushed red pepper flakes
- ¼ tsp. pepper
- 2⅔ cups hot cooked brown rice
- 3 green onions, thinly sliced

1. In a large skillet, cook beef and garlic over medium heat until beef is no longer pink, 6-8 minutes, breaking up beef into crumbles. Meanwhile, in a small bowl, mix brown sugar, soy sauce, oil and seasonings.
2. Stir sauce into beef; heat through. Serve with rice. Sprinkle with sliced green onions.
Freeze option: Freeze cooled meat mixture in freezer containers. To use, partially thaw mixture in refrigerator overnight. Heat through in a saucepan, stirring occasionally.
½ cup beef mixture with ⅔ cup rice: 413 cal., 13g fat (4g sat. fat), 71mg chol., 647mg sod., 46g carb. (14g sugars, 3g fiber), 27g pro.
Diabetic exchanges: 3 starch, 3 lean meat, ½ fat.

Pressure-Cooker Spicy Pork & Squash Ragu

This recipe is a marvelously spicy combo perfect for cooler fall weather—so satisfying after a day spent outdoors.
—Monica Osterhaus, Paducah, KY

Prep: 20 min.
Cook: 15 min. + releasing
Makes: 10 servings

- 2 cans (14½ oz. each) stewed tomatoes, undrained
- 1 pkg. (12 oz.) frozen cooked winter squash, thawed
- 1 large sweet onion, cut into ½-in. pieces
- 1 medium sweet red pepper, cut into ½-in. pieces
- ¾ cup reduced-sodium chicken broth
- 1½ tsp. crushed red pepper flakes
- 2 lbs. boneless country-style pork ribs
- 1 tsp. salt
- ¼ tsp. garlic powder
- ¼ tsp. pepper
  Hot cooked pasta
  Shaved Parmesan cheese, optional

1. Combine the first 6 ingredients in a 6-qt. electric pressure cooker. Sprinkle ribs with salt, garlic powder and pepper; place in pressure cooker. Lock lid; close pressure-release valve. Adjust to pressure-cook on high for 15 minutes. Let pressure release naturally for 10 minutes; quick-release any remaining pressure.
2. Remove cover; stir to break pork into smaller pieces. Serve with pasta. If desired, top with Parmesan cheese.
Freeze option: Freeze cooled ragu in freezer containers. To use, partially thaw in the refrigerator overnight. Heat through in a saucepan, stirring occasionally.
1 cup ragu: 196 cal., 8g fat (3g sat. fat), 52mg chol., 469mg sod., 13g carb. (6g sugars, 2g fiber), 18g pro.
Diabetic exchanges: 2 lean meat, 1 starch.

Pressure-Cooker Beef Daube Provencal

My dish is perfect on chilly nights, especially after we have been out chopping wood. The melt-in-your-mouth goodness makes it a staple in my menu rotation.
—Brenda Ryan, Marshall, MO

Prep: 30 min.
Cook: 30 min. + releasing
Makes: 8 servings

- 1 **boneless beef chuck roast or venison roast (about 2 lbs.), cut into 1-in. cubes**
- 1½ **tsp. salt, divided**
- ½ **tsp. coarsely ground pepper, divided**
- 2 **tsp. olive oil**
- 2 **cups chopped carrots**
- 1½ **cups chopped onion**
- 12 **garlic cloves, crushed**
- 1 **Tbsp. tomato paste**
- 1 **cup dry red wine**
- 1 **can (14½ oz.) diced tomatoes, undrained**
- ½ **cup beef broth**
- 1 **tsp. chopped fresh rosemary**
- 1 **tsp. chopped fresh thyme**
- 1 **bay leaf**
  Dash ground cloves
  Mashed potatoes or hot cooked pasta

1. Sprinkle beef with ½ tsp. salt and ¼ tsp. pepper. Select saute setting on a 6-qt. electric pressure cooker. Adjust for medium heat; add oil. When oil is hot, brown the beef in batches.
2. Add carrots, onions and garlic to pressure cooker; cook and stir until golden brown, 4-6 minutes. Add tomato paste; cook and stir until fragrant, about 1 minute. Add wine, stirring to loosen the browned bits. Return beef to pressure cooker. Add tomatoes, broth, rosemary, thyme, bay leaf, cloves and remaining 1 tsp. salt and ¼ tsp. pepper. Press cancel.
3. Lock lid; close pressure-release valve. Adjust to pressure-cook on high for 30 minutes. Let pressure release naturally for 10 minutes; quick-release any remaining pressure. A thermometer inserted in the beef should read at least 160°. Discard bay leaf. Serve with mashed potatoes or hot cooked pasta. If desired, sprinkle with additional thyme.
Freeze option: Place the beef and vegetables in freezer containers; top with cooking juices. Cool and freeze. To use, partially thaw in refrigerator overnight. Heat through in a covered saucepan, stirring gently and adding broth if necessary.

1 cup beef mixture: 248 cal., 12g fat (4g sat. fat), 74mg chol., 652mg sod., 10g carb. (5g sugars, 2g fiber), 24g pro.
Diabetic exchanges: 3 lean meat, 1 vegetable.

Sweet Onion & Sausage Spaghetti

This wholesome pasta dish gets tossed with light cream, basil and tomatoes for a quick, fresh-tasting meal in minutes.

—Mary Relyea, Canastota, NY

- -

Takes: 30 min. • **Makes:** 4 servings

    6   oz. uncooked whole wheat
        spaghetti
    ¾   lb. Italian turkey sausage links,
        casings removed
    2   tsp. olive oil
    1   sweet onion, thinly sliced
    1   pint cherry tomatoes, halved
    ½   cup loosely packed fresh basil
        leaves, thinly sliced
    ½   cup half-and-half cream
        Shaved Parmesan cheese,
        optional

1. Cook the spaghetti according to package directions. Meanwhile, in a large nonstick skillet over medium heat, cook the sausage in oil for 5 minutes. Add onion; cook until meat is no longer pink and onion is tender, 8-10 minutes longer.

2. Stir in tomatoes and basil; heat through. Add cream; bring to a boil. Drain spaghetti; toss with sausage mixture. Garnish with Parmesan cheese if desired.

1½ cups: 334 cal., 12g fat (4g sat. fat), 46mg chol., 378mg sod., 41g carb. (8g sugars, 6g fiber), 17g pro. **Diabetic exchanges:** 2½ starch, 2 lean meat, 1 vegetable, 1 fat.

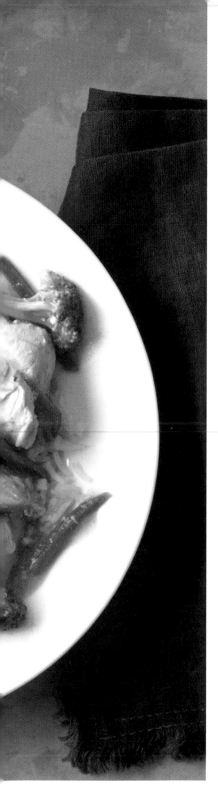

Pressure-Cooker Garlic Chicken & Broccoli

This simple riff on a classic Chinese chicken dish proves you can savor the takeout taste you crave while still eating right.
—Connie Krupp, Racine, WI

- -

Prep: 15 min. • **Cook:** 5 min.
Makes: 8 servings

2   lbs. boneless skinless chicken breasts, cut into 1-in. pieces
4   cups fresh broccoli florets
4   medium carrots, julienned
1   can (8 oz.) sliced water chestnuts, drained
6   garlic cloves, minced
3   cups reduced-sodium chicken broth
¼   cup reduced-sodium soy sauce
2   Tbsp. brown sugar
2   Tbsp. sesame oil
2   Tbsp. rice vinegar
½   tsp. salt
½   tsp. pepper
⅓   cup cornstarch
⅓   cup water
    Hot cooked rice

1. Place the first 5 ingredients in a 6-qt. electric pressure cooker. In a large bowl, mix broth, soy sauce, brown sugar, sesame oil, vinegar, salt and pepper; pour over the chicken mixture. Lock lid; close the pressure-release valve. Adjust to pressure-cook on high for 3 minutes. Quick-release pressure. Press the cancel button. A thermometer inserted in chicken should read at least 165°.

2. Remove chicken and vegetables; keep warm. In a small bowl, mix cornstarch and water until smooth; stir into cooking juices. Select saute setting and adjust for low heat. Simmer, stirring constantly, until thickened, 1-2 minutes. Serve with chicken, vegetables and cooked rice.

Freeze option: Place chicken and vegetables in freezer containers; top with sauce. Cool and freeze. To use, partially thaw in the refrigerator overnight. Microwave, covered, on high in a microwave-safe dish until heated through, stirring gently. Add broth or water if necessary.

1 cup: 241 cal., 6g fat (1g sat. fat), 63mg chol., 798mg sod., 19g carb. (8g sugars, 3g fiber), 26g pro.
Diabetic exchanges: 3 lean meat, 1 vegetable, ½ starch, ½ fat.

Ginger Veggie Brown Rice Pasta

Once I discovered brown rice pasta, I never looked back. Tossed with ginger, veggies and rotisserie chicken, it tastes like a deconstructed egg roll!
—Tiffany Ihle, Bronx, NY

Takes: 30 min. • **Makes:** 8 servings

- 2 cups uncooked brown rice elbow pasta
- 1 Tbsp. coconut oil
- ½ small red onion, sliced
- 2 tsp. ginger paste
- 2 tsp. garlic paste
- 1½ cups chopped fresh Brussels sprouts
- ½ cup chopped red cabbage
- ½ cup shredded carrots
- ½ medium sweet red pepper, chopped
- ½ tsp. salt
- ¼ tsp. ground ancho chile pepper
- ¼ tsp. coarsely ground pepper
- 1 rotisserie chicken, skin removed, shredded
- 2 green onions, chopped

1. In a Dutch oven, cook pasta according to package directions.

2. Meanwhile, in a large skillet, heat coconut oil over medium heat. Add red onion, ginger paste and garlic paste; saute 2 minutes. Stir in next 7 ingredients; cook until vegetables are crisp-tender, 4-6 minutes. Add chicken; heat through.

3. Drain pasta, reserving 1 cup pasta water. Return pasta to Dutch oven. Add vegetable mixture; toss to coat, adding enough reserved pasta water to moisten pasta. Sprinkle with green onions before serving.

Note: You may substitute an equal volume of minced fresh garlic and ginger for the pastes. Canola or olive oil may be substituted for coconut oil.

1 cup: 270 cal., 7g fat (3g sat. fat), 55mg chol., 257mg sod., 29g carb. (2g sugars, 2g fiber), 21g pro.

Diabetic exchanges: 3 lean meat, 2 starch, 1 fat.

Hungarian Goulash

Here's a cherished heirloom recipe from my family. My grandmother made this for my mother when she was a child, who made it for us to enjoy. Paprika and caraway add wonderful flavor and sour cream gives it a creamy richness.
—Marcia Doyle, Pompano, FL

- -

Prep: 20 min. • **Cook:** 7 hours
Makes: 12 servings

- 3 **medium onions, chopped**
- 2 **medium carrots, chopped**
- 2 **medium green peppers, chopped**
- 3 **lbs. beef stew meat**
- ¾ **tsp. salt, divided**
- ¾ **tsp. pepper, divided**
- 2 **Tbsp. olive oil**
- 1½ **cups reduced-sodium beef broth**
- ¼ **cup all-purpose flour**
- 3 **Tbsp. paprika**
- 2 **Tbsp. tomato paste**
- 1 **tsp. caraway seeds**
- 1 **garlic clove, minced**
  Dash sugar
- 12 **cups uncooked whole wheat egg noodles**
- 1 **cup reduced-fat sour cream**

1. Place the onions, carrots and green peppers in a 5-qt. slow cooker. Sprinkle meat with ½ tsp. salt and ½ tsp. pepper. In a large skillet, brown meat in oil in batches. Transfer to slow cooker.
2. Add broth to skillet, stirring to loosen browned bits from pan. Combine the flour, paprika, tomato paste, caraway seeds, garlic, sugar and remaining salt and pepper; stir into skillet. Bring to a boil; cook and stir for 2 minutes or until thickened. Pour over meat. Cover and cook on low for 7-9 hours or until the meat is tender.
3. Cook the noodles according to package directions. Stir sour cream into slow cooker. Drain noodles; serve with goulash.
⅔ cup goulash with 1 cup noodles: 388 cal., 13g fat (4g sat. fat), 78mg chol., 285mg sod., 41g carb. (5g sugars, 7g fiber), 31g pro.
Diabetic exchanges: 3 lean meat, 2 starch, 1 vegetable, 1 fat.

Hearty Turkey & Rice

We love this recipe, especially when we want a comforting dinner fast. The sauce is also excellent on tortilla chips, which we serve on the side.
—Joan Hallford,
North Richland Hills, TX

- -

Takes: 25 min. • **Makes:** 4 servings

- 1½ **cups instant brown rice**
- 1 **lb. extra-lean ground turkey**
- 1 **medium onion, chopped**
- 1½ **cups salsa**
- 1 **can (8 oz.) no-salt-added tomato sauce**
- 1 **tsp. reduced-sodium chicken bouillon granules**
- ¼ **tsp. salt**
- ¼ **cup shredded reduced-fat cheddar cheese**
- ¼ **cup reduced-fat sour cream**
  Optional toppings: chopped tomatoes, baked tortilla chips and sliced ripe olives

1. Cook rice according to package directions. Meanwhile, in a large nonstick skillet coated with cooking spray, cook turkey and onion over medium heat 6-8 minutes or until turkey is no longer pink and onion is tender, breaking up turkey into crumbles. Add salsa, tomato sauce, bouillon and salt; heat through.
2. Serve with rice, cheese, sour cream and, if desired, toppings of your choice.
Freeze option: Freeze cooled turkey mixture in airtight freezer containers. To use, partially thaw in refrigerator overnight. Heat mixture through in a saucepan, stirring occasionally and adding a little water or chicken broth if necessary.
1 cup turkey mixture with ¾ cup rice: 354 cal., 5g fat (2g sat. fat), 55mg chol., 732mg sod., 40g carb. (10g sugars, 3g fiber), 34g pro.

Caribbean Shrimp & Rice Bowl

I had a similar rice bowl on vacation and re-created this lighter version at home. It takes me back to the islands every time I make it. Grill the shrimp for a more smoky flavor.
—Lauren Katz, Ashburn, VA

- -

Takes: 20 min. • **Makes:** 4 servings

- 1   medium ripe avocado, peeled and pitted
- ⅓   cup reduced-fat sour cream
- ¼   tsp. salt
- 1   can (15 oz.) black beans, rinsed and drained
- 1   can (8 oz.) unsweetened crushed pineapple, undrained
- 1   medium mango, peeled and cubed
- ½   cup salsa
- 1   pkg. (8.8 oz.) ready-to-serve brown rice
- 1   lb. uncooked shrimp (31-40 per lb.), peeled and deveined
- 1   tsp. Caribbean jerk seasoning
- 1   Tbsp. canola oil
- 2   green onions, sliced
      Lime wedges

1. For avocado cream, mash the avocado with sour cream and salt until smooth. In a small saucepan, combine beans, pineapple, mango and salsa; heat through, stirring occasionally. Prepare rice according to package directions.

2. Toss shrimp with jerk seasoning. In a large skillet, heat oil over medium-high heat. Add shrimp; cook and stir until shrimp turn pink, 2-3 minutes.

3. Divide the rice and bean mixture among 4 bowls. Top with shrimp and green onions. Serve the dish with avocado cream and lime wedges.

1 serving: 498 cal., 14g fat (2g sat. fat), 145mg chol., 698mg sod., 62g carb. (23g sugars, 9g fiber), 29g pro.

Ginger Chicken & Quinoa Stew

This Asian-inspired one-pot chicken dinner is healthy and tasty. Serve it hot, cold or at room temperature.
—Doris Kwon, Newport Coast, CA

- -

Prep: 25 min. • **Cook:** 3½ hours
Makes: 8 servings

2	lbs. boneless skinless chicken thighs, cut into 1-in. pieces
1	cup quinoa, rinsed
1	medium onion, cut into 1-in. pieces
1	medium sweet yellow pepper, cut into 1-in. pieces
1	medium sweet red pepper, cut into 1-in. pieces
2	cups chicken broth
½	cup honey
⅓	cup reduced-sodium soy sauce
¼	cup mirin (sweet rice wine) or sherry
1	Tbsp. minced fresh gingerroot
2	garlic cloves, minced
¼	to 1 tsp. crushed red pepper flakes
1	can (8 oz.) unsweetened pineapple chunks, drained
3	green onions, thinly sliced
2	tsp. sesame seeds

1. Place the chicken in a 4- or 5-qt. slow cooker. Top with quinoa, onion and peppers. In a small bowl, whisk the broth, honey, soy sauce, mirin, ginger, garlic and red pepper flakes; pour into slow cooker.
2. Cook, covered, on low 3½- 4 hours or until the chicken is tender. Serve with pineapple, green onions and sesame seeds.
1 cup: 373 cal., 10g fat (3g sat. fat), 77mg chol., 696mg sod., 43g carb. (26g sugars, 3g fiber), 26g pro.

Meal-in-One WONDERS

Some nights, simplicity is key. Start here for quick options that cook all in one pot or full meals served all in one dish.

Asparagus Ham Dinner

I've been making this light meal for my family for years now, and it's always a hit. With asparagus, tomato, pasta and chunks of ham, it's a tempting blend of tastes and textures.

—Rhonda Zavodny, David City, NE

Takes: 25 min. • **Makes:** 6 servings

- 2 cups uncooked corkscrew or spiral pasta
- ¾ lb. fresh asparagus, cut into 1-in. pieces
- 1 medium sweet yellow pepper, julienned
- 1 Tbsp. olive oil
- 6 medium tomatoes, diced
- 6 oz. boneless fully cooked ham, cubed
- ¼ cup minced fresh parsley
- ½ tsp. salt
- ½ tsp. dried oregano
- ½ tsp. dried basil
- ⅛ to ¼ tsp. cayenne pepper
- ¼ cup shredded Parmesan cheese

Cook the pasta according to the package directions. Meanwhile, in a large cast-iron or other heavy skillet, saute asparagus and yellow pepper in oil until crisp-tender. Add tomatoes and ham; heat through. Drain pasta; add to mixture. Stir in parsley and seasonings. Sprinkle with cheese.

1⅓ cups: 204 cal., 5g fat (1g sat. fat), 17mg chol., 561mg sod., 29g carb. (5g sugars, 3g fiber), 12g pro.
Diabetic exchanges: 1½ starch, 1 lean meat, 1 vegetable, ½ fat.

Turkey Sausage & Spinach Orecchiette

It was fun to come up with this recipe on my own and even more fun when my picky husband loved it! Little ear-shaped orecchiette pasta is delicious with spicy turkey sausage.
—Andrea Phillips, Lakeville, MN

- -

Takes: 30 min. • **Makes:** 4 servings

- ½   lb. uncooked orecchiette or small tube pasta
- 3   hot Italian turkey sausage links, casings removed
- ¼   cup chopped onion
- 2   garlic cloves, minced
- ¼   tsp. crushed red pepper flakes
- 3   cups fresh spinach
- ½   cup shredded Asiago cheese
- ¼   cup grated Parmesan cheese
- ¼   cup rinsed and drained cannellini beans
- ¼   cup chopped roasted sweet red pepper
- ½   tsp. Italian seasoning
     Additional shredded Asiago cheese, optional

1. Cook orecchiette according to package directions.
2. In a large skillet, cook and stir the sausage, onion, garlic and pepper flakes over medium heat for 6-8 minutes or until sausage is no longer pink; drain. Add the spinach, Asiago cheese, Parmesan, beans, red pepper and Italian seasoning; cook just until spinach is wilted, stirring occasionally.
3. Drain orecchiette; add to sausage mixture and toss to combine. Sprinkle with additional Asiago cheese if desired.
1¼ cups: 382 cal., 11g fat (4g sat. fat), 47mg chol., 593mg sod., 47g carb. (3g sugars, 3g fiber), 22g pro.

Slow-Cooked Ropa Vieja

I tasted some the best food on a trip to Cuba a few years back. One dish, ropa vieja, stuck out more than the rest. I tried several variations of the specialty, and when I returned home I decided to make my own homemade version. I went through five trials before coming to this recipe. For a spicier version, add hot peppers. For a tangier version, add 2 Tbsp. lemon juice or green olives. For a heartier broth, add more tomato paste. For a sweeter version, add more carrots. The possibilities are endless!
—Joshua Boyer, Traverse City, MI

- -

Prep: 35 min. • **Cook:** 8 hours
Makes: 6 servings

- 1   beef flank steak (2 lbs.)
- ½   tsp. salt
- ½   tsp. pepper
- 2   cups beef broth
- ½   cup dry vermouth
- ½   cup dry red wine or additional beef broth
- 1   can (6 oz.) tomato paste
- 1   large onion, thinly sliced
- 1   large carrot, sliced
- 1   small sweet red pepper, thinly sliced
- 1   Cubanelle or mild banana pepper, thinly sliced
- 3   springs fresh oregano
     Hot cooked rice
     Optional: Additional fresh oregano, lime wedges and sliced green olives with pimientos

1. Cut steak into 6 pieces; sprinkle with salt and pepper. Heat a large skillet over medium-high heat; brown meat in batches. Transfer meat to a 5- or 6-qt. slow cooker. Add broth, vermouth, wine and tomato paste to pan. Cook 2-3 minutes, stirring to loosen browned bits from pan. Pour over meat.
2. Top with onion, carrot, red pepper, Cubanelle pepper and fresh oregano. Cook, covered, on low until meat is tender, 8-10 hours. Remove oregano sprigs; discard. Remove meat; shred with 2 forks. Return to slow cooker; heat through. Serve with rice and, if desired, additional oregano, lime wedges and green olives.
1 serving: 278 cal., 11g fat (5g sat. fat), 72mg chol., 611mg sod., 10g carb. (5g sugars, 2g fiber), 32g pro.
Diabetic exchanges: 4 lean meat, 1 vegetable.

Chunky Cod Stir-Fry

Here's a flavorful new way to serve fish. Good-for-you cod is accented with crunchy vegetables, peanuts and a simple sauce.

—Dorothy Colette, Bourbonnais, IL

- -

Takes: 30 min. • **Makes:** 4 servings

2	tsp. cornstarch
⅓	cup chicken broth
2	Tbsp. sherry or additional chicken broth
2	Tbsp. reduced-sodium soy sauce
⅛	tsp. crushed red pepper flakes
1	garlic clove, minced
1	Tbsp. canola oil
1	pkg. (16 oz.) frozen stir-fry vegetable blend, thawed
1	small sweet red pepper, julienned
1	lb. cod, cut into 1-in. cubes
¼	cup chopped peanuts
3	cups cooked long grain rice

1. In a bowl, combine the first 5 ingredients; set aside. In a large nonstick skillet or wok, stir-fry garlic in oil for 30 seconds. Add mixed vegetables and red pepper; stir-fry until crisp-tender, 4-5 minutes.
2. Remove and keep warm. Add half of the cod to skillet; gently stir-fry until fish flakes easily with a fork, 3-5 minutes. Remove and keep warm. Repeat with remaining cod.
3. Stir broth mixture and add to the pan. Bring to a boil; cook and stir for 2 minutes or until thickened. Return vegetables and fish to the pan. Add peanuts. Gently stir to coat. Cover and cook until heated through, about 1 minute. Serve over rice.
1 serving: 419 cal., 9g fat (1g sat. fat), 43mg chol., 507mg sod., 54g carb. (6g sugars, 4g fiber), 27g pro.

Contest-Winning Greek Pasta Bake

When I take this tempting casserole to potlucks, I always come home with an empty pan! It's healthy and hearty and made with everyday ingredients. Add a simple salad of field greens and a crusty loaf of artisan bread for a quick weeknight meal.

—Anne Taglienti, Kennett Square, PA

- -

Prep: 20 min. • **Bake:** 25 min.
Makes: 8 servings

3⅓	cups uncooked whole grain spiral or penne pasta
4	cups cubed cooked chicken breast
1	can (29 oz.) tomato sauce
1	can (14½ oz.) no-salt-added diced tomatoes, drained
1	pkg. (10 oz.) frozen chopped spinach, thawed and squeezed dry
2	cans (2¼ oz. each) sliced ripe olives, drained
¼	cup thinly sliced red onion
¼	cup chopped green pepper
1	tsp. dried basil
1	tsp. dried oregano
1	cup shredded mozzarella cheese
½	cup crumbled feta cheese Optional: Chopped fresh oregano or fresh basil

1. Cook pasta according to package directions; drain. In a large bowl, combine pasta, chicken, tomato sauce, tomatoes, spinach, olives, onion, green pepper, basil and oregano.
2. Transfer to a 13x9-in. baking dish coated with cooking spray. Sprinkle with cheeses. Bake, uncovered, at 400° until heated through and cheese is melted. If desired, sprinkle with oregano or basil.
Freeze option: If the pasta in the unbaked casserole is still hot, allow to cool completely. Cover and freeze. To use, partially thaw in refrigerator overnight. Remove from refrigerator 30 minutes before baking. Preheat oven to 400°. Bake the casserole as directed, increasing baking time as necessary to heat through and for a thermometer inserted in center to read 165°.
½ cup: 398 cal., 10g fat (3g sat. fat), 67mg chol., 832mg sod., 47g carb. (5g sugars, 9g fiber), 34g pro.
Diabetic exchanges: 3 lean meat, 3 very lean meat, 2½ starch, 1 vegetable, ½ fat.

Spicy Mongolian Beef Salad

More than just a plate of greens, this beef salad is sure to satisfy. Even my meat-loving husband devours it!
—Marla Clark, Albuquerque, NM

- -

Takes: 30 min. • **Makes:** 4 servings

- ¼ cup olive oil
- 2 Tbsp. rice vinegar
- 1 Tbsp. reduced-sodium soy sauce
- 1 Tbsp. sesame oil
- 2 tsp. minced fresh gingerroot
- 1 small garlic clove, minced
- 1 tsp. sugar

BEEF

- 1 Tbsp. reduced-sodium soy sauce
- 2 garlic cloves, minced
- 2 tsp. sugar
- 1 to 2 tsp. crushed red pepper flakes
- 1 tsp. sesame oil
- 1 beef top sirloin steak (1 lb.), cut into ¼-in. strips
- 1 Tbsp. olive oil

SALAD

- 8 cups torn mixed salad greens
- 1 cup shredded carrots
- ½ cup thinly sliced cucumber
- 4 radishes, thinly sliced

1. For dressing, whisk together first 7 ingredients.

2. Mix first 5 beef ingredients; toss with beef strips. In a large cast-iron or other heavy skillet, heat olive oil over medium-high heat; stir-fry the beef mixture until browned, 2-3 minutes. Remove from pan.

3. Combine salad ingredients; divide among 4 plates. Top with beef. Drizzle with dressing.

1 serving: 396 cal., 26g fat (5g sat. fat), 46mg chol., 550mg sod., 15g carb. (7g sugars, 3g fiber), 27g pro.

Chicken Veggie Packets

People think I go to a lot of trouble when I serve these packets. They're wrong! Individual aluminum foil pouches are a cinch to assemble and retain the juices during baking to keep the herbed chicken moist and tender. It saves time and cleanup is a breeze.
—Edna Shaffer, Beulah, MI

- -

Takes: 30 min. • **Makes:** 4 servings

- 4 boneless skinless chicken breast halves (4 oz. each)
- ½ lb. sliced fresh mushrooms
- 1½ cups fresh baby carrots
- 1 cup pearl onions
- ½ cup julienned sweet red pepper
- ¼ tsp. pepper
- 3 tsp. minced fresh thyme
- ½ tsp. salt, optional
  Lemon wedges, optional

1. Preheat oven to 375°. Flatten chicken breasts to ½-in. thickness; place each on a piece of heavy-duty foil (about 12 in. square). Layer the mushrooms, carrots, onions and red pepper over chicken; sprinkle with pepper, thyme and, if desired, salt.

2. Fold foil around chicken and vegetables and seal tightly. Place on a baking sheet. Bake until chicken juices run clear, about 20 minutes. If desired, serve with lemon wedges.

1 serving: 175 cal., 3g fat (1g sat. fat), 63mg chol., 100mg sod., 11g carb. (6g sugars, 2g fiber), 25g pro.
Diabetic exchanges: 3 lean meat, 2 vegetable.

Ginger Salmon with Green Beans

I developed this flavor-packed dinner for a busy friend who is following a clean-eating diet.
—Nicole Stevens, Charleston, SC

- -

Takes: 30 min. • **Makes:** 2 servings

- ¼ cup lemon juice
- 2 Tbsp. rice vinegar
- 3 garlic cloves, minced
- 2 tsp. minced fresh gingerroot
- 2 tsp. honey
- ⅛ tsp. salt
- ⅛ tsp. pepper
- 2 salmon fillets (4 oz. each)
- 1 medium lemon, thinly sliced

GREEN BEANS
- ¾ lb. fresh green beans, trimmed
- 2 Tbsp. water
- 2 tsp. olive oil
- ½ cup finely chopped onion
- 3 garlic cloves, minced
- ⅛ tsp. salt

1. Preheat oven to 325°. Mix first 7 ingredients.

2. Place each salmon fillet on an 18x12-in. piece of heavy-duty foil; fold up edges of foil to create a rim around the fish. Spoon lemon juice mixture over salmon; top with lemon slices. Carefully fold foil around fish, sealing tightly.

3. Place packets in a 15x10x1-in. pan. Bake until fish just begins to flake easily with a fork, 15-20 minutes. Open foil carefully to allow steam to escape.

4. Meanwhile, place green beans, water and oil in a large skillet; bring to a boil. Reduce heat; simmer, covered, 5 minutes. Stir in remaining ingredients; cook, uncovered, until beans are crisp-tender, stirring occasionally. Serve with salmon.

1 serving: 357 cal., 15g fat (3g sat. fat), 57mg chol., 607mg sod., 35g carb. (18g sugars, 8g fiber), 24g pro. **Diabetic exchanges:** 3 lean meat, 1 starch, 1 vegetable, 1 fat.

Sausage-Topped White Pizza

I love to cook, and I learned most of what I know from Nana and Mom. Pizza is one of my favorite dishes to prepare. I switched up this recipe to make it my own.
—Tracy Brown, River Edge, NJ

- -

Takes: 30 min. • **Makes:** 6 servings

2   hot Italian turkey sausage links, casings removed
1   cup reduced-fat ricotta cheese
¼   tsp. garlic powder
1   prebaked 12-in. thin whole wheat pizza crust
1   medium sweet red pepper, julienned
1   small onion, halved and thinly sliced
½   tsp. Italian seasoning
¼   tsp. freshly ground pepper
¼   tsp. crushed red pepper flakes, optional
½   cup shredded part-skim mozzarella cheese
2   cups arugula or baby spinach

1. Preheat oven to 450°. In a large skillet, cook and crumble sausage over medium-high heat until no longer pink, 4-6 minutes. Mix the ricotta cheese and garlic powder.
2. Place crust on a baking sheet; spread with ricotta cheese mixture. Top with sausage, red pepper and onion; sprinkle with seasonings, then with mozzarella cheese.
3. Bake on a lower oven rack until the edge is lightly browned and cheese is melted, 8-10 minutes. Top with arugula.
1 piece: 242 cal., 8g fat (4g sat. fat), 30mg chol., 504mg sod., 28g carb. (5g sugars, 4g fiber), 16g pro.
Diabetic exchanges: 2 starch, 2 medium-fat meat.

Spicy Sausage & Rice Skillet

The spicy sausage in this quick skillet dish gives it a kick, and the sliced apples are a pleasant, tart surprise.
—Jamie Jones, Madison, GA

- -

Takes: 30 min. • **Makes:** 6 servings

- 1 pkg. (12 oz.) fully cooked spicy chicken sausage links, halved lengthwise and cut into ½-in. slices
- 1 Tbsp. olive oil
- 2 medium yellow summer squash, chopped
- 2 medium zucchini, chopped
- 1 large sweet red pepper, chopped
- 1 medium onion, chopped
- 1 medium tart apple, cut into ¼-in. slices
- 1 garlic clove, minced
- ½ tsp. salt
- 1 pkg. (8.80 oz.) ready-to-serve brown rice
- 1 can (15 oz.) black beans, rinsed and drained
- ¼ to ½ cup water

1. In a large nonstick skillet, cook sausage over medium-high heat, turning occasionally, until lightly browned. Remove from skillet.
2. In the same skillet, heat oil over medium-high heat. Saute squash, zucchini, pepper, onion, apple, garlic and salt until vegetables are tender, 5-7 minutes. Add rice, beans, ¼ cup water and sausage; cook and stir until heated through, about 5 minutes, adding more water if needed.
1⅓ cups: 285 cal., 8g fat (2g sat. fat), 43mg chol., 668mg sod., 34g carb. (9g sugars, 6g fiber), 17g pro.
Diabetic exchanges: 2 starch, 2 lean meat, 1 vegetable, ½ fat.

Cantonese Pork

This Cantonese-style recipe is our favorite way to prepare pork loin. We love it with fried rice and veggies, but it's also delicious sliced and served cold as an appetizer. Try dipping cold slices in a mixture of soy sauce, hot mustard and sesame seeds.
—Carla Mendres, Winnipeg, MB

- -

Prep: 10 min. + marinating
Cook: 3 hours • **Makes:** 10 servings

- 3 Tbsp. honey
- 2 Tbsp. soy sauce
- 1 Tbsp. sesame oil
- 1 Tbsp. Chinese cooking wine or mirin (sweet rice wine)
- 4 garlic cloves, crushed
- 1 tsp. minced fresh gingerroot
- 1 tsp. hoisin sauce
- 1 tsp. oyster sauce
- 1 tsp. Chinese five-spice powder
- 1 tsp. salt
- 1 tsp. red food coloring, optional
- 1 boneless pork loin roast (about 4 lbs.)

1. In a large shallow bowl, combine the first 10 ingredients and, if desired, red food coloring. Cut pork roast lengthwise in half. Add pork to marinade; turn to coat. Cover and refrigerate at least 24 hours.
2. Transfer pork and marinade to a 5-qt. slow cooker. Cook, covered, on low 3-4 hours or until a thermometer inserted in roast reads 145° and meat is tender. Let roast stand for 10-15 minutes before slicing.
5 oz. cooked pork: 262 cal., 10g fat (3g sat. fat), 91mg chol., 498mg sod., 6g carb. (5g sugars, 0 fiber), 36g pro.
Diabetic exchanges: 5 lean meat.

Country French Pork with Prunes & Apples

The classic flavors of herbes de Provence, apples and dried plums make this easy slow-cooked pork taste like a hearty meal at a rustic French cafe. For a traditional pairing, serve the pork with braised lentils.
—Suzanne Banfield, Basking Ridge, NJ

- -

Prep: 20 min.
Cook: 4 hours + standing
Makes: 10 servings

2	Tbsp. all-purpose flour
1	Tbsp. herbes de Provence
1½	tsp. salt
¾	tsp. pepper
1	boneless pork loin roast (3 to 4 lbs.)
2	Tbsp. olive oil
2	medium onions, halved and thinly sliced
1	cup apple cider or unsweetened apple juice
1	cup beef stock
2	bay leaves
2	large tart apples, peeled, cored and chopped
1	cup pitted dried plums (prunes)

1. Mix flour, herbes de Provence, salt and pepper; rub over pork. In a large skillet, heat oil over medium-high heat. Brown roast on all sides. Place roast in a 5- or 6-qt. slow cooker. Add onions, apple cider, beef stock and bay leaves.

2. Cook, covered, on low 3 hours. Add apples and dried plums. Cook, covered, on low 1-1½ hours longer or until apples and pork are tender. Remove roast, onions, apples and plums to a serving platter, discarding bay leaves; tent with foil. Let stand 15 minutes before slicing.

4 oz. cooked pork with ¾ cup fruit mixture: 286 cal., 9g fat (3g sat. fat), 68mg chol., 449mg sod., 22g carb. (13g sugars, 2g fiber), 28g pro.

Slow-Cooker Thai Peanut Chicken with Noodles

I serve this Thai favorite with noodles mixed into the sauce, but it's also wonderful served over rice. Garnish with green onion or cilantro for a pop of color and fresh flavor.
—Catherine Cebula, Littleton, MA

- -

Prep: 35 min. • **Cook:** 2½ hours
Makes: 6 servings

- 1½ lbs. boneless skinless chicken breasts, cut into ¾-in. cubes
- 1 medium onion, chopped
- ¾ cup salsa
- ¼ cup creamy peanut butter
- 2 Tbsp. black bean sauce
- 1 Tbsp. reduced-sodium soy sauce
- 8 oz. uncooked linguine
- 1 Tbsp. canola oil
- ½ lb. sliced baby portobello mushrooms
  Thinly sliced green onions, optional

1. Place the chicken and onion in a 4-qt. slow cooker. Combine salsa, peanut butter, bean sauce and soy sauce; add to slow cooker. Cook, covered, on low 2½-3½ hours, until chicken is tender.
2. Meanwhile, prepare the pasta according to package directions. In a large skillet, heat oil over medium-high heat. Add mushrooms; cook and stir until tender, 6-8 minutes. Drain pasta; stir into slow cooker. Stir in mushrooms. If desired, sprinkle with green onions.

1⅓ cups: 378 cal., 11g fat (2g sat. fat), 63mg chol., 436mg sod., 37g carb. (5g sugars, 2g fiber), 32g pro.
Diabetic exchanges: 4 lean meat, 2 starch, 2 fat, 1 vegetable.

Southwestern Spaghetti

Chili powder and cumin give a mild Mexican flavor to this colorful one-skillet supper. With chunks of fresh zucchini, it's a nice change of pace from typical spaghetti dishes.
—Beth Coffee, Hartford City, IN

- -

Takes: 30 min. • **Makes:** 5 servings

- ¾ lb. lean ground beef (90% lean)
- 2¼ cups water
- 1 can (15 oz.) tomato sauce
- 2 tsp. chili powder
- ½ tsp. garlic powder
- ½ tsp. ground cumin
- ⅛ tsp. salt
- 1 pkg. (7 oz.) thin spaghetti, broken into thirds
- 1 lb. zucchini (about 4 small), cut into chunks
- ½ cup shredded cheddar cheese

1. In a large skillet, cook beef over medium heat until no longer pink; drain. Remove beef and set aside. In the same skillet, combine water, tomato sauce, chili powder, garlic powder, cumin and salt; bring to a boil. Stir in spaghetti; return to a boil. Boil for 6 minutes.
2. Add zucchini. Cook 4-5 minutes longer or until spaghetti and zucchini are tender, stirring several times. Stir in beef and heat through. Sprinkle with cheese.

1 cup: 340 cal., 11g fat (5g sat. fat), 54mg chol., 600mg sod., 38g carb. (5g sugars, 4g fiber), 24g pro.
Diabetic exchanges: 2 starch, 2 lean meat, 2 vegetable, ½ fat.

Spanish Chicken Rice

This meaty dish is a snap to put on the table, especially when using leftover cooked chicken.

—Patricia Rutherford, Winchester, IL

- -

Takes: 30 min. • **Makes:** 2 servings

⅔	cup finely chopped onion
¼	cup sliced fresh mushrooms
1¼	cups cubed cooked chicken breast
2	plum tomatoes, peeled and chopped
½	cup cooked long grain rice
½	cup reduced-sodium tomato juice
½	cup reduced-sodium chicken broth
⅓	cup frozen peas
1	Tbsp. chopped pimientos
⅛	tsp. dried tarragon
⅛	tsp. dried savory
	Pinch pepper

In a skillet coated with cooking spray, saute onion and mushrooms for 4 minutes or until tender. Place in an ungreased 1-qt. baking dish. Stir in the remaining ingredients. Cover and bake at 375° for 15-20 minutes or until liquid is absorbed.

1½ cups: 254 cal., 3g fat (1g sat. fat), 67mg chol., 264mg sod., 25g carb. (8g sugars, 4g fiber), 30g pro.
Diabetic exchanges: 3 lean meat, 1 starch, 1 vegetable.

Italian Sausage Veggie Skillet

We love Italian sausage sandwiches, and this stovetop dish is a fun riff on that same concept. If you like some heat, use hot peppers in place of the sweet peppers.

—Tina Howells, Salem, OH

- -

Takes: 30 min. • **Makes:** 6 servings

4	cups uncooked whole wheat spiral pasta
1	lb. Italian turkey sausage, casings removed
1	medium onion, chopped
1	garlic clove, minced
2	medium zucchini, chopped
1	large sweet red pepper, chopped
1	large sweet yellow pepper, chopped
1	can (28 oz.) diced tomatoes, drained
¼	tsp. salt
¼	tsp. pepper

1. Cook pasta according to package directions; drain.
2. Meanwhile, in large skillet, cook sausage and onion over medium-high heat until sausage is no longer pink, 5-7 minutes. Add garlic and cook 1 minute longer. Add zucchini and peppers; cook until crisp-tender, 3-5 minutes. Add tomatoes, salt and pepper. Cook and stir until vegetables are tender and begin to release their juices, 5-7 minutes. Serve with pasta.

1⅓ cups: 251 cal., 6g fat (1g sat. fat), 28mg chol., 417mg sod., 35g carb. (4g sugars, 6g fiber), 16g pro.
Diabetic exchanges: 2 vegetable, 2 lean meat, 1½ starch.

Lemon Pork with Mushrooms

This is my family's favorite healthy dish, but you'd never guess it's good for you. A little squeeze of lemon gives these crispy seasoned chops a bright boost.

—Christine Datian, Las Vegas, NV

Takes: 30 min. • **Makes:** 4 servings

- 1 large egg, lightly beaten
- 1 cup seasoned bread crumbs
- 8 thin boneless pork loin chops (2 oz. each)
- ¼ tsp. salt
- ⅛ tsp. pepper
- 1 Tbsp. olive oil
- 1 Tbsp. butter
- ½ lb. sliced fresh mushrooms
- 2 garlic cloves, minced
- 2 tsp. grated lemon zest
- 1 Tbsp. lemon juice
  Lemon wedges, optional

1. Place egg and bread crumbs in separate shallow bowls. Sprinkle pork chops with salt and pepper; dip in egg, then coat with crumbs, pressing to adhere.

2. In a large skillet, heat oil over medium heat. In batches, cook pork until golden brown, 2-3 minutes per side. Remove from pan; keep warm.

3. Wipe pan clean. In skillet, heat butter over medium heat; saute fresh mushrooms until tender, 2-3 minutes. Stir in garlic, lemon zest and lemon juice; cook and stir 1 minute. Serve over pork. If desired, serve with lemon wedges.

1 serving: 331 cal., 15g fat (5g sat. fat), 109mg chol., 601mg sod., 19g carb. (2g sugars, 1g fiber), 28g pro. **Diabetic exchanges:** 3 lean meat, 1½ fat, 1 starch.

Salmon with Tomato-Goat Cheese Couscous

Rich with goat cheese and tomato, this recipe works for a weeknight supper or an elegant company dinner, and is easy to adjust to accommodate any number of guests.

—Toni Roberts, La Canada, CA

Takes: 30 min. • **Makes:** 4 servings

- 4 salmon fillets (5 oz. each)
- ¼ tsp. salt
- ¼ tsp. garlic salt
- ¼ tsp. pepper
- 1 Tbsp. olive oil
- 1 cup chicken stock
- ¾ cup uncooked whole wheat couscous
- 2 plum tomatoes, chopped
- 4 green onions, chopped
- ¼ cup crumbled goat cheese

1. Sprinkle salmon with salt, garlic salt and pepper. Heat oil in a large skillet over medium-high heat; add salmon skin side up and cook 3 minutes. Turn fish and cook an additional 4 minutes or until fish flakes easily with a fork. Remove from heat and keep warm.

2. In a large saucepan, bring stock to a boil. Stir in couscous. Remove from heat; let stand, covered, until stock is absorbed, about 5 minutes. Stir in tomatoes, green onions and goat cheese. Serve with salmon.

1 fillet with 1 cup couscous mixture: 414 cal., 19g fat (4g sat. fat), 80mg chol., 506mg sod., 31g carb. (2g sugars, 6g fiber), 32g pro. **Diabetic exchanges:** 4 lean meat, 2 starch, 1 fat.

Lemon Chicken & Rice

On our busy ranch, we need meals we can put on the table quickly. This hearty all-in-one dish, with its delicate lemon flavor, fits the bill. We love that it's budget-friendly, too.
—Kat Thompson, Prineville, OR

Takes: 30 min. • **Makes:** 4 servings

- 2 Tbsp. butter
- 1 lb. boneless skinless chicken breasts, cut into strips
- 1 medium onion, chopped
- 1 large carrot, thinly sliced
- 2 garlic cloves, minced
- 1 Tbsp. cornstarch
- 1 can (14½ oz.) chicken broth
- 2 Tbsp. lemon juice
- ¼ tsp. salt
- 1 cup frozen peas
- 1½ cups uncooked instant rice

1. In a large cast-iron or other heavy skillet, heat butter over medium-high heat; saute chicken, onion, carrot and garlic until chicken is no longer pink, 5-7 minutes.

2. In a small bowl, mix cornstarch, broth, lemon juice and salt until smooth. Gradually add to skillet; bring to a boil. Cook and stir until thickened, 1-2 minutes.

3. Stir in peas; return to a boil. Stir in rice. Remove from heat; let stand, covered, 5 minutes.

1 serving: 370 cal., 9g fat (4g sat. fat), 80mg chol., 746mg sod., 41g carb. (4g sugars, 3g fiber), 29g pro.
Diabetic exchanges: 3 starch, 3 lean meat, 1½ fat.

TIMESAVING TIP

Be sure to rinse your rice well with cold water before adding it to the skillet. This helps separate the grains so they don't clump. Rice that isn't rinsed is more starchy and mushy, and could make the dish gummy.

Fish & Fries

Dine as though you're in a traditional British pub. These baked fish fillets have a fuss-free coating that's healthy but just as crunchy and golden as the deep-fried kind. Simply seasoned, the crispy fries are perfect on the side.
—Janice Mitchell, Aurora, CO

- -

Prep: 10 min. • **Bake:** 35 min.
Makes: 4 servings

- 1 **lb. potatoes (about 2 medium)**
- 2 **Tbsp. olive oil**
- ¼ **tsp. pepper**

FISH

- ⅓ **cup all-purpose flour**
- ¼ **tsp. pepper**
- 1 **large egg**
- 2 **Tbsp. water**
- ⅔ **cup crushed cornflakes**
- 1 **Tbsp. grated Parmesan cheese**
- ⅛ **tsp. cayenne pepper**
- 1 **lb. haddock or cod fillets**
  Tartar sauce, optional

1. Preheat oven to 425°. Peel and cut potatoes lengthwise into ½-in.-thick slices; cut slices into ½-in.-thick sticks.

2. In a bowl, toss potatoes with oil and pepper. Transfer to a 15x10x1-in. baking pan coated with cooking spray. Bake fries, uncovered, 25-30 minutes or until golden brown and crisp, stirring once.

3. Meanwhile, in a shallow bowl, mix flour and pepper. In another shallow bowl, whisk egg with water. In a third bowl, toss cornflakes with the cheese and cayenne. Dip fish in flour mixture to coat both sides; shake off excess. Dip fish in egg mixture, then in the cornflake mixture, patting to help coating adhere.

4. Place on a baking sheet coated with cooking spray. Bake until fish just begins to flake easily with a fork, 10-12 minutes. Serve with fries and, if desired, tartar sauce.

1 serving: 376 cal., 9g fat (2g sat. fat), 120mg chol., 228mg sod., 44g carb. (3g sugars, 2g fiber), 28g pro.
Diabetic exchanges: 3 starch, 3 lean meat, 1½ fat.

Spinach & Shrimp Fra Diavolo

This quick dish is spicy, garlicky, saucy and loaded with delicious shrimp. Plus, with the addition of spinach, you're also getting a serving of veggies. When you need a perfect low-fat weeknight meal that is easy to pull together, this is it. You can substitute arugula or kale for the spinach if you'd like.

—Julie Peterson, Crofton, MD

- -

Takes: 30 min. • **Makes:** 4 servings

- 2 Tbsp. olive oil
- 1 medium onion, chopped
- 5 garlic cloves, minced
- ½ to 1 tsp. crushed red pepper flakes
- 1 cup dry white wine
- 1 can (14½ oz.) diced tomatoes, undrained
- 1 can (8 oz.) tomato sauce
- 3 Tbsp. minced fresh basil or 1 Tbsp. dried basil
- 1 tsp. dried oregano
- ¼ tsp. salt
- ¼ tsp. pepper
- 1 lb. uncooked shrimp (26-30 per lb.), peeled and deveined
- 3 cups finely chopped fresh spinach
  Grated Parmesan cheese, optional

1. In a large skillet, heat the oil over medium-high heat. Add onion; cook and stir until tender, 5-7 minutes. Add minced garlic and pepper flakes; cook 1 minute longer. Stir in wine. Bring to a boil; cook until liquid is reduced by half. Stir in tomatoes, tomato sauce, basil, oregano, salt and pepper. Cook and stir until the sauce is slightly thickened, about 10 minutes.

2. Add shrimp and spinach; cook and stir until shrimp turn pink and spinach is wilted, 3-5 minutes. If desired, sprinkle with cheese.

1½ cups: 235 cal., 9g fat (1g sat. fat), 138mg chol., 727mg sod., 14g carb. (6g sugars, 4g fiber), 22g pro.
Diabetic exchanges: 3 lean meat, 2 vegetable, 1½ fat.

Smoked Sausage with Pasta

Loaded with sausage, mushrooms, tomatoes and basil, this quick recipe satisfies the toughest critics. It's one of my husband's favorite dishes, and he has no idea it's lower in fat. Add a green salad for a delicious meal.
—Ruth Ann Ruddell, Shelby Township, MI

- -

Takes: 30 min. • **Makes:** 4 servings

4	oz. uncooked angel hair pasta
½	lb. smoked turkey kielbasa, cut into ½-in. slices
2	cups sliced fresh mushrooms
2	garlic cloves, minced
4½	tsp. minced fresh basil or 1½ tsp. dried basil
1	Tbsp. olive oil
2	cups julienned seeded plum tomatoes
⅛	tsp. salt
⅛	tsp. pepper
	Grated Parmesan cheese, optional

Cook pasta according to package directions. Meanwhile, in a large nonstick skillet, saute the sausage, mushrooms, garlic and basil in oil until mushrooms are tender. Drain pasta; add to the sausage mixture. Add the tomatoes, salt and pepper; toss gently. Heat through. If desired, top with additional fresh basil and grated Parmesan cheese.

1 cup: 232 cal., 7g fat (2g sat. fat), 35mg chol., 639mg sod., 27g carb. (5g sugars, 2g fiber), 15g pro.
Diabetic exchanges: 2 lean meat, 1½ starch, 1 vegetable, ½ fat.

Grilled Shrimp & Tomatoes with Linguine

This pasta dish came about one night when I started making up dinner as I went along, using ingredients I had on hand. We knew it was a keeper with the very first bite.
—Lisa Bynum, Brandon, MS

- -

Takes: 30 min. • **Makes:** 4 servings

- 8 oz. uncooked linguine
- 16 cherry tomatoes
- 2 Tbsp. olive oil
- 1 lb. uncooked large shrimp, peeled and deveined
- ½ tsp. pepper
- ¼ tsp. salt
- ¼ tsp. garlic powder
- ¼ tsp. Italian seasoning
- 2 Tbsp. butter
- ¼ cup grated Parmesan cheese
- 2 Tbsp. torn fresh basil

1. In a large saucepan, cook linguine according to package directions. Meanwhile, thread tomatoes onto metal or soaked wooden skewers; brush with 1 Tbsp. oil. Thread shrimp onto skewers; brush with remaining oil. Mix seasonings; sprinkle over the shrimp.

2. Grill shrimp, covered, over medium heat until shrimp turn pink, 3-4 minutes on each side. Grill tomatoes, covered, over medium heat 2-3 minutes or until slightly softened, turning occasionally.

3. Drain linguine, reserving ¼ cup pasta water. In same saucepan, melt butter over medium heat. Add the linguine, cheese and reserved pasta water, tossing to combine. Remove shrimp and tomatoes from skewers; serve with pasta. Sprinkle with basil.

1 serving: 445 cal., 17g fat (6g sat. fat), 158mg chol., 416mg sod., 45g carb. (4g sugars, 3g fiber), 29g pro.

Summer Turkey Kabobs

These kabobs let you enjoy the classic flavors of Thanksgiving any time of year! We grill them in the summer.
—Angela Mathews, Fayetteville, NY

- -

Takes: 30 min. • **Makes:** 6 kabobs

- 2 small yellow summer squash
- 2 small zucchini
- 1 can (about 15 oz.) whole potatoes, drained
- 2 Tbsp. olive oil
- 1 pkg. (20 oz.) turkey breast tenderloins
- ½ tsp. pepper
- ¼ tsp. salt
- 1 pkg. (5 oz.) torn mixed salad greens
- 1 cup salad croutons
- ½ cup red wine vinaigrette

1. Trim ends of yellow squash and zucchini; cut crosswise into 1-in. slices. Place slices in a large bowl; add potatoes. Pour oil over mixture, tossing to coat.

2. Cut turkey into 24 cubes; add to vegetables. Sprinkle with pepper and salt; toss again.

3. On 6 metal or soaked wooden skewers, alternately thread turkey cubes, squash, zucchini and potatoes. Grill, covered, over medium heat, turning occasionally, until turkey is no longer pink and vegetables are crisp-tender, 12-15 minutes. Serve on greens with croutons. Drizzle with vinaigrette.

1 kabob: 274 cal., 13g fat (1g sat. fat), 38mg chol., 720mg sod., 15g carb. (3g sugars, 2g fiber), 26g pro.
Diabetic exchanges: 2 lean meat, 1 vegetable, 1 fat, ½ starch.

Curried Chicken Skillet

This protein-packed skillet dish is loaded with bright flavor. A little curry and fresh ginger make the veggies, chicken and quinoa pop.
—Ruth Hartunian-Alumbaugh, Willimantic, CT

Takes: 30 min. • **Makes:** 4 servings

- 1⅓ cups plus ½ cup reduced-sodium chicken broth, divided
- ⅔ cup quinoa, rinsed
- 1 Tbsp. canola oil
- 1 medium sweet potato, diced
- 1 medium onion, chopped
- 1 celery rib, chopped
- 1 cup frozen peas
- 2 garlic cloves, minced
- 1 tsp. minced fresh gingerroot
- 3 tsp. curry powder
- ¼ tsp. salt
- 2 cups shredded cooked chicken

1. In a small saucepan, bring 1⅓ cups broth to a boil. Add quinoa. Reduce heat; simmer, covered, until liquid is absorbed, 12-15 minutes.

2. In a large skillet, heat the oil over medium-high heat; saute the sweet potato, onion and celery until potato is tender, 10-12 minutes. Add peas, garlic, ginger and seasonings; cook and stir 2 minutes. Stir in chicken and remaining broth; heat through. Stir in quinoa.

2 cups: 367 cal., 11g fat (2g sat. fat), 62mg chol., 450mg sod., 39g carb. (8g sugars, 6g fiber), 29g pro.
Diabetic exchanges: 3 lean meat, 2½ starch, ½ fat.

TIMESAVING TIP

Twelve ounces uncooked boneless chicken can be used if you don't have cooked chicken handy. Cut it into cubes or strips and saute it before cooking the vegetables. Remove it while the vegetables are sauteing so it doesn't overcook.

Apple-Onion Pork Tenderloin

This slightly sweet and tender pork roast is quick enough to make on a weeknight, but I often serve it on special occasions. It tastes amazing served with mashed potatoes or over egg noodles.
—Trisha Kruse, Eagle, ID

Takes: 30 min. • **Makes:** 4 servings

- 2 Tbsp. canola oil, divided
- 1 pork tenderloin (1 lb.), cut in half
- 3 Tbsp. honey mustard
- 2 medium apples, thinly sliced
- 1 large onion, halved and thinly sliced
- ½ cup white wine or apple cider
- ⅛ tsp. salt
- ⅛ tsp. pepper

1. Preheat oven to 425°. In an ovenproof skillet, heat 1 Tbsp. oil over medium-high heat. Brown the tenderloin halves on all sides; remove pan from heat. Spread honey mustard over pork; roast in oven until a thermometer reads 145°, 15-20 minutes.
2. Meanwhile, in another skillet, heat remaining oil over medium heat; saute the apples and onion 7 minutes. Stir in wine; bring to a boil. Reduce the heat; simmer, uncovered, until apples and onion are tender, 5-8 minutes. Stir in salt and pepper.
3. Remove pork from oven; let stand 5 minutes before slicing. Serve with apple mixture.

3 oz. cooked pork with ½ cup apple mixture: 294 cal., 12g fat (2g sat. fat), 64mg chol., 218mg sod., 20g carb. (13g sugars, 3g fiber), 24g pro.
Diabetic exchanges: 3 lean meat, 1½ fat, ½ starch, ½ fruit.

Comforting Barley & Pumpkin Beef Stew

There's nothing more comforting than a bowl of beef stew unless, of course, it's loaded with barley. And thanks to pumpkin and seasonings, this stew's flavor is as amazing as it's texture. To make it meatless, replace the beef with mushrooms and use vegetable broth instead of beef broth.
—Colleen Delawder, Herndon, VA

Prep: 30 min. • **Cook:** 6 hours
Makes: 9 servings (3½ qt.)

- ¼ cup all-purpose flour
- 3 Tbsp. cornstarch
- 1½ tsp. salt, divided
- 1½ tsp. pepper, divided
- 1½ lbs. beef stew meat
- 3 Tbsp. olive oil
- 1 large sweet onion, finely chopped
- 2 cartons (32 oz. each) beef broth
- 1 can (15 oz.) pumpkin
- 1 cup medium pearl barley
- 1 tsp. dried thyme
- ¼ tsp. garlic powder
- ¼ tsp. crushed red pepper flakes
  Optional: Additional red pepper flakes and minced fresh parsley

In a shallow dish, mix the flour, cornstarch, 1 tsp. salt and 1 tsp. pepper. Add beef, a few pieces at a time, and toss to coat. In a large skillet, heat oil over medium-high heat; brown meat in batches. Transfer meat to a 5- or 6-qt. slow cooker; leave drippings in the pan. In the same skillet, cook and stir onion in pan drippings until tender, 6-8 minutes; add to slow cooker. Stir in the broth, pumpkin, barley, thyme, garlic powder, red pepper flakes, and remaining salt and pepper. Cook, covered, on low until meat is tender, 6-8 hours. If desired, serve with additional red pepper flakes and parsley.

1½ cups: 211 cal., 8g fat (2g sat. fat), 35mg chol., 819mg sod., 20g carb. (3g sugars, 4g fiber), 15g pro.

Beef Barley Skillet

This versatile dish goes together fast since it's made with quick-cooking barley. You can make it with ground turkey or chicken, and any color bell pepper that you have on hand.
—Irene Tetreault, South Hadley, MA

- -

Takes: 30 min. • **Makes:** 4 servings

- 1 lb. lean ground beef (90% lean)
- 1 small onion, chopped
- ¼ cup chopped celery
- ¼ cup chopped green pepper
- 1 can (14½ oz.) diced tomatoes, undrained
- 1½ cups water
- ¾ cup quick-cooking barley
- ½ cup chili sauce
- 1 tsp. Worcestershire sauce
- ½ tsp. dried marjoram
- ⅛ tsp. pepper
- Chopped parsley, optional

In a large skillet, cook ground beef, onion, celery and green pepper over medium-high heat until beef is no longer pink and the vegetables are tender, 5-7 minutes; crumble beef; drain. Stir in the next 7 ingredients. Bring to a boil; reduce heat. Simmer, uncovered, until barley is tender, 5-10 minutes. If desired, top with chopped parsley.

1½ cups: 362 cal., 10g fat (4g sat. fat), 71mg chol., 707mg sod., 41g carb. (11g sugars, 8g fiber), 27g pro.
Diabetic exchanges: 3 lean meat, 2 starch, 1 vegetable.

TIMESAVING TIP

Barley is a flavorful, chewy alternative to white rice. Pearl barley has the double outer hull and bran layer removed. Quick-cooking barley, used in this recipe, is precooked pearl barley.

Spinach & Mushroom Smothered Chicken

Chicken breasts stay nice and moist tucked under a blanket of melted cheese. It's extra special to serve but not tricky to make.
—Katrina Wagner, Grain Valley, MO

- -

Takes: 30 min. • **Makes:** 4 servings

1½	tsp. olive oil
1¾	cups sliced fresh mushrooms
3	green onions, sliced
3	cups fresh baby spinach
2	Tbsp. chopped pecans
4	boneless skinless chicken breast halves (4 oz. each)
½	tsp. rotisserie chicken seasoning
2	slices reduced-fat provolone cheese, halved

1. Preheat grill or broiler. In a large skillet, heat oil over medium-high heat; saute mushrooms and green onions until tender. Stir in spinach and pecans until spinach is wilted. Remove from heat; keep warm.

2. Sprinkle chicken with seasoning. Grill, covered, on an oiled grill rack over medium heat or broil 4 in. from heat on a greased broiler pan until a thermometer reads 165°, about 4-5 minutes per side. Top with the cheese; grill or broil until cheese is melted. To serve, top chicken with mushroom mixture.

1 serving: 203 cal., 9g fat (2g sat. fat), 68mg chol., 210mg sod., 3g carb. (1g sugars, 2g fiber), 27g pro.
Diabetic exchanges: 3 lean meat, 1 vegetable, 1 fat.

Pineapple-Ginger Chicken Stir-Fry

I found the original recipe for this stir-fry on a can of pineapple in the 1980s. After making it for several years, I lightened up the ingredients and adapted it to a quick skillet meal. We've enjoyed it this way ever since!
—Sue Gronholz, Beaver Dam, WI

- -

Takes: 30 min. • **Makes:** 4 servings

- 1 can (20 oz.) unsweetened pineapple chunks
- 1 Tbsp. cornstarch
- 3 Tbsp. reduced-sodium soy sauce
- 2 Tbsp. honey
- ¼ tsp. ground cinnamon
- 2 Tbsp. canola oil, divided
- 1 lb. boneless skinless chicken breasts, cut into 1-in. cubes
- 1 small onion, chopped
- 1 Tbsp. minced fresh gingerroot
- 2 garlic cloves, minced
  Hot cooked brown rice
  Minced fresh cilantro, optional

1. Drain pineapple, reserving juice. Mix cornstarch, soy sauce, honey, cinnamon and reserved juice until smooth. In a skillet, heat 1 Tbsp. oil over medium-high heat; saute the chicken until lightly browned, 4-6 minutes. Remove from pan.

2. In same pan, saute onion, ginger and garlic in the remaining oil until crisp-tender, about 2 minutes. Stir cornstarch mixture; add to pan with chicken and pineapple chunks. Bring to a boil, stirring constantly; cook and stir until the sauce is thickened and the chicken is cooked through, 5-7 minutes.

3. Serve with rice. If desired, sprinkle with cilantro.

1 cup chicken mixture: 316 cal., 10g fat (1g sat. fat), 63mg chol., 487mg sod., 31g carb. (26g sugars, 1g fiber), 25g pro.
Diabetic exchanges: 3 lean meat, 1½ starch, 1½ fat, ½ fruit.

Slow-Cooker Chicken Taco Salad

We use this delicious chicken in several meals, including tacos, sandwiches, omelets and enchiladas. My kids love helping me measure the seasonings and fill the slow cooker.
—Karie Houghton, Lynnwood, WA

- -

Prep: 10 min. • **Cook:** 3 hours
Makes: 6 servings

- 3 tsp. chili powder
- 1 tsp. each ground cumin, seasoned salt and pepper
- ½ tsp. each white pepper, ground chipotle pepper and paprika
- ¼ tsp. dried oregano
- ¼ tsp. crushed red pepper flakes
- 1½ lbs. boneless skinless chicken breasts
- 1 cup chicken broth
- 9 cups torn romaine
  Optional toppings: Sliced avocado, shredded cheddar cheese, chopped tomato or halved cherry tomatoes, sliced green onions and salad dressing of choice

1. Mix seasonings; rub over chicken. Place in a 3-qt. slow cooker. Add broth. Cook, covered, on low until chicken is tender, 3-4 hours.
2. Remove chicken; cool slightly. Shred with 2 forks. Serve over romaine; top as desired.
1¾ cups: 143 cal., 3g fat (1g sat. fat), 63mg chol., 516mg sod., 4g carb. (1g sugars, 2g fiber), 24g pro.
Diabetic exchanges: 3 lean meat, 1 vegetable.

Saucy Mediterranean Chicken with Rice

The hints of Mediterranean flavor in this quick and easy chicken dish make it a favorite in our family.
—Tabitha Alloway, Edna, KS

- -

Takes: 30 min. • **Makes:** 4 servings

¾	cup water
3	Tbsp. tomato paste
2	Tbsp. lemon juice
¾	tsp. salt
1	tsp. chili powder
½	tsp. garlic powder
½	tsp. ground ginger
¼	tsp. ground fennel seed
¼	tsp. ground turmeric
1	tsp. ground coriander, optional
3	Tbsp. olive oil
1	medium onion, chopped
1	lb. boneless skinless chicken breasts, cut into 1-in. cubes
3	cups hot cooked rice Minced fresh parsley, optional

1. In a small bowl, mix the water, tomato paste, lemon juice, salt, chili powder, garlic powder, ginger, fennel, turmeric and, if desired, coriander until smooth.

2. In a large skillet, heat the oil over medium-high heat. Add onions; cook and stir until tender. Stir in chicken; brown 3-4 minutes. Pour the water mixture into pan.

3. Bring to a boil. Reduce the heat; simmer, uncovered, until chicken is no longer pink, 8-10 minutes. Serve with rice. If desired, top with parsley.

¾ cup chicken mixture with ¾ cup rice: 394 cal., 13g fat (2g sat. fat), 63mg chol., 527mg sod., 40g carb. (3g sugars, 2g fiber), 27g pro.
Diabetic exchanges: 3 lean meat, 2½ starch, 2 fat.

Shrimp with Warm German-Style Coleslaw

We love anything that's tangy or has bacon. With fennel and tarragon, this dish boasts a savory herb flavor. I use the medley from Minute Rice if I don't have time to make my own.
—Ann Sheehy, Lawrence, MA

- -

Takes: 30 min. • **Makes:** 4 servings

- 6 bacon strips
- 2 Tbsp. canola oil, divided
- 3 cups finely shredded green cabbage
- ½ cup finely shredded carrot (1 medium carrot)
- 1 cup finely shredded red cabbage, optional
- ½ cup finely shredded fennel bulb, optional
- 6 green onions, finely chopped
- 3 Tbsp. minced fresh parsley
- 2 Tbsp. minced fresh tarragon or 2 tsp. dried tarragon
- ¼ tsp. salt
- ⅛ tsp. pepper
- ¼ cup red wine vinegar
- 1 lb. uncooked shrimp (26-30 per lb.), peeled and deveined
- 3 cups hot cooked rice or multigrain medley

1. In a large skillet, cook bacon over medium heat until crisp. Remove to paper towels to drain. Pour off pan drippings, discarding all but 2 Tbsp. Crumble bacon.
2. In same skillet, heat 1 Tbsp. drippings with 1 Tbsp. oil over medium heat. Add green cabbage, carrot and, if desired, red cabbage and fennel; cook and stir until the vegetables are just tender, 1-2 minutes. Remove to a bowl. Stir in the green onions, parsley, tarragon, salt and pepper; toss with vinegar. Keep warm.
3. Add remaining drippings and remaining oil to skillet. Add shrimp; cook and stir over medium heat until shrimp turn pink, 2-3 minutes. Remove from heat.

4. To serve, spoon rice and coleslaw into soup bowls. Top with shrimp; sprinkle with crumbled bacon.
1 serving: 472 cal., 20g fat (5g sat. fat), 156mg chol., 546mg sod., 44g carb. (2g sugars, 3g fiber), 28g pro.

Sweet & Sour Sausage Stir-Fry

Who couldn't use a stir-fry that's low in prep time, yet bursting with flavor? My quick recipe is achievable on even your busiest nights.
—Wendy Wendler, Indian Harbour Beach, FL

- -

Takes: 30 min. • **Makes:** 4 servings

- 1 pkg. (14 oz.) smoked turkey sausage, cut into ½-in. slices
- 2 small onions, quartered and separated
- 1 cup shredded carrots
- 1 can (8 oz.) unsweetened pineapple chunks, undrained
- 1 Tbsp. cornstarch
- ½ to 1 tsp. ground ginger
- ⅓ cup cold water
- 2 Tbsp. reduced-sodium soy sauce
  Hot cooked rice, optional

1. Stir-fry sausage in a large nonstick skillet for 3-4 minutes or until lightly browned. Add onions and carrots; stir-fry until crisp-tender. Drain pineapple, reserving juice. Add pineapple to sausage mixture.
2. Combine cornstarch and ginger. Stir in water, soy sauce and reserved pineapple juice until smooth. Add to the skillet. Bring to a boil; cook and stir for 1-2 minutes or until mixture is thickened. Serve over rice if desired.
1 cup: 197 cal., 5g fat (2g sat. fat), 62mg chol., 1283mg sod., 19g carb. (13g sugars, 2g fiber), 17g pro.

Half-Homemade
STAPLES

Pressed for time? Take advantage of shortcut ingredients—
canned goods, store-bought dough, frozen veggies and more.

Bacon-Corn Stuffed Peppers

Filled with corn, salsa, green onions, mozzarella cheese and bacon, these grilled pepper halves are sure to liven up your next cookout. They have a wonderful taste and give a fun twist to the usual corn on the cob.

—Mitzi Sentiff, Annapolis, MD

- -

Prep: 20 min. • **Grill:** 25 min.
Makes: 4 servings

2	cups frozen corn, thawed
⅓	cup salsa
6	green onions, chopped
1	medium green pepper, halved and seeded
1	medium sweet red pepper, halved and seeded
¼	cup shredded part-skim mozzarella cheese
2	bacon strips, cooked and crumbled
	Additional salsa, optional

1. In a large bowl, combine the corn, salsa and onions. Spoon into pepper halves. Place each stuffed pepper half on a piece of heavy-duty foil (about 18x12 in.). Fold foil around peppers and seal tightly.

2. Grill, covered, over medium heat until peppers are crisp-tender, 25-30 minutes. Carefully open packets to allow steam to escape. Sprinkle with cheese and bacon. Return to the grill until cheese is melted, 3-5 minutes. Serve with additional salsa if desired.

1 stuffed pepper half: 130 cal., 4g fat (1g sat. fat), 9mg chol., 207mg sod., 21g carb. (5g sugars, 3g fiber), 6g pro.
Diabetic exchanges: 1 starch, 1 vegetable, ½ fat.

Chipotle Citrus-Glazed Turkey Tenderloins

This simple skillet recipe makes it easy to cook turkey on a weeknight. The combination of sweet, spicy and smoky flavors from orange, peppers and molasses is amazing.
—Darlene Morris, Franklinton, LA

- -

Takes: 30 min.
Makes: 4 servings (½ cup sauce)

- 4 turkey breast tenderloins (5 oz. each)
- ¼ tsp. salt
- ¼ tsp. pepper
- 1 Tbsp. canola oil
- ¾ cup orange juice
- ¼ cup lime juice
- ¼ cup packed brown sugar
- 1 Tbsp. molasses
- 2 tsp. minced chipotle peppers in adobo sauce
- 2 Tbsp. minced fresh cilantro

1. Sprinkle turkey tenderloins with salt and pepper. In a large skillet, brown turkey in oil on all sides.
2. Meanwhile, in a small bowl, whisk juices, brown sugar, molasses and chipotle peppers; add to skillet. Reduce heat and simmer until the turkey reaches 165°, 12-16 minutes. Transfer turkey to a cutting board; let rest for 5 minutes.
3. Simmer glaze until thickened, about 4 minutes. Slice turkey and serve with glaze. Top with cilantro.
4 oz. cooked turkey with 2 Tbsp. glaze: 274 cal., 5g fat (0 sat. fat), 56mg chol., 252mg sod., 24g carb. (22g sugars, 0 fiber), 35g pro.

Chicken & Waffles

My first experience with chicken and waffles sent my taste buds into orbit. I first made the dish as appetizers, but we love it as a main course, too.
—Lisa Renshaw, Kansas City, MO

- -

Takes: 25 min. • **Makes:** 4 servings

- 12 frozen crispy chicken strips (about 18 oz.)
- ½ cup honey
- 2 tsp. hot pepper sauce
- 8 frozen waffles, toasted

1. Bake chicken strips according to package directions. Meanwhile, in a small bowl, mix honey and pepper sauce.
2. Cut chicken into bite-sized pieces; serve on toasted waffles. Drizzle with honey mixture.
1 serving: 643 cal., 22g fat (3g sat. fat), 32mg chol., 958mg sod., 93g carb. (39g sugars, 6g fiber), 21g pro.

> **TIMESAVING TIP**
>
> For a fruity southern twist, use peach preserves instead of the honey.

Turkey Alfredo Pizza

A longtime family favorite, this thin-crust pizza is both tasty and nutritious. It's an excellent way to use up leftover turkey, too.
—Edie DeSpain, Logan, UT

- -

Takes: 25 min. • **Makes:** 6 servings

- 1 prebaked 12-in. thin pizza crust
- 1 garlic clove, peeled and halved
- ¾ cup reduced-fat Alfredo sauce, divided
- 1 pkg. (10 oz.) frozen chopped spinach, thawed and squeezed dry
- 2 tsp. lemon juice
- ¼ tsp. salt
- ⅛ tsp. pepper
- 2 cups shredded cooked turkey breast
- ¾ cup shredded Parmesan cheese
- ½ tsp. crushed red pepper flakes

1. Place the crust on a baking sheet; rub with cut sides of garlic. Discard garlic. Spread ½ cup Alfredo sauce over crust.

2. In a bowl, combine the spinach, lemon juice, salt and pepper; spoon evenly over sauce. Top with turkey; drizzle with remaining Alfredo sauce. Sprinkle with Parmesan cheese and pepper flakes.

3. Bake at 425° until ingredients are heated through and cheese is melted, 11-13 minutes.

1 piece: 300 cal., 9g fat (4g sat. fat), 60mg chol., 823mg sod., 27g carb. (2g sugars, 2g fiber), 25g pro.
Diabetic exchanges: 3 lean meat, 2 starch, ½ fat.

Tex-Mex Pork Chops

These easy, flavorful chops won a contest for me. Salsa, cumin and green chiles give these chops the kick they need to be called Tex-Mex.
—Jo Ann Dalrymple, Claremore, OK

- -

Takes: 20 min. • **Makes:** 6 servings

    Butter-flavored cooking spray
1 **small onion, chopped**
6 **boneless pork loin chops**
    (5 oz. each)
1 **cup salsa**
1 **can (4 oz.) chopped green**
    chiles
½ **tsp. ground cumin**
¼ **tsp. pepper**

1. In a large skillet coated with butter-flavored cooking spray, saute onion until tender. Add pork chops; cook over medium heat until a thermometer reads 145°, 5-6 minutes on each side.

2. Combine salsa, chiles, cumin and pepper; pour over pork. Bring to a boil. Reduce heat; cover and simmer until heated through.

1 pork chop: 223 cal., 8g fat (3g sat. fat), 68mg chol., 433mg sod., 9g carb. (3g sugars, 5g fiber), 32g pro. **Diabetic exchanges:** 4 lean meat, 1 vegetable.

Spicy Salmon Patties

Made with canned salmon, these patties are good hot or cold. I usually serve them on buns with slices of ripe tomato, sweet red onion, and red and green bell pepper.
—Barbara Coston, Little Rock, AR

- -

Takes: 30 min. • **Makes:** 4 servings

- 2 slices whole wheat bread
- 12 miniature pretzels
- 2 tsp. Italian seasoning
- 2 tsp. salt-free spicy seasoning blend
- ½ tsp. pepper
- 2 large eggs, lightly beaten
- 1 can (14¾ oz.) salmon, drained, bones and skin removed
- ½ cup finely chopped onion
- ⅓ cup finely chopped green pepper
- 1 Tbsp. finely chopped jalapeno pepper
- 2 garlic cloves, minced
- 2 Tbsp. olive oil

1. Place the first 5 ingredients in a blender or food processor; cover and process until mixture resembles fine crumbs.

2. In a bowl, combine eggs, salmon, onion, green pepper, jalapeno, garlic and ½ cup crumb mixture. Shape into eight ½-in.-thick patties. Coat with remaining crumb mixture.

3. In a large nonstick skillet over medium heat, cook patties in oil until golden brown, 4-5 minutes on each side.

2 patties: 339 cal., 18g fat (3g sat. fat), 176mg chol., 607mg sod., 13g carb. (2g sugars, 2g fiber), 30g pro. **Diabetic exchanges:** 4 lean meat, 2 fat, 1 starch.

Cheesy Summer Squash Flatbreads

When you want a meatless meal with Mediterranean style, these flatbreads smothered with squash, hummus and mozzarella deliver the goods.
—Matthew Hass, Ellison Bay, WI

- -

Takes: 30 min. • **Makes:** 4 servings

- 3 small yellow summer squash, sliced ¼ in. thick
- 1 Tbsp. olive oil
- ½ tsp. salt
- 2 cups fresh baby spinach, coarsely chopped
- 2 naan flatbreads
- ⅓ cup roasted red pepper hummus
- 1 carton (8 oz.) fresh mozzarella cheese pearls
  Pepper

1. Preheat oven to 425°. Toss squash with oil and salt; spread evenly in a 15x10x1-in. baking pan. Roast until tender, 8-10 minutes. Transfer to a bowl; stir in spinach.

2. Place naan on a baking sheet; spread with hummus. Top with squash mixture and cheese. Bake on a lower oven rack just until the cheese is melted, 4-6 minutes. Sprinkle with pepper.

½ topped flatbread: 332 cal., 20g fat (9g sat. fat), 47mg chol., 737mg sod., 24g carb. (7g sugars, 3g fiber), 15g pro.

Quick Tacos al Pastor

My husband and I tried pork and pineapple tacos at a truck stand in Hawaii. Something about them was so tasty, I decided to make my own version at home.
—Lori McLain, Denton, TX

- -

Takes: 25 min. • **Makes:** 4 servings

- 1 pkg. (15 oz.) refrigerated pork roast au jus
- 1 cup well-drained unsweetened pineapple chunks, divided
- 1 Tbsp. canola oil
- ½ cup enchilada sauce
- 8 corn tortillas (6 in.), warmed
- ½ cup finely chopped onion
- ¼ cup chopped fresh cilantro
  Optional: Crumbled queso fresco, salsa verde and lime wedges

1. Coarsely shred pork, reserving juices. In a small bowl, crush half the pineapple with a fork.

2. In a large nonstick skillet, heat oil over medium-high heat. Add whole pineapple chunks; cook until lightly browned, 2-3 minutes, turning occasionally. Remove from pan.

3. Add enchilada sauce and the crushed pineapple to same skillet; stir in pork and reserved juices. Cook over medium-high heat until liquid is evaporated, 4-6 minutes, stirring occasionally.

4. Serve in tortillas with pineapple chunks, onion and cilantro. If desired, top with queso fresco and salsa, and serve with lime wedges.

2 tacos: 317 cal., 11g fat (3g sat. fat), 57mg chol., 573mg sod., 36g carb. (12g sugars, 5g fiber), 24g pro. **Diabetic exchanges:** 3 lean meat, 2 starch, 1 fat.

Ziti Bake

My children aren't crazy for many of my casseroles, but they give a cheer when they hear we're having this classic dish for supper. Even the leftovers are devoured.
—Charity Burkholder, Pittsboro, IN

- -

Prep: 20 min. • **Bake:** 50 min.
Makes: 6 servings

- 3 cups uncooked ziti or small tube pasta
- 1¾ cups meatless spaghetti sauce, divided
- 1 cup 4% cottage cheese
- 1½ cups shredded part-skim mozzarella cheese, divided
- 1 large egg, lightly beaten
- 2 tsp. dried parsley flakes
- ½ tsp. dried oregano
- ¼ tsp. garlic powder
- ⅛ tsp. pepper

1. Cook pasta according to package directions. Meanwhile, in a large bowl, combine ¾ cup spaghetti sauce, cottage cheese, 1 cup mozzarella cheese, egg, parsley, oregano, garlic powder and pepper. Drain pasta; stir into cheese mixture.

2. In a greased 8-in. square baking dish, spread ¼ cup spaghetti sauce. Top with pasta mixture, remaining sauce and mozzarella cheese.

3. Cover and bake at 375° for 45 minutes. Uncover; bake until a thermometer reads 160°, 5-10 minutes longer.

1½ cups: 297 cal., 9g fat (5g sat. fat), 52mg chol., 639mg sod., 37g carb. (8g sugars, 3g fiber), 18g pro.

Chicken Chop Suey with a Twist

If you're in for a busy evening, here's an ideal way to ensure you can still have a healthy and satisfying supper. It's tasty, traditional and easy, too!
—Melody Littlewood, Royal City, WA

- -

Prep: 20 min. • **Cook:** 5½ hours
Makes: 9 servings

1½ lbs. boneless skinless chicken
  thighs, cut into 2-in. pieces
8 oz. sliced fresh mushrooms
2 celery ribs, sliced
1 medium onion, chopped
1 can (14 oz.) bean sprouts,
  rinsed and drained
1 can (8 oz.) bamboo shoots,
  drained
1 can (8 oz.) sliced water
  chestnuts, drained
1 can (14½ oz.) reduced-
  sodium chicken broth
½ cup reduced-sodium
  soy sauce

1 Tbsp. minced fresh gingerroot
¼ tsp. crushed red pepper flakes
2 Tbsp. cornstarch
2 Tbsp. cold water
½ cup frozen shelled edamame
  Hot cooked rice

1. Place chicken in a 4- or 5-qt. slow cooker. Top with mushrooms, celery, onion, bean sprouts, bamboo shoots and water chestnuts. In a small bowl, combine the broth, soy sauce, ginger and pepper flakes. Pour over chicken and vegetables. Cover and cook on low until chicken is tender, 5-6 hours.
2. Combine cornstarch and water until smooth; gradually stir into chop suey. Add edamame, cover and cook on high until thickened, about 30 minutes. Serve with rice.
1 cup: 178 cal., 6g fat (2g sat. fat), 50mg chol., 739mg sod., 12g carb. (3g sugars, 3g fiber), 19g pro.
Diabetic exchanges: 2 lean meat, 1 vegetable.

TIMESAVING TIP

Edamame is a type of soybean. Popular in many Asian foods, the beans are harvested early before they are processed and become hard. The young beans are parboiled and frozen to retain their freshness and can be found in the freezer of grocery and health food stores. A good source of fiber, protein, calcium and vitamin C, edamame is a tasty addition to soups, salads, sandwiches, soups and main dishes or eaten alone as a healthy snack.

Coconut-Crusted Turkey Strips

My granddaughter shared these baked turkey strips with me. With a plum dipping sauce, they're just the thing for a light dinner.
—Agnes Ward, Stratford, ON

- -

Takes: 30 min. • **Makes:** 6 servings

- 2 **large egg whites**
- 2 **tsp. sesame oil**
- ½ **cup sweetened shredded coconut, toasted**
- ½ **cup dry bread crumbs**
- 2 **Tbsp. sesame seeds, toasted**
- ½ **tsp. salt**
- 1½ **lbs. turkey breast tenderloins, cut into ½-in. strips**
  Cooking spray

DIPPING SAUCE

- ½ **cup plum sauce**
- ⅓ **cup unsweetened pineapple juice**
- 1½ **tsp. prepared mustard**
- 1 **tsp. cornstarch**

1. Preheat oven to 425°. In a shallow bowl, whisk egg whites and oil. In another shallow bowl, mix coconut, bread crumbs, sesame seeds and salt. Dip turkey in egg mixture, then in coconut mixture, patting to help coating adhere.

2. Place on baking sheets coated with cooking spray; spritz the turkey with cooking spray. Bake until turkey is no longer pink, 10-12 minutes, turning once during cooking.

3. Meanwhile, in a small saucepan, mix sauce ingredients. Bring to a boil; cook and stir 1-2 minutes or until thickened. Serve turkey with sauce.

Note: To toast coconut, bake in a shallow pan in a 350°; oven for 5-10 minutes or cook in a skillet over low heat until golden brown, stirring occasionally.

3 oz. cooked turkey with 2 Tbsp. sauce: 278 cal., 8g fat (3g sat. fat), 56mg chol., 519mg sod., 22g carb. (11g sugars, 1g fiber), 30g pro.
Diabetic exchanges: 3 lean meat, 1½ starch, ½ fat.

Stuffed Vegetarian Shells

When my aunt first told me about these shells, they sounded like a lot of work—but the recipe whips up in no time. Sometimes I add a little cooked bacon to the ricotta filling.
—Amelia Hopkin, Salt Lake City, UT

- -

Prep: 20 min. • **Bake:** 30 min.
Makes: 8 servings

24	uncooked jumbo pasta shells
1	carton (15 oz.) part-skim ricotta cheese
3	cups frozen chopped broccoli, thawed and drained
1	cup shredded part-skim mozzarella cheese
2	large egg whites
1	Tbsp. minced fresh basil or 1 tsp. dried basil
½	tsp. garlic salt
¼	tsp. pepper
1	jar (26 oz.) meatless spaghetti sauce
2	Tbsp. shredded Parmesan cheese

1. Cook pasta according to package directions. In a large bowl, combine the ricotta, broccoli, mozzarella, egg whites and seasonings. Drain pasta and rinse in cold water.

2. Spread half the spaghetti sauce into a 13x9-in. baking dish coated with cooking spray. Stuff pasta shells with ricotta mixture; arrange over spaghetti sauce. Pour remaining sauce over pasta shells.

3. Cover and bake at 375° for 25 minutes. Uncover; sprinkle with Parmesan cheese. Bake until heated through, about 5 minutes longer.

3 stuffed shells: 279 cal., 8g fat (5g sat. fat), 26mg chol., 725mg sod., 36g carb. (8g sugars, 4g fiber), 18g pro.
Diabetic exchanges: 2½ starch, 2 lean meat.

TIMESAVING TIP

To amp up the heat in this tropical jerk chicken, add 1 habanero or Scotch bonnet pepper, seeded and minced.

Red Pepper Chicken

Chicken breasts are cooked with black beans, red peppers and juicy tomatoes in this southwestern supper. We love it served with rice cooked in chicken broth.
—Piper Spiwak, Vienna, VA

- -

Prep: 15 min. • **Cook:** 6 hours
Makes: 4 servings

- 4   **boneless skinless chicken breast halves (4 oz. each)**
- 1   **can (15 oz.) no-salt-added black beans, rinsed and drained**
- 1   **can (14½ oz.) Mexican stewed tomatoes, undrained**
- 1   **jar (12 oz.) roasted sweet red peppers, drained and cut into strips**
- 1   **large onion, chopped**
  Pepper to taste
  Hot cooked rice

Place chicken in a 3-qt. slow cooker. In a bowl, combine beans, tomatoes, red peppers, onion and pepper. Pour over chicken. Cover and cook on low until chicken is tender, about 6 hours. Serve with rice.

1 serving: 288 cal., 3g fat (1g sat. fat), 63mg chol., 657mg sod., 28g carb. (8g sugars, 7g fiber), 30g pro.
Diabetic exchanges: 3 lean meat, 1½ starch, 1 vegetable.

Jerk Chicken with Tropical Couscous

Caribbean cuisine brightens up our weeknights thanks to its bold colors and flavors. Ready in less than 30 minutes, this chicken is one of my go-to meals.
—Jeanne Holt, St. Paul, MN

- -

Takes: 25 min. • **Makes:** 4 servings

1 can (15.25 oz.) mixed tropical fruit
1 lb. boneless skinless chicken breasts, cut into 2½-in. strips
3 tsp. Caribbean jerk seasoning
1 Tbsp. olive oil
½ cup chopped sweet red pepper
1 Tbsp. finely chopped seeded jalapeno pepper
⅓ cup thinly sliced green onions (green portion only)
1½ cups reduced-sodium chicken broth
3 Tbsp. chopped fresh cilantro, divided
1 Tbsp. lime juice
¼ tsp. salt
1 cup uncooked whole wheat couscous
Lime wedges

1. Drain mixed fruit, reserving ¼ cup syrup. Chop fruit.

2. Toss chicken with jerk seasoning. In a large cast-iron or other heavy skillet, heat oil over medium-high heat; saute chicken until no longer pink, 4-5 minutes. Remove from pan, reserving drippings.

3. In same pan, saute peppers and green onions in drippings 2 minutes. Add the broth, 1 Tbsp. cilantro, lime juice, salt, reserved syrup and chopped fruit; bring to a boil. Stir in couscous; reduce heat to low. Place chicken on top; cook, covered, until the liquid is absorbed and chicken is heated through, about 3-4 minutes. Sprinkle with the remaining cilantro. Serve with lime wedges.

Note: Wear disposable gloves when cutting hot peppers; the oils can burn skin. Avoid touching your face.

1½ cups: 411 cal., 7g fat (1g sat. fat), 63mg chol., 628mg sod., 57g carb. (19g sugars, 7g fiber), 31g pro.

READER REVIEW
"Really tasty, and great for summer in the hot, muggy Midwest. It's good either hot or cold. I love it exactly as written, though I leave out the jalapeno pepper to reduce the heat when I make it for my family."
—ELLENMAAS, TASTEOFHOME.COM

Honey Chicken Stir-Fry

I'm a new mom, and my schedule is dependent upon our young son, so I like meals that can be ready in as little time as possible. This all-in-one stir-fry with a hint of sweetness from honey is a big timesaver.

—Caroline Sperry, Allentown, MI

- -

Takes: 30 min. • **Makes:** 4 servings

- 2 tsp. cornstarch
- 1 Tbsp. cold water
- 3 tsp. olive oil, divided
- 1 lb. boneless skinless chicken breasts, cut into 1-in. pieces
- 1 garlic clove, minced

- 3 Tbsp. honey
- 2 Tbsp. reduced-sodium soy sauce
- ⅛ tsp. salt
- ⅛ tsp. pepper
- 1 pkg. (16 oz.) frozen broccoli stir-fry vegetable blend Hot cooked rice, optional

1. Mix cornstarch and water until smooth. In a large nonstick skillet, heat 2 tsp. oil over medium-high heat; stir-fry chicken and garlic 1 minute. Add honey, soy sauce, salt and pepper; cook and stir until chicken is no longer pink, 2-3 minutes. Remove from pan.
2. In same pan, stir-fry vegetable blend in remaining oil just until tender, 4-5 minutes. Return chicken to pan. Stir cornstarch mixture and add to pan; bring to a boil. Cook and stir until thickened, about 1 minute. Serve with rice if desired.

1 cup stir-fry: 249 cal., 6g fat (1g sat. fat), 63mg chol., 455mg sod., 21g carb. (15g sugars, 3g fiber), 25g pro.
Diabetic exchanges: 3 lean meat, 2 vegetable, ½ starch.

Maple-Glazed Pork Tenderloin

My husband and I think this roasted pork tenderloin tastes like a fancy restaurant dish, but it couldn't be simpler to make at home. The maple glaze makes it extra special. Add Brussels sprouts or your favorite veggie to make it a complete meal.
—Colleen Mercier, Salmon Arm, BC

Takes: 30 min. • **Makes:** 4 servings

- ¾ tsp. salt
- ¾ tsp. rubbed sage
- ½ tsp. pepper
- 2 pork tenderloins (¾ lb. each)
- 1 tsp. butter
- ¼ cup maple syrup
- 3 Tbsp. cider vinegar
- 1¾ tsp. Dijon mustard

1. Preheat oven to 425°. Mix the seasonings; sprinkle over pork. In a large nonstick skillet, heat butter over medium heat; brown tenderloins on all sides. Transfer to a foil-lined 15x10x1-in. pan. Roast 10 minutes.

2. Meanwhile, for glaze, in same skillet, mix the syrup, vinegar and mustard; bring to a boil, stirring to loosen browned bits from pan. Cook and stir until slightly thickened, 1-2 minutes; remove from heat.

3. Brush 1 Tbsp. glaze over pork tenderloins; continue roasting until a thermometer inserted in pork reads 145°, 7-10 minutes, brushing halfway through with remaining glaze. Let stand 5 minutes before slicing.

5 oz. cooked pork: 264 cal., 7g fat (3g sat. fat), 98mg chol., 573mg sod., 14g carb. (12g sugars, 0 fiber), 34g pro.

Diabetic exchanges: 5 lean meat, 1 starch.

Thai Chicken Thighs

Thanks to the slow cooker, this traditional Thai dish with peanut butter, jalapeno peppers and chili sauce becomes incredibly easy to make. If you want to crank up the spice a little bit, use more jalapeno peppers.
—*Taste of Home* Test Kitchen

- -

Prep: 25 min. • **Cook:** 5 hours
Makes: 8 servings

8	bone-in chicken thighs (about 3 lbs.), skin removed
½	cup salsa
¼	cup creamy peanut butter
2	Tbsp. lemon juice
2	Tbsp. reduced-sodium soy sauce
1	Tbsp. chopped seeded jalapeno pepper
2	tsp. Thai chili sauce
1	garlic clove, minced
1	tsp. minced fresh gingerroot
2	green onions, sliced
2	Tbsp. sesame seeds, toasted Hot cooked basmati rice, optional

1. Place chicken in a 3-qt. slow cooker. In a small bowl, combine salsa, peanut butter, lemon juice, soy sauce, jalapeno, Thai chili sauce, garlic and ginger; pour over chicken.
2. Cover and cook on low until the chicken is tender, 5-6 hours. Sprinkle with green onions and sesame seeds. Serve with rice if desired.
Note: Wear disposable gloves when cutting hot peppers; the oils can burn skin. Avoid touching your face.
1 chicken thigh with ¼ cup sauce: 261 cal., 15g fat (4g sat. fat), 87mg chol., 350mg sod., 5g carb. (2g sugars, 1g fiber), 27g pro.
Diabetic exchanges: 4 lean meat, 1 fat, ½ starch.

Turkey Lo Mein

I substituted turkey for pork in this classic Chinese recipe. It was a hit at our church potluck, and my husband and two children love it, too.
—Leigh Lundy, York, NE

- -

Takes: 30 min. • **Makes:** 6 servings

1	lb. lean ground turkey
2	medium carrots, thinly sliced
1	medium onion, chopped
½	tsp. garlic powder
2	pkg. (3 oz. each) chicken ramen noodles
1½	cups water
6	cups shredded cabbage
1	cup frozen peas, thawed
¼	cup reduced-sodium soy sauce

1. In a large skillet, cook and crumble turkey with carrots, onion and garlic powder over medium-high heat meat is until no longer pink, 5-7 minutes.
2. Break up noodles and add to skillet; stir in contents of seasoning packets and water. Bring to a boil. Reduce heat; simmer, covered, 3-5 minutes. Add the remaining ingredients; cook and stir until cabbage is crisp-tender, 1-3 minutes.
1⅓ cups: 294 cal., 11g fat (4g sat. fat), 52mg chol., 1024mg sod., 28g carb. (3g sugars, 4g fiber), 21g pro.

Chinese Cashew Chicken Pizza

I make this quick weeknight dinner recipe when I'm craving takeout pizza and Chinese food. I take advantage of shortcuts, like premade pizza crust and rotisserie chicken, to cut down on my time in the kitchen.
—Joseph Sciascia, San Mateo, CA

- -

Takes: 30 min. • **Makes:** 8 servings

1	prebaked 12-in. pizza crust or flatbread
1	Tbsp. sesame oil
¾	cup hoisin sauce
2	tsp. chili garlic sauce
1½	cups shredded cooked chicken
4	green onions, chopped, divided
½	cup chopped sweet red pepper
⅓	cup shredded carrots
½	cup chopped cashews
3	Tbsp. chopped fresh cilantro
1¼	cups shredded mozzarella cheese

1. Preheat oven to 425°. Place pizza crust on a pizza pan; brush with sesame oil. In a small bowl, combine hoisin sauce and chili garlic sauce; brush ⅓ cup over crust. Toss the remaining mixture with chicken; sprinkle over crust. Top with 2 chopped green onions, red pepper, carrots, cashews and cilantro. Sprinkle the mozzarella over top.

2. Bake until the cheese is lightly browned, 12-15 minutes. Let stand 5 minutes; sprinkle with remaining 2 green onions.

1 piece: 357 cal., 15g fat (5g sat. fat), 38mg chol., 876mg sod., 37g carb. (9g sugars, 2g fiber), 19g pro.

Easy Chana Masala

I love this quick, healthy Indian-inspired dish so much I always make sure to have the ingredients stocked in my pantry. It makes weeknight dinners feel a little more special.
—Janeen Judah, Houston, TX

- -

Takes: 30 min. • **Makes:** 4 servings

- 1 Tbsp. canola oil
- ½ cup finely chopped onion
- 1 Tbsp. minced fresh gingerroot
- 2 garlic cloves, minced
- 1 jalapeno pepper, seeded and finely chopped, optional
- ½ tsp. salt
- 1 tsp. garam masala
- ½ tsp. ground coriander
- ½ tsp. ground cumin
- 1 can (15 oz.) diced tomatoes, undrained
- 1 can (15 oz.) chickpeas or garbanzo beans, rinsed and drained
- 3 cups hot cooked brown rice
- ¼ cup plain yogurt
- Minced fresh cilantro

1. In a large skillet, heat the oil over medium heat. Add onion, ginger, garlic and, if desired, jalapeno; cook and stir until onion is softened and lightly browned, 4-5 minutes. Add salt and spices; cook and stir 1 minute.

2. Stir in tomatoes and garbanzo beans; bring to a boil. Reduce heat; simmer, covered, until flavors are blended, 12-15 minutes, stirring occasionally. Serve with rice. Top with yogurt and cilantro.

Freeze option: Freeze cooled garbanzo bean mixture in freezer containers. To use, partially thaw in refrigerator overnight. Heat through in a saucepan, stirring occasionally; add water if necessary.

¾ cup garbanzo bean mixture with ¾ cup rice: 359 cal., 8g fat (1g sat. fat), 2mg chol., 616mg sod., 64g carb. (8g sugars, 9g fiber), 10g pro.

Meatless Chili Mac

I found this recipe in a newspaper years ago. It's been a hit at our house ever since. It's fast, flavorful and appeals to everyone, even die-hard meat lovers.
—Cindy Ragan,
North Huntingdon, PA

- -

Prep: 15 min. • **Cook:** 25 min.
Makes: 8 servings

- 1 large onion, chopped
- 1 medium green pepper, chopped
- 1 Tbsp. olive oil
- 1 garlic clove, minced
- 2 cups water
- 1½ cups uncooked elbow macaroni
- 1 can (16 oz.) mild chili beans, undrained
- 1 can (15½ oz.) great northern beans, rinsed and drained
- 1 can (14½ oz.) diced tomatoes, undrained
- 1 can (8 oz.) tomato sauce
- 4 tsp. chili powder
- 1 tsp. ground cumin
- ½ tsp. salt
- ½ cup fat-free sour cream

1. In a Dutch oven, saute onion and green pepper in oil until tender. Add garlic; cook 1 minute longer. Stir in water, macaroni, beans, tomatoes, tomato sauce, chili powder, cumin and salt.
2. Bring to a boil. Reduce heat; cover and simmer for 15-20 minutes or until macaroni is tender. Top each serving with 1 Tbsp. sour cream.
1¼ cups: 206 cal., 3g fat (1g sat. fat), 1mg chol., 651mg sod., 37g carb. (6g sugars, 9g fiber), 10g pro.
Diabetic exchanges: 2 starch, 1 vegetable, 1 lean meat.

Slow-Cooker Chicken & Black Bean Tacos

My husband and I love Mexican food. Place the toppings in separate bowls on the buffet table so guests and kids can assemble their own.
—Laura Rodriguez, Willoughby, OH

- -

Prep: 20 min. • **Cook:** 4¼ hours
Makes: 6 servings

- 1 can (8 oz.) crushed pineapple
- ½ cup salsa
- 2 green onions, sliced
- 1 tsp. grated lime zest
- ¼ cup lime juice
- ½ tsp. chili powder
- ¼ tsp. garlic powder
- ¼ tsp. ground cumin
- ⅛ tsp. each salt, cayenne pepper and pepper
- 1 lb. boneless skinless chicken thighs
- 1 can (15 oz.) black beans, rinsed and drained
- 12 flour tortillas (6 in.), warmed
  Toppings: Shredded Mexican cheese blend, shredded lettuce, peeled medium ripe avocado and hot sauce

1. In a small bowl, combine the first 5 ingredients; stir in seasonings. Place chicken in a 3-qt. slow cooker; add pineapple mixture. Cook, covered, on low 4-5 hours or until chicken is tender.
2. Remove chicken; cool slightly. Shred meat with 2 forks; return to slow cooker. Stir in beans. Cook, covered, on low 15-20 minutes longer or until heated through. Using a slotted spoon, serve chicken mixture in tortillas with toppings.
2 tacos: 387 cal., 12g fat (2g sat. fat), 50mg chol., 757mg sod., 47g carb. (9g sugars, 3g fiber), 24g pro.
Diabetic exchanges: 3 starch, 3 lean meat.

One-Pot Chicken Pesto Pasta

When my garden basil explodes, I use it to make pesto. I freeze the pesto in small containers to save for the right opportunity, like this saucy one-pot chicken with pasta.

—Kimberly Fenwick, Hobart, IN

- -

Takes: 30 min. • **Makes:** 4 servings

1 lb. boneless skinless chicken thighs, cut into 1-in. pieces
1 tsp. salt-free seasoning blend
2 tsp. olive oil
1 can (14½ oz.) reduced-sodium chicken broth
2 Tbsp. lemon juice
1 cup uncooked gemelli or spiral pasta
2 cups fresh broccoli florets
1 cup frozen peas
⅓ cup prepared pesto

1. Toss chicken with seasoning blend. In a large nonstick skillet, heat oil over medium-high heat. Add chicken and brown evenly; remove from pan.
2. In same pan, combine broth and lemon juice; bring to a boil, stirring to loosen browned bits from pan. Stir in pasta; return to a boil. Reduce heat; simmer, covered, 10 minutes.
3. Add broccoli; cook, covered, 5 minutes. Return chicken to pan; cook, covered, until the pasta is tender and the chicken is no longer pink, 2-3 minutes longer, stirring occasionally. Add peas; heat through. Stir in pesto.
1 cup: 404 cal., 18g fat (4g sat. fat), 76mg chol., 646mg sod., 29g carb. (4g sugars, 4g fiber), 30g pro. **Diabetic exchanges:** 3 lean meat, 2 starch, 2 fat.

Pork Chops & Beans

This hearty combination of tender pork chops and two kinds of beans makes a satisfying slow-cooked meal.

—Dorothy Pritchett, Wills Point, TX

- -

Prep: 15 min. • **Cook:** 5 hours
Makes: 4 servings

4 pork loin chops (½ in. thick)
¼ tsp. salt
¼ tsp. pepper
1 Tbsp. canola oil
2 medium onions, chopped
2 garlic cloves, minced
¼ cup chili sauce
1½ tsp. brown sugar
1 tsp. prepared mustard
1 can (16 oz.) kidney beans, rinsed and drained
1¾ cups frozen lima beans, thawed

1. Sprinkle pork chops with salt and pepper. In a large skillet, heat oil over medium-high heat. Brown chops on both sides. Transfer to a 3-qt. slow cooker. Discard drippings, reserving 1 Tbsp. drippings in skillet. Add onions; cook and stir until tender. Add garlic; cook and stir 1 minute. Stir in chili sauce, brown sugar and mustard. Pour over chops.
2. Cook, covered, on low 4 hours or until meat is almost tender. Stir in beans. Cook, covered, 1-2 hours longer or until heated through.
1 serving: 297 cal., 5g fat (1g sat. fat), 14mg chol., 607mg sod., 45g carb. (10g sugars, 11g fiber), 19g pro. **Diabetic exchanges:** 3 starch, 3 lean meat.

Creamy Chicken & Thyme

Thyme gives this simple chicken dish its unique flavor. I lightened up the original recipe by using reduced-fat sour cream, but you'd never guess based on the rich, creamy flavor.
—Harriet Johnson, Champlin, MN

- -

Takes: 30 min. • **Makes:** 4 servings

- 4 boneless skinless chicken breast halves (4 oz. each)
- 1 can (14½ oz.) reduced-sodium chicken broth
- 1 Tbsp. all-purpose flour
- ½ cup reduced-fat sour cream
- ½ tsp. dried parsley flakes
- ¼ tsp. salt
- ¼ tsp. dill weed
- ¼ tsp. dried thyme
- ⅛ tsp. onion salt
- ⅛ tsp. pepper
- Hot cooked egg noodles, optional

1. Place chicken breast halves in a large nonstick skillet. Add ½ cup of broth. Cover and simmer until juices run clear, 10-12 minutes, turning once. Remove chicken from pan; keep warm. Add remaining broth to skillet and bring to a boil; reduce heat to low.

2. In a small bowl, combine the flour and sour cream. Whisk into pan. Stir in the parsley, salt, dill weed, thyme, onion salt and pepper. Simmer, uncovered, until slightly thickened, about 5 minutes. If desired, serve with hot cooked noodles.

1 serving: 167 cal., 5g fat (2g sat. fat), 66mg chol., 575mg sod., 4g carb. (3g sugars, 0 fiber), 27g pro.
Diabetic exchanges: 3 lean meat, ½ fat.

Snapper with Spicy Pineapple Glaze

Ginger and cayenne spice these tangy red snapper fillets. Sweet pineapple preserves round out the delectable combination of flavors.
—*Taste of Home* Test Kitchen

- -

Takes: 30 min. • **Makes:** 4 servings

- ½ cup pineapple preserves
- 2 Tbsp. rice vinegar
- 2 tsp. minced fresh gingerroot
- 2 garlic cloves, minced
- ¾ tsp. salt, divided
- ¼ tsp. cayenne pepper
- 4 red snapper fillets (6 oz. each)
- 3 tsp. olive oil

1. In a small bowl, combine the preserves, vinegar, ginger, garlic, ½ tsp. salt and cayenne; set aside. Place fillets on a broiler pan coated with cooking spray. Rub fillets with oil; sprinkle with remaining salt.

2. Broil 4-6 in. from the heat for 5 minutes. Baste with half of the glaze. Broil 5-7 minutes longer or until fish flakes easily with a fork. Baste with remaining glaze.

1 fillet: 304 cal., 6g fat (1g sat. fat), 63mg chol., 552mg sod., 27g carb. (24g sugars, 0 fiber), 35g pro.
Diabetic exchanges: 5 lean meat, 2 starch.

Meatless
MONDAYS

Whether it's a Monday night ritual or any day of the week, you won't be able to get enough of these flavorful meatless options!

Cauliflower Tikka Masala

I'm a vegetarian and sometimes find it challenging to find new recipes. Here is my easy version of tikka masala. I love the convenience of making it in my pressure cooker.
—Garima Arora, Charlotte, NC

- -

Prep: 45 min. • **Cook:** 15 min.
Makes: 4 servings

- 2 Tbsp. canola oil
- 1 large head cauliflower, cut into florets
- 1 tsp. ground mustard
- ½ tsp. paprika
- ½ tsp. ground turmeric
- ½ tsp. garam masala

MASALA

- 2 Tbsp. canola oil
- 1 small onion, chopped
- ¼ cup salted cashews
- 4 cardamom pods
- 2 whole cloves
- 1 can (14½ oz.) diced tomatoes, undrained
- ½ cup water
- 1½ tsp. minced garlic
- 1½ tsp. minced fresh gingerroot
- ¼ cup 2% milk or water
- 2 Tbsp. almond flour
- 1 Tbsp. ground fenugreek
- 1 Tbsp. maple syrup
- ½ tsp. salt
- ½ tsp. garam masala
- ¼ to ½ tsp. cayenne pepper
- 2 Tbsp. plain yogurt
  Fresh cilantro leaves

1. Select saute setting on a 6-qt. electric pressure cooker. Adjust for medium heat; add oil. When oil is hot, cook and stir cauliflower, mustard, paprika, turmeric and garam masala until crisp-tender, 6-8 minutes. Remove and keep warm.
2. For masala, add oil to pressure cooker. When hot, add onion, cashews, cardamom and cloves. Cook and stir until onion is tender, 4-5 minutes. Add tomatoes and ½ cup water. Press cancel. Lock lid; close pressure-release valve. Adjust to pressure-cook on high for 5 minutes. Let pressure release naturally for 5 minutes; quick-release any remaining pressure. Discard cardamom and cloves. Cool sauce slightly; transfer to a food processor. Process until smooth. Return to pressure cooker.
3. Select saute setting and adjust for low heat. Add garlic and ginger; cook and stir 1 minute. Add milk, almond flour, fenugreek, maple syrup, salt, garam masala and cayenne; simmer, uncovered, until mixture is slightly thickened, 10-12 minutes, stirring occasionally. Press cancel. Stir in yogurt and cauliflower; heat through. Sprinkle with cilantro leaves.
1¼ cups: 312 cal., 22g fat (3g sat. fat), 3mg chol., 573mg sod., 26g carb. (13g sugars, 7g fiber), 8g pro.

Air-Fryer Spinach Feta Turnovers

These quick turnovers are one of my wife's favorite entrees. Refrigerated dough makes preparation a snap!
—David Baruch, Weston, FL

Takes: 30 min. • **Makes:** 4 servings

- 2   large eggs
- 1   pkg. (10 oz.) frozen spinach, thawed, squeezed dry and chopped
- ¾   cup crumbled feta cheese
- 2   garlic cloves, minced
- ¼   tsp. pepper
- 1   tube (13.8 oz.) refrigerated pizza crust
      Refrigerated tzatziki sauce, optional

1. Preheat air fryer to 425°. In a bowl, whisk eggs; set aside 1 Tbsp. of eggs. Combine spinach, feta cheese, garlic, pepper and remaining beaten eggs.
2. Unroll pizza crust; roll into a 12-in. square. Cut into four 6-in. squares. Top each square with about ⅓ cup spinach mixture. Fold into a triangle and pinch edges to seal. Cut slits in top; brush with reserved egg.
3. In batches if necessary, place triangles in a single layer on greased tray in air-fryer basket. Cook until golden brown, 10-12 minutes. If desired, serve with tzatziki sauce.

1 turnover: 361 cal., 9g fat (4g sat. fat), 104mg chol., 936mg sod., 51g carb. (7g sugars, 4g fiber), 17g pro.

TIMESAVING TIP

There's no need to add oil to your air fryer if the recipe doesn't call for it, but you may want to lightly spritz your food with oil before air-frying. This will give it the crispy, golden exterior that makes deep-fried food so delicious.

Mushroom & Brown Rice Hash with Poached Eggs

I made my mother's famous roast beef hash healthier by using cremini mushrooms instead of beef, and brown rice instead of potatoes. It's ideal for a light main dish.
—Lily Julow, Lawrenceville, GA

- -

Takes: 30 min. • **Makes:** 4 servings

- 2 **Tbsp. olive oil**
- 1 **lb. sliced baby portobello mushrooms**
- ½ **cup chopped sweet onion**
- 1 **pkg. (8.8 oz.) ready-to-serve brown rice**
- 1 **large carrot, grated**
- 2 **green onions, thinly sliced**
- ½ **tsp. salt**
- ¼ **tsp. pepper**
- ¼ **tsp. caraway seeds**
- 4 **large eggs, cold**

1. In a large skillet, heat oil over medium-high heat; saute mushrooms until lightly browned, 5-7 minutes. Add sweet onion; cook 1 minute. Add rice and carrot; cook and stir until the vegetables are tender, 4-5 minutes. Stir in green onions, salt, pepper and caraway seeds; heat through.
2. Meanwhile, place 2-3 in. of water in a large saucepan or skillet with high sides. Bring to a boil; adjust heat to maintain a gentle simmer. Break cold eggs, 1 at a time, into a small bowl; holding bowl close to surface of water, slip egg into water.
3. Cook, uncovered, until whites are completely set and yolks begin to thicken but are not hard, 3-5 minutes. Using a slotted spoon, lift eggs out of water. Serve over rice mixture.
1 serving: 282 cal., 13g fat (3g sat. fat), 186mg chol., 393mg sod., 26g carb. (4g sugars, 3g fiber), 13g pro.

Cumin Quinoa Patties

These easy veggie burgers have an amazing taste, and the addition of quinoa makes the texture to die for. Pan frying them adds a perfect crunch that brings it to the next level. The mixture can be made ahead of time, and it freezes very well. Enjoy!
—Beth Klein, Arlington, VA

- -

Takes: 30 min. • **Makes:** 4 servings

- 1 **cup water**
- ½ **cup quinoa, rinsed**
- 1 **medium carrot, cut into 1-in. pieces**
- 1 **cup canned cannellini beans, rinsed and drained**
- ¼ **cup panko bread crumbs**
- 3 **green onions, chopped**
- 1 **large egg, lightly beaten**
- 3 **tsp. ground cumin**
- ¼ **tsp. salt**
- ⅛ **tsp. pepper**
- 2 **Tbsp. olive oil**
  Optional: Sour cream, salsa and minced fresh cilantro

1. In a small saucepan, bring water to a boil. Add quinoa. Reduce heat; simmer, covered, until the liquid is absorbed, 12-15 minutes. Remove from heat; fluff with a fork.
2. Meanwhile, place carrot in a food processor; pulse until coarsely chopped. Add beans; process until chopped. Transfer mixture to a large bowl. Mix in cooked quinoa, bread crumbs, green onions, beaten egg and seasonings. Shape mixture into 8 patties.
3. In a large skillet, heat oil over medium heat. Add the patties; cook until a thermometer reads 160°, 3-4 minutes on each side, turning carefully. If desired, serve with optional ingredients.
2 patties: 235 cal., 10g fat (1g sat. fat), 47mg chol., 273mg sod., 28g carb. (2g sugars, 5g fiber), 8g pro.
Diabetic exchanges: 2 starch, 1½ fat, 1 lean meat.

Portobello Polenta Stacks

My friends and I have recently started growing portobello mushrooms from kits we found at a farmers market. We love to try new recipes like this one with our harvest.
—Breanne Heath, Chicago, IL

- -

Takes: 30 min. • **Makes:** 4 servings

- 1 **Tbsp. olive oil**
- 3 **garlic cloves, minced**
- 2 **Tbsp. balsamic vinegar**
- 4 **large portobello mushrooms (about 5 in.), stems removed**
- ¼ **tsp. salt**
- ¼ **tsp. pepper**
- 1 **tube (18 oz.) polenta, cut into 12 slices**
- 4 **slices tomato**
- ½ **cup grated Parmesan cheese**
- 2 **Tbsp. minced fresh basil**

1. Preheat oven to 400°. In a small saucepan, heat oil over medium heat. Add garlic; cook and stir until tender, 1-2 minutes (do not allow to brown). Stir in vinegar; remove from heat.

2. Place mushrooms in a 13x9-in. baking dish, gill side up. Brush with vinegar mixture; sprinkle with salt and pepper. Top with polenta and tomato slices; sprinkle with cheese.

3. Bake, uncovered, until mushrooms are tender, 20-25 minutes. Sprinkle with basil.

1 serving: 219 cal., 6g fat (2g sat. fat), 9mg chol., 764mg sod., 32g carb. (7g sugars, 3g fiber), 7g pro.
Diabetic exchanges: 1½ starch, 1 vegetable, 1 lean meat, 1 fat.

TIMESAVING TIP

Popular in many vegan and vegetarian diets as a meat substitute (particularly in dishes such as fajitas, tacos and burgers) portobellos are mild in flavor, but meaty in texture and big in size—making it easy to substitute for meat.

Spicy Veggie Pasta Bake

My dad often cooked with a cast-iron skillet. Whenever I cook with mine, I'm reminded of his amazing culinary skills. I keep the tradition going with my veggie pasta.
—Sonya Goergen, Moorhead, MN

- -

Takes: 30 min. • **Makes:** 6 servings

- 3 **cups uncooked spiral pasta**
- 1 **medium yellow summer squash**
- 1 **small zucchini**
- 1 **medium sweet red pepper**
- 1 **medium green pepper**
- 1 **Tbsp. olive oil**
- 1 **small red onion, halved and sliced**
- 1 **cup sliced fresh mushrooms**
- ½ **tsp. salt**
- ¼ **tsp. pepper**
- ¼ **tsp. crushed red pepper flakes**
- 1 **jar (24 oz.) spicy marinara sauce**
- 8 **oz. fresh mozzarella cheese pearls**
  Optional: Grated Parmesan cheese and julienned fresh basil

1. Preheat oven to 375°. Cook pasta according to package directions for al dente; drain.

2. Cut squash, zucchini and peppers into ¼-in. julienned strips. In a 12-in. cast-iron or other ovenproof skillet, heat oil over medium-high heat. Add onion, mushrooms and julienned vegetables; cook and stir until crisp-tender, 5-7 minutes. Stir in seasonings. Add marinara sauce and pasta; toss to combine. Top with cheese pearls.

3. Transfer to oven; bake, uncovered, until cheese is melted, 10-15 minutes. If desired, sprinkle with Parmesan cheese and basil before serving.

1⅓ cups: 420 cal., 13g fat (6g sat. fat), 32mg chol., 734mg sod., 57g carb. (12g sugars, 5g fiber), 17g pro.

Makeover Macaroni & Cheese

This is one of my family's favorites. Creamy, cheesy and comforting, this lightened-up five-ingredient classic will become a must-have at your house, too!
—Nancy Langrock, Southbury, CT

- -

Takes: 30 min. • **Makes:** 8 servings

- 1 **pkg. (16 oz.) elbow macaroni**
- 2 **Tbsp. all-purpose flour**
- 2 **cups fat-free milk**
- 1 **pkg. (16 oz.) reduced-fat Velveeta, cubed**
- 1 **cup shredded sharp cheddar cheese, divided**

1. Cook macaroni according to package directions. Meanwhile, in a large saucepan, combine flour and milk until smooth. Bring to a boil; cook and stir for 2 minutes or until thickened. Stir in process cheese and ½ cup cheddar cheese until smooth. Drain macaroni; stir into cheese sauce.

2. Remove from the heat; sprinkle with remaining cheese. Cover and let stand for 5 minutes or until cheese is melted.

1 cup: 403 cal., 11g fat (6g sat. fat), 36mg chol., 944mg sod., 54g carb. (9g sugars, 2g fiber), 23g pro.

Garbanzo-Vegetable Green Curry

My son loves anything with coconut milk, so I always keep some on hand for weeknight meals like this one. For a milder version, use red or yellow curry paste instead of green.
—Marie Parker, Milwaukee, WI

- -

Takes: 20 min. • **Makes:** 6 servings

3	cups frozen cauliflower
2	cans (15 oz. each) garbanzo beans or chickpeas, rinsed and drained
1	can (13.66 oz.) coconut milk
¼	cup green curry paste
½	tsp. salt
2	tsp. cornstarch
1	Tbsp. cold water
1½	cups frozen peas
2	pkg. (8.8 oz. each) ready-to-serve long grain rice
½	cup lightly salted cashews

1. In a large skillet, combine the cauliflower, beans, coconut milk, curry paste and salt. Bring to a boil; cook, uncovered, 5-6 minutes or until cauliflower is tender.

2. Combine cornstarch and water until smooth; gradually stir into skillet. Stir in peas. Bring to a boil. Cook and stir for 2 minutes or until thickened.

3. Meanwhile, prepare rice according to the package directions. Sprinkle cauliflower mixture with cashews. Serve with rice.

1 cup with ⅔ cup rice: 516 cal., 24g fat (13g sat. fat), 0 chol., 646mg sod., 63g carb. (7g sugars, 10g fiber), 15g pro.

Pinto Bean Tostadas

Ready-to-go pinto beans and crispy corn tortillas prove how easy it is to make a healthy meal. Sometimes I add some chopped leftover meat to the tostadas, but they're equally satisfying just as they are.
—Lily Julow, Lawrenceville, GA

- -

Takes: 30 min. • **Makes:** 6 servings

¼	cup sour cream
¾	tsp. grated lime zest
¼	tsp. ground cumin
½	tsp. salt, divided
2	Tbsp. canola oil, divided
2	garlic cloves, minced
2	cans (15 oz. each) pinto beans, rinsed and drained
1	to 2 tsp. hot pepper sauce
1	tsp. chili powder
6	corn tortillas (6 in.)
2	cups shredded lettuce
½	cup salsa
¾	cup crumbled feta cheese or queso fresco
	Lime wedges

1. In a small bowl, mix sour cream, lime zest, cumin and ¼ tsp. salt. In a large saucepan, heat 1 Tbsp. oil over medium heat. Add garlic; cook and stir just until fragrant, about 45 seconds. Stir in beans, pepper sauce, chili powder and remaining salt; heat mixture through, stirring occasionally. Keep warm.

2. Brush both sides of tortillas with remaining oil. Place a large skillet over medium-high heat. Add tortillas in 2 batches; cook until lightly browned and crisp, 2-3 minutes on each side.

3. To serve, arrange beans and lettuce over tostada shells; top with salsa, sour cream mixture and cheese. Serve with lime wedges.

1 tostada: 291 cal., 10g fat (3g sat. fat), 14mg chol., 658mg sod., 38g carb. (4g sugars, 8g fiber), 11g pro.
Diabetic exchanges: 2½ starch, 1 lean meat, 1 fat.

Gnocchi Alfredo

This gnocchi is one of my go-tos for company and potlucks. It's pure comfort food, especially in the cold weather months.

—Jessica Silva, East Berlin, CT

- -

Takes: 25 min. • **Makes:** 5 servings

- 2 lbs. potato gnocchi
- 3 Tbsp. butter, divided
- 1 Tbsp. plus 1½ tsp. all-purpose flour
- 1½ cups whole milk
- ½ cup grated Parmesan cheese
  Dash ground nutmeg
- ½ lb. sliced baby portobello mushrooms
  Minced fresh parsley, optional

1. Cook gnocchi according to package directions; drain. Meanwhile, in a small saucepan, melt 1 Tbsp. butter. Stir in flour until smooth; gradually whisk in milk. Bring to a boil, stirring constantly; cook and stir 1-2 minutes or until thickened. Remove from heat; stir in cheese and nutmeg until blended. Keep warm.

2. In a large heavy skillet, melt remaining butter over medium heat. Heat 5-7 minutes or until golden brown, stirring constantly. Immediately add mushrooms and gnocchi; cook and stir 4-5 minutes or until mushrooms are tender and gnocchi are lightly browned. Serve with sauce. If desired, sprinkle with minced fresh parsley.

Note: Look for potato gnocchi in the pasta or frozen foods section.

1 cup gnocchi mixture with ⅓ cup sauce: 529 cal., 14g fat (8g sat. fat), 46mg chol., 996mg sod., 81g carb. (15g sugars, 5g fiber), 19g pro.

READER REVIEW

"I sauteed onion, garlic and some fresh chopped spinach along with the mushrooms. We all loved it! This is a keeper!"

—KENNEDY22, TASTEOFHOME.COM

Zucchini-Parmesan Bake

When my garden is overflowing with zucchini, I turn to this recipe as a tasty way to use it up.
—Shannon Davis, Mason, MI

- -

Takes: 30 min. • **Makes:** 6 servings

- **3** large eggs
- **½** cup canola oil
- **3** cups shredded zucchini (about 1 lb.)
- **1** cup reduced-fat biscuit/ baking mix
- **½** cup shredded Parmesan cheese

1. Preheat oven to 375°. In a bowl, whisk eggs and oil until blended. Stir in remaining ingredients.

2. Transfer to a greased 10-in. ovenproof skillet. Bake 25-30 minutes or until golden brown.

1 piece: 314 cal., 24g fat (4g sat. fat), 111mg chol., 387mg sod., 17g carb. (2g sugars, 1g fiber), 8g pro.

Grilled Flatbread Veggie Pizza

We pile veggies onto flatbread for a fun way to eat healthier. Our go-to recipe for weeknights easily changes with different veggies or meats.
—Darla Andrews, Boerne, TX

Takes: 25 min. • **Makes:** 4 servings

1	Tbsp. butter
½	lb. sliced baby portobello mushrooms
1	large green pepper, julienned
4	cups fresh baby spinach (about 4 oz.)
¼	tsp. salt
⅛	tsp. pepper
2	naan flatbreads or 4 whole pita breads
2	Tbsp. olive oil
¼	cup prepared pesto
2	plum tomatoes, sliced
2	cups shredded part-skim mozzarella cheese

1. In a large skillet, heat butter over medium-high heat. Add mushrooms and green pepper; cook and stir until tender, 5-7 minutes. Add the spinach, salt and pepper; cook and stir until spinach is wilted, 2-3 minutes.
2. Brush both sides of flatbreads with oil. Grill flatbreads, covered, over medium heat 2-3 minutes on 1 side or until lightly browned.
3. Remove from grill. Spread grilled sides with pesto; top with vegetable mixture, tomatoes and mozzarella. Return to grill; cook, covered, until cheese is melted, 2-3 minutes longer. Cut pizzas in half before serving.
½ pizza: 426 cal., 28g fat (11g sat. fat), 47mg chol., 1005mg sod., 25g carb. (6g sugars, 3g fiber), 20g pro.

Creamy Pasta with Florets

Cottage cheese is the surprising base for the wonderfully creamy sauce that coats the pasta and veggies in this side dish. My husband, who doesn't like to compromise good taste for low-fat foods, didn't even realize this recipe was lower in fat.
—Barbara Toher, Lexington, KY

Takes: 30 min. • **Makes:** 4 servings

1	cup 1% cottage cheese
½	cup 1% milk
¼	cup reduced-fat sour cream
¼	cup grated Parmesan cheese
½	tsp. salt
⅛	tsp. cayenne pepper
5	cups broccoli florets
4	cups cauliflowerets
4	oz. uncooked angel hair pasta
3	garlic cloves, minced
2	tsp. olive oil
2½	cups sliced fresh mushrooms

1. In a blender or food processor, combine the cottage cheese, milk, sour cream, Parmesan cheese, salt and cayenne; cover and process until smooth. Set aside.
2. In a saucepan, bring 1 in. of water to a boil; place the broccoli and cauliflower in a steamer basket over boiling water. Cover and steam for 3-4 minutes or until crisp-tender. Meanwhile, cook pasta according to the package directions; drain.
3. In a large nonstick skillet, saute garlic in oil for 2 minutes. Add the mushrooms; saute 5 minutes longer. Stir in the broccoli, cauliflower, pasta and cottage cheese mixture; heat through.
2 cups: 260 cal., 4g fat (2g sat. fat), 10mg chol., 699mg sod., 38g carb. (9g sugars, 6g fiber), 20g pro.
Diabetic exchanges: 2½ starch, 1 medium-fat meat.

Saucy Vegetable Tofu

This is my daughter Tonya's favorite meal. Sometimes we make it with rigatoni and call it Riga-Tonya. Either way, it's a quick way to prepare your kids some yummy vegetables.
—Sandra Eckert, Pottstown, PA

- -

Takes: 20 min. • **Makes:** 6 servings

8 oz. uncooked whole wheat spiral pasta
1 large onion, coarsely chopped
1 large green or sweet red pepper, coarsely chopped
1 medium zucchini, halved lengthwise and sliced
1 Tbsp. olive oil
1 pkg. (16 oz.) firm tofu, drained and cut into ½-in. cubes
2 cups meatless spaghetti sauce

1. Cook pasta according to package directions. Meanwhile, in a large skillet, saute the onion, pepper and zucchini in oil until crisp-tender.
2. Stir in tofu and spaghetti sauce; heat through. Drain pasta; serve with tofu mixture.

1¼ cups tofu mixture with ⅔ cup pasta: 274 cal., 7g fat (1g sat. fat), 0 chol., 380mg sod., 41g carb. (9g sugars, 7g fiber), 14g pro.
Diabetic exchanges: 2 starch, 2 lean meat, 1 vegetable, ½ fat.

Slow-Cooker Veggie Lasagna

This veggie-licious alternative to traditional lasagna makes use of slow-cooker convenience. I suggest using chunky spaghetti sauce.
—Laura Davister, Little Suamico, WI

- -

Prep: 25 min. • **Cook:** 3½ hours
Makes: 2 servings

½ cup shredded part-skim mozzarella cheese
3 Tbsp. 1% cottage cheese
2 Tbsp. grated Parmesan cheese
2 Tbsp. egg substitute
½ tsp. Italian seasoning
⅛ tsp. garlic powder
¾ cup meatless spaghetti sauce
½ cup sliced zucchini
2 no-cook lasagna noodles
4 cups fresh baby spinach
½ cup sliced fresh mushrooms

1. Cut two 18x3-in. strips of heavy-duty foil; crisscross so they resemble an X. Place strips on the bottom and up sides of a 1½-qt. slow cooker. Coat the strips with cooking spray.
2. In a small bowl, combine the first 6 ingredients. Spread 1 Tbsp. spaghetti sauce on the bottom of prepared slow cooker. Top with half of the zucchini and a third of the cheese mixture.
3. Break noodles into 1-in. pieces; sprinkle half of the noodles over cheese mixture. Spread with 1 Tbsp. sauce. Top with half of the spinach and half of the mushrooms. Repeat layers. Top with remaining cheese mixture and spaghetti sauce.
4. Cover and cook on low until noodles are tender, 3½-4 hours.

1 piece: 259 cal., 8g fat (4g sat. fat), 23mg chol., 859mg sod., 29g carb. (9g sugars, 4g fiber), 19g pro.
Diabetic exchanges: 2 lean meat, 2 medium-fat meat, ½ starch, 1 vegetable, ½ fat.

Beans & Rice Dinner

On cold or rainy days, this comforting dish fills the tummy. Sometimes I use pinto beans instead of kidney beans or white rice instead of brown. Add rolls and a green salad, and your dinner's done!

—Lorraine Caland, Shuniah, ON

- -

Takes: 30 min. • **Makes:** 4 servings

- 1 Tbsp. canola oil
- 2 celery ribs, chopped
- 1 medium green pepper, chopped
- 1 medium onion, chopped
- 1 can (28 oz.) diced tomatoes, undrained
- 1 can (16 oz.) kidney beans, rinsed and drained
- 2 cups cooked brown rice
- 2 tsp. Worcestershire sauce
- 1½ tsp. chili powder
- ¼ tsp. pepper
- ¼ cup shredded cheddar cheese
- ¼ cup reduced-fat sour cream
- 2 green onions, chopped

1. In a large nonstick skillet, heat oil over medium-high heat. Add celery, green pepper and onion; cook and stir until tender.

2. Stir in the tomatoes, beans, rice, Worcestershire sauce, chili powder and pepper; bring to a boil. Reduce heat; simmer, covered, until heated through, 7-9 minutes. Top with cheddar cheese, sour cream and green onions.

1½ cups: 354 cal., 8g fat (3g sat. fat), 13mg chol., 549mg sod., 58g carb. (13g sugars, 12g fiber), 15g pro.

Quick Italian Veggie Skillet

When you're not sure what to serve for dinner, Italian flavors are a good starting point. I combine cannellini and garbanzo beans for this snappy rice dish.

—Sonya Labbe, West Hollywood, CA

- -

Takes: 25 min. • **Makes:** 4 servings

- 1 can (15 oz.) no-salt-added garbanzo beans or chickpeas, rinsed and drained
- 1 can (15 oz.) no-salt-added cannellini beans, rinsed and drained
- 1 can (14½ oz.) no-salt-added stewed tomatoes, undrained
- 1 cup vegetable broth
- ¾ cup uncooked instant rice
- 1 tsp. Italian seasoning
- ¼ tsp. crushed red pepper flakes, optional
- 1 cup marinara sauce
- ¼ cup grated Parmesan cheese Minced fresh basil

In a large skillet, combine the first 6 ingredients and, if desired, pepper flakes; bring to a boil. Reduce heat; simmer, covered, until rice is tender, 7-9 minutes. Stir in marinara sauce; heat through, stirring occasionally. Top with cheese and basil.

1⅓ cups: 342 cal., 4g fat (1g sat. fat), 6mg chol., 660mg sod., 59g carb. (10g sugars, 11g fiber), 16g pro.

Pressure-Cooker Stuffed Peppers

Here's a good-for-you dinner that's also a meal-in-one classic. Add a salad and, in just moments, call everyone to the table.
—Michelle Gurnsey, Lincoln, NE

- -

Prep: 15 min.
Cook: 5 min. + releasing
Makes: 4 servings

- 4 medium sweet red peppers
- 1 can (15 oz.) black beans, rinsed and drained
- 1 cup shredded pepper jack cheese
- ¾ cup salsa
- 1 small onion, chopped
- ½ cup frozen corn
- ⅓ cup uncooked converted long grain rice
- 1¼ tsp. chili powder
- ½ tsp. ground cumin
  Reduced-fat sour cream, optional

1. Place trivet insert and 1 cup water in a 6-qt. electric pressure cooker.
2. Cut and discard the tops from peppers; remove seeds. In a large bowl, mix beans, cheese, salsa, onion, corn, rice, chili powder and cumin; spoon into peppers. Set peppers on trivet.
3. Lock lid; close pressure-release valve. Adjust to pressure-cook on high for 5 minutes. Let pressure release naturally. If desired, serve with sour cream.

1 stuffed pepper: 333 cal., 10g fat (5g sat. fat), 30mg chol., 582mg sod., 45g carb. (8g sugars, 8g fiber), 15g pro.
Diabetic exchanges: 2 starch, 2 vegetable, 2 lean meat, 1 fat.

The best way to prevent eggplant from soaking up all the oil is to salt the slices. Place in a colander and sprinkle both sides with salt. Allow them to sit for 45 minutes to an hour, until you see drops of water on the surface of the slices. Rinse the eggplant slices under cold running water, gently rubbing the surface with your fingers to remove any excess salt. Place them on a paper-towel-lined baking sheet and press into them with a towel until they're completely dry on the surface.

One-Pan Tuscan Ravioli

Sometimes I use chickpeas instead of cannellini beans, grated Asiago or provolone instead of Parmesan, and all zucchini if I don't have eggplant. There are so many delicious ways to switch things up!

—Sonya Labbe, West Hollywood, CA

- -

Takes: 25 min. • **Makes:** 4 servings

- 1 Tbsp. olive oil
- 2 cups cubed eggplant (½ in.)
- 1 can (14½ oz.) Italian diced tomatoes, undrained
- 1 can (14½ oz.) reduced-sodium chicken broth
- 1 medium zucchini, halved lengthwise and cut into ½-in. slices
- 1 pkg. (9 oz.) refrigerated cheese ravioli
- 1 can (15 oz.) cannellini beans, rinsed and drained
  Shredded Parmesan cheese
  Thinly sliced fresh basil

1. In a large skillet, heat oil over medium heat; saute eggplant until lightly browned, 2-3 minutes.
2. Stir in tomatoes, broth and zucchini; bring to a boil. Add ravioli; cook, uncovered, over medium heat until ravioli are tender, 7-9 minutes, stirring occasionally. Stir in beans; heat through. Sprinkle with cheese and basil.
1½ cups: 376 cal., 10g fat (4g sat. fat), 36mg chol., 1096mg sod., 56g carb. (11g sugars, 8g fiber), 16g pro.

Pasta with Roasted Garlic & Tomatoes

Here's a simple sauce with just four ingredients, and it's savory enough for a fancy party. I use bow tie pasta, but penne works, too.

—Aysha Schurman, Ammon, ID

- -

Takes: 20 min. • **Makes:** 4 servings

1½	lbs. cherry tomatoes
12	garlic cloves, peeled
3	Tbsp. olive oil
3	cups uncooked bow tie pasta
4	oz. (½ cup) cream cheese, softened
½	tsp. salt

1. Preheat oven to 450°. In a bowl, toss tomatoes and garlic cloves with oil; transfer to a greased 15x10x1-in. baking pan. Roast 14-16 minutes or until very soft. Meanwhile, cook pasta according to package directions.
2. Cool the tomato mixture slightly. Reserve 12 tomatoes for serving with pasta. Transfer remaining tomato mixture to a food processor. Add cream cheese and salt; process until smooth. Transfer to a large bowl.
3. Drain pasta; add to tomato mixture and toss to coat. Top with reserved tomatoes.
1 cup: 441 cal., 22g fat (8g sat. fat), 32mg chol., 401mg sod., 52g carb. (7g sugars, 4g fiber), 12g pro.

Vegetarian Bean Tacos

We love Mexican food but I was looking for a healthier option for my family. These meatless tacos are a great alternative. We devour the tacos whenever I make them.

—Amanda Petrucelli, Plymouth, IN

- -

Takes: 25 min. • **Makes:** 4 servings

1	Tbsp. canola oil
1	medium onion, chopped
1	jalapeno pepper, seeded and finely chopped
2	garlic cloves, minced
1	Tbsp. chili powder
2	tsp. ground cumin
1	tsp. ground coriander
1	can (16 oz.) refried beans
1	can (15 oz.) black beans, rinsed and drained
1	can (14½ oz.) no-salt-added diced tomatoes, drained
4	whole wheat tortillas (8 in.), warmed
	Optional toppings: Shredded lettuce, shredded cheddar cheese, cubed avocado, sour cream and salsa

1. In a large nonstick skillet coated with cooking spray, heat oil over medium heat. Add the onion and jalapeno; cook and stir until tender. Add the garlic and seasonings; cook 1 minute longer. Stir in beans and tomatoes; heat through.
2. Serve bean mixture in tortillas with toppings as desired.
Note: Wear disposable gloves when cutting hot peppers; the oils can burn skin. Avoid touching your face.
1 taco: 413 cal., 9g fat (1g sat. fat), 9mg chol., 774mg sod., 66g carb. (8g sugars, 16g fiber), 17g pro.

Sage-Pecan Butternut Squash Ravioli

I am in love with this ravioli recipe! The sauce is delicious with any pasta, but I like the wow factor of squash ravioli. The flavor is sweet, salty, nutty, buttery and savory all at the same time. Give it a try!

—Barbara Miller, Oakdale, MN

- -

Takes: 25 min. • **Makes:** 4 servings

- 1 pkg. (18 oz.) frozen butternut squash ravioli or 2 pkg. (9 oz. each) refrigerated cheese ravioli
- ¾ cup chopped pecans or walnuts
- 3 Tbsp. butter
- ¼ cup packed brown sugar
- ½ tsp. salt
- ¼ tsp. ground nutmeg
- Dash cayenne pepper
- ¼ cup heavy whipping cream
- 2 Tbsp. minced fresh sage or 2 tsp. rubbed sage
- Shaved or shredded Parmesan cheese

1. Cook ravioli according to package directions.
2. Meanwhile, in a large dry skillet, toast pecans over medium-low heat 1-2 minutes or until lightly browned, stirring occasionally. Stir in butter until melted. Stir in brown sugar, salt, nutmeg and cayenne. Remove from heat; stir in cream and sage.
3. Drain ravioli; add to skillet and toss to coat. Top with cheese.

1 cup: 568 cal., 32g fat (11g sat. fat), 44mg chol., 637mg sod., 63g carb. (19g sugars, 5g fiber), 11g pro.

Sun-Dried Tomato Linguine

At my house, this dish is known as Gus's Special Pasta. My oldest child claimed it as his own when he was 8. I am always happy to oblige his desire for this cheesy, garlicky dish.

—Courtney Gaylord, Columbus, IN

- -

Takes: 25 min. • **Makes:** 6 servings

- 1 pkg. (16 oz.) linguine
- 1 jar (7 oz.) julienned oil-packed sun-dried tomatoes
- 6 garlic cloves, minced
- 1 Tbsp. lemon juice
- ½ cup minced fresh parsley
- 1½ cups crumbled feta cheese
- 1½ cups grated Parmesan cheese

1. In a 6-qt. stockpot, cook linguine according to package directions for al dente. Drain, reserving ½ cup pasta water; return linguine to pot.
2. Meanwhile, drain sun-dried tomatoes, reserving 2 Tbsp. oil. In a small microwave-safe bowl, combine garlic and reserved oil; microwave on high 45 seconds. Stir in the drained tomatoes and lemon juice.
3. Add tomato mixture to linguine. Toss with parsley, cheeses and enough pasta water to moisten.

1⅓ cups: 542 cal., 21g fat (8g sat. fat), 32mg chol., 726mg sod., 68g carb. (3g sugars, 6g fiber), 23g pro.

Feta-Stuffed Portobello Mushrooms

My husband adores mushrooms, and portobellos have loads of room for stuffing with feta cheese and pesto. Plan for one mushroom per person.
—Amy Martell, Canton, PA

- -

Takes: 20 min. • **Makes:** 4 servings

4	large portobello mushrooms (4 to 4½ in.)
2	Tbsp. olive oil
1	garlic clove, minced
¼	tsp. salt
1	cup (4 oz.) crumbled feta cheese
½	cup prepared pesto

1. Remove and discard stems from mushrooms; with a spoon, scrape and remove gills. In a small bowl, combine oil and garlic; brush over mushrooms. Sprinkle with salt. In a small bowl, combine feta cheese and pesto.

2. Place mushrooms on a piece of greased heavy-duty foil (about 12-in. square). Grill mushrooms, stem side up, covered, over medium heat or broil 4 in. from heat 8-10 minutes or until mushrooms are tender. Spoon cheese mixture over mushrooms; grill, covered, 2-3 minutes or until filling is heated through.

1 stuffed mushroom: 273 cal., 22g fat (5g sat. fat), 15mg chol., 783mg sod., 9g carb. (3g sugars, 3g fiber), 9g pro.

Saucy Mac & Cheese

I love the curly noodles in this creamy recipe. Cavatappi is a corkscrew pasta, also sold under the name cellentani, but any type of spiral pasta will work. This dish is fun to make and looks so pretty topped with extra cheese and crunchy, golden crumbs. I add ground pepper to my serving.
—Sara Martin, Brookfield, WI

- -

Takes: 25 min. • **Makes:** 4 servings

2	cups cavatappi or spiral pasta
3	Tbsp. butter, divided
⅓	cup panko bread crumbs
2	Tbsp. all-purpose flour
1½	cups 2% milk
¾	lb. Velveeta, cubed
¼	cup shredded cheddar cheese

1. Cook pasta according to package directions. Meanwhile, in a large nonstick skillet, melt 1 Tbsp. butter over medium-high heat. Add bread crumbs; cook and stir until golden brown. Remove to a small bowl and set aside.

2. In the same skillet, melt remaining butter. Stir in flour until smooth. Gradually add milk; bring to a boil. Cook and stir until thickened, about 2 minutes. Reduce the heat. Stir in Velveeta until melted.

3. Drain pasta; add to cheese mixture. Cook and stir until heated through, 3-4 minutes. Sprinkle with cheddar cheese and bread crumbs.

1¼ cups: 661 cal., 36g fat (21g sat. fat), 121mg chol., 1267mg sod., 58g carb. (11g sugars, 2g fiber), 27g pro.

Tortellini with Asparagus & Lemon

This is a terrific warm-weather dish, loaded with fresh flavors. I make mine meatless, but you could slice grilled chicken if you want extra protein.
—Crystal Schlueter, Northglenn, CO

- -

Takes: 30 min. • **Makes:** 4 servings

- 2 pkg. (9 oz. each) refrigerated cheese tortellini
- 3 Tbsp. butter
- 1 Tbsp. olive oil
- 2 cups cut fresh asparagus (2-in. pieces)
- 3 garlic cloves, minced
- ⅛ tsp. pepper
- 2 tsp. chopped chives
- 1 tsp. minced fresh parsley
- ½ tsp. chopped fresh dill
- ½ tsp. grated lemon zest
- 2 Tbsp. lemon juice
- ⅔ cup crumbled feta cheese
- ⅓ cup grated Parmesan cheese

1. Cook tortellini according to the package directions. Meanwhile, in a large skillet, heat butter and oil over medium-high heat. Add asparagus; cook and stir 3-4 minutes or until crisp-tender. Add garlic and pepper; cook 1 minute longer.

2. Remove from heat; stir in herbs, lemon zest and lemon juice. Drain tortellini; transfer to a large bowl. Stir in cheeses and asparagus mixture.

1¼ cups: 594 cal., 28g fat (15g sat. fat), 94mg chol., 843mg sod., 64g carb. (5g sugars, 5g fiber), 24g pro.

Southwestern Vegetables & Rice

Short on time? Here's a spicy supper made from everyday ingredients that comes together in minutes.
—*Taste of Home* Test Kitchen

- -

Takes: 20 min. • **Makes:** 4 servings

- 1 can (14½ oz.) fire-roasted diced tomatoes, undrained
- 1 pkg. (12 oz.) frozen vegetarian meat crumbles, thawed
- 1 pkg. (10.8 oz.) frozen southwestern corn, thawed
- 1 can (10¾ oz.) condensed tomato soup, undiluted
- 1 cup water
- 1 tsp. ground cumin
- ¼ tsp. salt
- 1 cup uncooked instant rice
- 1 cup shredded Monterey Jack cheese

In a Dutch oven, combine the first 7 ingredients. Bring to a boil. Stir in rice. Remove from the heat; cover and let stand for 5-7 minutes or until rice is tender. Sprinkle with cheese.

1½ cups: 502 cal., 15g fat (6g sat. fat), 25mg chol., 1629mg sod., 62g carb. (16g sugars, 7g fiber), 29g pro.

Garden Vegetable Gnocchi

When we go meatless, we toss gnocchi (my husband's favorite pasta) with veggies and a dab of prepared pesto. I use zucchini in this 30-minute dish, too.
—Elisabeth Larsen, Pleasant Grove, UT

- -

Takes: 30 min. • **Makes:** 4 servings

- 2 medium yellow summer squash, sliced
- 1 medium sweet red pepper, chopped
- 8 oz. sliced fresh mushrooms
- 1 Tbsp. olive oil
- ¼ tsp. salt
- ¼ tsp. pepper
- 1 pkg. (16 oz.) potato gnocchi
- ½ cup Alfredo sauce
- ¼ cup prepared pesto
  Chopped fresh basil, optional

1. Preheat oven to 450°. In a greased 15x10x1-in. baking pan, toss the vegetables with oil, salt and pepper. Roast until tender, 18-22 minutes, stirring once.
2. Meanwhile, in a large saucepan, cook gnocchi according to package directions. Drain and return to pan.
3. Stir in roasted vegetables, Alfredo sauce and pesto. If desired, sprinkle with basil.
1½ cups: 402 cal., 14g fat (4g sat. fat), 17mg chol., 955mg sod., 57g carb. (12g sugars, 5g fiber), 13g pro.

Thai Pasta with Spicy Peanut Sauce

We love how the whole wheat pasta and crisp, raw vegetables blend with this rich and creamy peanut sauce. The addition of fresh lime juice really brightens the flavor of the dish. Some folks eat it hot, but my husband and I prefer to wait until it's closer to room temperature.
—Donna McCallie, Lake Park, FL

- -

Takes: 30 min. • **Makes:** 6 servings

- 1 pkg. (12 oz.) whole wheat linguine
- 1 jar (11½ oz.) Thai peanut sauce
- 2 Tbsp. lime juice
- 2 cups bean sprouts
- 1 large cucumber, peeled, seeded and chopped
- 2 medium carrots, julienned
- 5 green onions, sliced
- 1 small sweet red pepper, julienned
- ½ cup minced fresh cilantro

1. Cook the linguine according to package directions. Drain; return to pan.
2. In a small bowl, combine peanut sauce and lime juice. Add peanut sauce mixture, vegetables and cilantro to pan; toss to coat.
1¾ cups: 410 cal., 12g fat (2g sat. fat), 0 chol., 452mg sod., 66g carb. (18g sugars, 8g fiber), 14g pro.

Make-Ahead GREATS

Conquer weekly meal prep with delicious make-ahead and freezer-friendly dishes. Your future self will thank you!

Italian-Style Salisbury Steaks

This is my husband's favorite recipe. If you like, you can top each serving with mozzarella or Parmesan cheese.
—Heather Nalley, Easley, SC

- -

Takes: 25 min. • **Makes:** 4 servings

- 1 large egg, beaten
- 1 tsp. Worcestershire sauce
- ½ cup seasoned bread crumbs
- ½ tsp. garlic powder
- ½ tsp. pepper
- 1 lb. ground beef
- 1 Tbsp. canola oil
- 1 can (14½ oz.) diced tomatoes with basil, oregano and garlic, undrained
- 1 can (8 oz.) Italian tomato sauce

1. In a large bowl, combine the first 5 ingredients. Crumble the beef over mixture and mix lightly but thoroughly. Shape into 4 oval patties. In a large skillet, brown patties in oil on both sides. Drain.

2. In a small bowl, combine diced tomatoes and tomato sauce. Pour over patties. Bring to a boil. Reduce heat; cover and simmer until meat is no longer pink, 10-15 minutes.

Freeze option: Freeze individual cooled steaks with some tomato mixture in resealable freezer bags. To use, partially thaw in refrigerator overnight. Microwave, covered, on high in a microwave-safe dish until heated through, stirring and adding a little water if necessary.

1 patty with ½ cup sauce : 359 cal., 20 g fat (6 g sat. fat), 123 mg chol., 1104 mg sod., 21 g carb. (7 g sugars, 2 g fiber), 26 g pro.

Pizza Meat Loaf Cups

Fix and freeze these moist little meat loaves packed with pizza flavor. Try reheating for an after-school snack or quick dinner. My family likes to drizzle extra pizza sauce on top.
—Susan Wollin, Marshall, WI

- -

Takes: 30 min. • **Makes:** 1 dozen

- 1 large egg, lightly beaten
- ½ cup pizza sauce
- ¼ cup seasoned bread crumbs
- ½ tsp. Italian seasoning
- 1½ lbs. ground beef
- 1½ cups shredded part-skim mozzarella cheese
  Optional: Additional pizza sauce and basil leaves

1. Preheat oven to 375°. In a large bowl, mix first 4 ingredients. Add beef; mix lightly but thoroughly. Divide into 12 portions; press each onto the bottom and up sides of a greased muffin cup. Add cheese to the centers.

2. Bake until meat is cooked through, 15-18 minutes. If desired, top with additional sauce and basil before serving.

Freeze option: Freeze cooled meat loaves in freezer containers. To use, partially thaw in the refrigerator overnight. Microwave, covered, on high in a microwave-safe dish until heated through, 2-3 minutes.

2 meat loaf cups: 327 cal., 20g fat (8g sat. fat), 119mg chol., 416mg sod., 6g carb. (2g sugars, 1g fiber), 29g pro.

Jiffy Ground Pork Skillet

Some people call it dinner hour, but busy cooks call it rush hour. Slow down with this super-easy meal. The only thing you'll have left over is time to share with your family at the table.
—Brigitte Schaller, Flemington, MO

Takes: 30 min. • **Makes:** 5 servings

- 1½ cups uncooked penne pasta
- 1 lb. ground pork
- ½ cup chopped onion
- 1 can (14½ oz.) stewed tomatoes, undrained
- 1 can (8 oz.) tomato sauce
- 1 tsp. Italian seasoning
- 1 medium zucchini, cut into ¼-in. slices

1. Cook pasta according to package directions. Meanwhile, in a large skillet, cook pork and onion over medium heat until meat is no longer pink; drain. Add tomatoes, tomato sauce and Italian seasoning. Bring to a boil. Reduce heat; cover and cook mixture for 5 minutes to allow flavors to blend.

2. Drain pasta; add to skillet. Stir in zucchini. Cover and cook until the zucchini is crisp-tender, 3-5 minutes.

Freeze option: Transfer individual portions of cooled pasta mixture to freezer containers. To use, partially thaw in refrigerator overnight. Heat through in a saucepan, stirring occasionally; add tomato sauce if necessary.

1⅓ cups: 317 cal., 14g fat (5g sat. fat), 61mg chol., 408mg sod., 27g carb. (7g sugars, 2g fiber), 21g pro.

Tacos on a Stick

It's as much fun to assemble these creative kabobs as it is to eat them. The whole family is sure to love this sensational southwestern twist on beef shish kabobs.
—Dixie Terry, Goreville, IL

Prep: 15 min. + marinating
Grill: 15 min. • **Makes:** 6 servings

- 1 envelope taco seasoning
- 1 cup tomato juice
- 2 Tbsp. canola oil
- 2 lbs. beef top sirloin steak, cut into 1-in. cubes
- 1 medium green pepper, cut into chunks
- 1 medium sweet red pepper, cut into chunks
- 1 large onion, cut into wedges
- 16 cherry tomatoes
  Salsa con queso or sour cream, optional

1. In a large shallow dish, combine taco seasoning, tomato juice and oil; mix well. Remove ½ cup for basting; refrigerate. Add beef and turn to coat. Cover; refrigerate for at least 5 hours.

2. Drain and discard marinade from beef. On metal or soaked wooden skewers, alternately thread beef, peppers, onion and tomatoes. Grill, uncovered, over medium heat for 3 minutes on each side. Baste with reserved marinade. Continue turning and basting until the meat reaches desired doneness, 8-10 minutes. If desired, serve with salsa con queso or sour cream.

1 serving: 277 cal., 10g fat (3g sat. fat), 61mg chol., 665mg sod., 12g carb. (4g sugars, 2g fiber), 34g pro.
Diabetic exchanges: 4 lean meat, 2 vegetable, 1 fat.

Slow-Cooked Beef Brisket

When my husband and I were both working full-time, this recipe's long cook time was ideal for our schedule. The beef brisket tastes so good after simmering all day in the slow cooker, and the chili sauce adds a unique touch to the gravy.

—Anna Stodolak, Volant, PA

- -

Prep: 10 min. • **Cook:** 8½ hours
Makes: 8 servings

1 large onion, sliced
1 fresh beef brisket (3 to 4 lbs.), cut in half
¼ tsp. pepper
1 jar (4½ oz.) sliced mushrooms, drained
¾ cup beef broth
½ cup chili sauce
¼ cup packed brown sugar
2 garlic cloves, minced
¼ cup all-purpose flour
¼ cup cold water

1. Place onion in a 5-qt. slow cooker. Rub brisket with pepper; place over onion. Top with mushrooms. In a small bowl, combine the broth, chili sauce, brown sugar and garlic; pour over brisket. Cover and cook on low for 8-10 hours or until meat is tender.
2. Remove brisket and keep warm. In a small bowl, combine the flour and water until smooth; stir into cooking juices. Cover and cook on high for 30 minutes or until thickened. Slice brisket; serve with gravy.
Note: This is a fresh beef brisket, not corned beef.

5 oz. cooked beef with ½ cup gravy: 284 cal., 7g fat (3g sat. fat), 72mg chol., 441mg sod., 17g carb. (11g sugars, 1g fiber), 36g pro.
Diabetic exchanges: 5 lean meat, 1 starch.

Pulled Pork Parfait

I tried a version of this meaty parfait at Miller Park, the then-home of my favorite baseball team, the Milwaukee Brewers. I take it up a notch by adding layers of corn and creamy mac and cheese. It truly is a full barbecue meal you can take on the go.
—Rachel Bernhard Seis, Milwaukee, WI

- -

Takes: 15 min. • **Makes:** 4 servings

- 1 pkg. (16 oz.) refrigerated fully cooked barbecued shredded pork
- 1 cup frozen corn
- 2 cups refrigerated mashed potatoes
- 2 cups prepared macaroni and cheese

1. In each of 4 1-pint wide-mouth canning jars, divide and layer ingredients in the following order: pulled pork, corn, mashed potatoes, and macaroni and cheese. Cover and freeze or refrigerate until ready to serve. When ready to serve, remove jar lids and microwave until heated through.

2. To serve from freezer, partially thaw in refrigerator overnight before microwaving.

1 serving: 349 cal., 8g fat (4g sat. fat), 45mg chol., 1116mg sod., 41g carb. (20g sugars, 1g fiber), 17g pro.

Classic Crab Cakes

Our region is known for good seafood, and crab cakes are a traditional favorite. I learned to make them from the chef of a restaurant where they were a best-seller. The crabmeat's flavor is sparked by the blend of other ingredients.
—Debbie Terenzini, Lusby, MD

- -

Takes: 20 min. • **Makes:** 8 servings

- 1 lb. fresh or canned crabmeat, drained, flaked and cartilage removed
- 2 to 2½ cups soft bread crumbs
- 1 large egg, beaten
- ¾ cup mayonnaise
- ⅓ cup each chopped celery, green pepper and onion
- 1 Tbsp. seafood seasoning
- 1 Tbsp. minced fresh parsley
- 2 tsp. lemon juice
- 1 tsp. Worcestershire sauce
- 1 tsp. prepared mustard
- ¼ tsp. pepper
- ⅛ tsp. hot pepper sauce
- 2 to 4 Tbsp. vegetable oil, optional
  Lemon wedges, optional

In a large bowl, combine the crab, bread crumbs, egg, mayonnaise, vegetables and seasonings. Shape into 8 patties. Broil or cook patties in a cast-iron or other ovenproof skillet in oil until golden brown, 4 minutes on each side. If desired, serve with lemon.

Freeze option: Freeze cooled crab cakes in freezer containers, separating the layers with waxed paper. To use, reheat the crab cakes on a baking sheet in a preheated 325° oven until heated through.

1 serving: 282 cal., 22g fat (3g sat. fat), 85mg chol., 638mg sod., 7g carb. (1g sugars, 1g fiber), 14g pro.

Applesauce Barbecue Chicken

You only need a few ingredients to create this sweet and peppery chicken. The subtle flavor of apple makes this tender barbecue dish stand out from the rest.
—Darla Andrews, Boerne, TX

Takes: 20 min. • **Makes:** 4 servings

- 4   boneless skinless chicken breast halves (6 oz. each)
- ½   tsp. pepper
- 1   Tbsp. olive oil
- ⅔   cup chunky applesauce
- ⅔   cup spicy barbecue sauce
- 2   Tbsp. brown sugar
- 1   tsp. chili powder

Sprinkle chicken with pepper. In a large skillet, brown chicken in oil on both sides. In a small bowl, combine remaining ingredients; pour over chicken. Cover and cook until a thermometer reads 165°, 7-10 minutes.

Freeze option: Cool chicken; transfer to a freezer container and freeze for up to 3 months. Thaw in refrigerator overnight. Cover and microwave chicken on high until heated through, 8-10 minutes, stirring once.

1 chicken breast half: 308 cal., 8g fat (2g sat. fat), 94mg chol., 473mg sod., 22g carb. (19g sugars, 1g fiber), 35g pro.

Cheddar Bean Burritos

My family goes meatless several nights a week, and this recipe is one of our favorites. I usually puree a can or two of chipotles in adobo and freeze in ice cube trays so I can use a small amount when I need it.
—Amy Bravo, Ames, IA

Takes: 25 min. • **Makes:** 6 servings

- 2   tsp. canola oil
- 1   Tbsp. minced chipotle pepper in adobo sauce
- 2   garlic cloves, minced
- 2   tsp. chili powder
- 1   tsp. ground cumin
- ⅛   tsp. salt
- 2   cans (15 oz. each) black beans, rinsed and drained
- 2   Tbsp. water
- ½   cup pico de gallo
- 6   flour tortillas (8 in.), warmed
- 1   cup shredded cheddar or Monterey Jack cheese
- ½   cup sour cream
    Optional: Additional pico de gallo and sour cream

1. In a large skillet, heat the oil over medium heat; saute chipotle pepper, garlic and seasonings 2 minutes. Stir in beans and water; bring to a boil. Reduce heat; simmer, uncovered, until flavors are blended, 5-7 minutes, stirring occasionally.

2. Coarsely mash bean mixture; stir in pico de gallo. Spoon onto tortillas; top with cheese and sour cream and roll up. If desired, serve with additional pico de gallo and sour cream.

Freeze option: Cool filling before making burritos. Individually wrap burritos in paper towels and foil; freeze in an airtight container. To use, remove foil; place a paper towel-wrapped burrito on a microwave-safe plate. Microwave on high until heated through, 4-6 minutes, turning once. Let stand 2 minutes.

1 burrito: 410 cal., 16g fat (7g sat. fat), 23mg chol., 726mg sod., 50g carb. (2g sugars, 8g fiber), 16g pro.

Cranberry Sweet-and-Sour Pork

This fresh take on the popular Asian-style dish is sure to get a thumbs up at the dinner table.
—Gert Snyder, West Montrose, ON

Takes: 20 min. • **Makes:** 6 servings

- 1 Tbsp. cornstarch
- ½ cup unsweetened pineapple juice
- 1 cup whole-berry cranberry sauce
- ½ cup barbecue sauce
- 1½ lbs. pork tenderloin, cut into ½-in. cubes
- 1 Tbsp. canola oil
- ½ tsp. salt
- ¼ tsp. pepper
- 1 medium green pepper, cut into strips
- ¾ cup pineapple tidbits
  Optional: Hot cooked rice, chow mein noodles or crispy wonton strips

1. In a small bowl, combine the cornstarch and pineapple juice until smooth. Stir in cranberry and barbecue sauces; set aside.

2. In a large skillet, stir-fry pork in oil until the meat is no longer pink, 3 minutes. Sprinkle with salt and pepper. Remove from pan and keep warm.

3. Add green pepper and pineapple to pan; stir-fry for 2 minutes. Stir cornstarch mixture and add to skillet. Bring to a boil. Cook and stir until thickened, 2 minutes. Add pork; heat through. Serve with rice, noodles or wonton strips if desired.

Freeze option: Place cooled meat mixture in freezer containers. To use, partially thaw in refrigerator overnight. Heat through slowly in a covered skillet, stirring occasionally; add water if necessary.

1¼ cups: 268 cal., 7g fat (2g sat. fat), 63mg chol., 444mg sod., 28g carb. (19g sugars, 1g fiber), 23g pro.

Slow-Cooked Flank Steak

My slow cooker gets lots of use, especially during the hectic summer months. I can fix this flank steak in the morning and forget about it until dinner. Serve with noodles and a tossed salad.
—Michelle Armistead, Keyport, NJ

Prep: 15 min. • **Cook:** 4 hours
Makes: 6 servings

- 1   beef flank steak (1½ lbs.)
- 1   Tbsp. canola oil
- 1   large onion, sliced
- ⅓   cup water
- 1   can (4 oz.) chopped green chiles
- 2   Tbsp. vinegar
- 1¼ tsp. chili powder
- 1   tsp. garlic powder
- ½   tsp. sugar
- ½   tsp. salt
- ⅛   tsp. pepper

In a skillet, brown steak in oil; transfer to a 5-qt. slow cooker. In same skillet, saute onion for 1 minute. Gradually add water, stirring to loosen browned bits from pan. Add all remaining ingredients; bring to a boil. Pour over flank steak. Cover and cook on low until the meat is tender, 4-5 hours. Slice the meat; serve with onion and pan juices.

3 oz. cooked beef: 199 cal., 11g fat (4g sat. fat), 48mg chol., 327mg sod., 4g carb. (2g sugars, 1g fiber), 20g pro.
Diabetic exchanges: 3 lean meat, ½ fat.

Red Clam Sauce

This recipe tastes as if it took all day. It's a classy way to jazz up pasta sauce!
—JoAnn Brown, Latrobe, PA

Prep: 25 min. • **Cook:** 3 hours
Makes: 4 servings

- 1 medium onion, chopped
- 1 Tbsp. canola oil
- 2 garlic cloves, minced
- 2 cans (6½ oz. each) chopped clams, undrained
- 1 can (14½ oz.) diced tomatoes, undrained
- 1 can (6 oz.) tomato paste
- ¼ cup minced fresh parsley
- 1 bay leaf
- 1 tsp. sugar
- 1 tsp. dried basil
- ½ tsp. dried thyme
  Additional minced fresh parsley, optional
- 6 oz. linguine, cooked and drained

1. In a small skillet, saute onion in oil until tender. Add the garlic; cook 1 minute longer.

2. Transfer to a 1½- or 2-qt. slow cooker. Stir in the clams, tomatoes, tomato paste, parsley, bay leaf, sugar, basil and thyme.

3. Cover and cook on low until heated through, 3-4 hours. Discard bay leaf. If desired, sprinkle with additional parsley. Serve with pasta.

Freeze option: Omit additional parsley. Cool before placing in a freezer container. Cover and freeze for up to 3 months. To use, thaw in the refrigerator overnight. Place in a large saucepan; heat through, stirring occasionally. Serve with pasta and, if desired, minced parsley.

1 cup sauce with ¾ cup cooked linguine: 305 cal., 5g fat (0 sat. fat), 15mg chol., 553mg sod., 53g carb. (14g sugars, 7g fiber), 15g pro.

Slow-Cooker Beef Barbacoa

I love this beef barbacoa because the meat is fall-apart tender and the sauce is smoky, slightly spicy and so flavorful. It's an amazing alternative to ground beef tacos or even pulled pork carnitas. It's also versatile. You can have a soft taco bar and let people make their own—or offer Mexican pizzas or rice bowls.
—Holly Sander, Lake Mary, FL

- -

Prep: 20 min. • **Cook:** 6 hours
Makes: 8 servings

1	beef rump or bottom round roast (3 lbs.)
½	cup minced fresh cilantro
⅓	cup tomato paste
8	garlic cloves, minced
2	Tbsp. chipotle peppers in adobo sauce plus 1 Tbsp. sauce
2	Tbsp. cider vinegar
4	tsp. ground cumin
1	Tbsp. brown sugar
1½	tsp. salt
1	tsp. pepper
1	cup beef stock
1	cup beer or additional stock
16	corn tortillas (6 in.)
	Pico de gallo
	Optional toppings: Lime wedges, queso fresco and additional cilantro

1. Cut roast in half. Mix the next 9 ingredients; rub over roast. Place in a 5-qt. slow cooker. Add stock and beer. Cook, covered, until the meat is tender, 6-8 hours.

2. Remove roast; shred with 2 forks. Reserve 3 cups of cooking juices; discard remaining juices. Skim fat from reserved juices. Return beef and reserved juices to slow cooker; heat through.

3. Serve beef with tortillas and pico de gallo. If desired, serve with lime wedges, queso fresco and additional cilantro.

Freeze option: Place shredded beef in freezer containers. Cool and freeze. To use, partially thaw in refrigerator overnight. Heat through in a covered saucepan, stirring gently; add broth if necessary.

2 filled tortillas: 361 cal., 10g fat (3g sat. fat), 101mg chol., 652mg sod., 28g carb. (4g sugars, 4g fiber), 38g pro. **Diabetic exchanges:** 5 lean meat, 2 starch.

TIMESAVING TIP

Barbacoa comes from the early indigenous Caribbean people's cooking style of slow-roasting cuts of meat seasoned with garlic, spices and chipotle peppers over an open fire. Its origins helped shape what we today call barbecue.

Italian Beef Patties

Make these pizza-flavored patties and watch the kids devour them! Give them a try on rice or with a side of deli pasta salad for a fast fix.
—Deanna Maciejewski,
Bridgeton, MO

- -

Takes: 25 min. • **Makes:** 6 servings

- ⅔ cup pizza sauce, divided
- 1 large egg, beaten
- ⅓ cup dry bread crumbs
- 2 tsp. dried minced onion
- ½ tsp. dried oregano
- ¼ tsp. salt
- ⅛ tsp. pepper
- 1½ lbs. ground beef
- 3 slices part-skim mozzarella cheese, halved

1. In a large bowl, combine ⅓ cup pizza sauce, egg, bread crumbs, onion, oregano, salt and pepper. Crumble beef over mixture and mix lightly but thoroughly. Shape into 6 patties. Place on a broiler pan coated with cooking spray.
2. Broil 6 in. from the heat until juices run clear, 5-6 minutes on each side, basting frequently with remaining pizza sauce. Top with cheese. Broil 1 minute longer or until the cheese is melted.
Freeze option: Prepare uncooked patties and freeze, covered, on a parchment-lined baking sheet until firm. Transfer patties to a large resealable plastic bag; return to freezer. To use, cook frozen patties and top with cheese as directed, increasing time as necessary for a thermometer to read 160°.
1 serving: 325 cal., 19g fat (8g sat. fat), 132mg chol., 365mg sod., 7g carb. (1g sugars, 1g fiber), 29g pro.

Maple-Pecan Pork Chops

For a standout dinner, start with this change-of-pace entree. Begin by simmering the chops in apple juice, then drizzle with sweet maple syrup and top with crunchy pecans.
—*Taste of Home* Test Kitchen

- -

Takes: 30 min.
Makes: 4 servings (1¼ cups sauce)

- 2 Tbsp. spicy brown mustard
- ½ tsp. pepper
- ½ cup maple syrup, divided
- 4 bone-in pork loin chops (¾ in. thick and 8 oz. each)
- 1 Tbsp. butter
- ½ cup unsweetened apple juice
- 1 cup pecan halves

1. Mix mustard, pepper and 2 tsp. syrup. Lightly drizzle over both sides of pork chops.

2. In a large nonstick skillet, heat butter over medium heat. Brown pork chops for 2-3 minutes on each side. Add apple juice. Reduce heat; simmer, covered, until thermometer reads 145°, 15-20 minutes. Remove chops; let stand 5 minutes, keeping them warm.
3. Add pecans and remaining syrup to skillet; cook and stir until blended, 1-2 minutes. Serve with pork chops.
Freeze option: Cool pork chops. Prepare maple sauce, but do not add pecans. Freeze pecans and pork chops with sauce in separate freezer containers. To use, thaw pecans; partially thaw pork chop mixture in refrigerator overnight. Heat through slowly in a covered skillet, turning occasionally, until a thermometer inserted in pork reads 165°. Remove chops to a platter. Add pecans to sauce; serve with chops.
1 pork chop with 5 Tbsp. sauce: 657 cal., 41g fat (10g sat. fat), 119mg chol., 199mg sod., 34g carb. (28g sugars, 3g fiber), 39g pro.

Meat Loaf Muffins

Serve these tangy meat loaf muffins for dinner or slice them up for a take-along sandwich lunch. They're just as flavorful after freezing.
—Cheryl Norwood, Canton, GA

- -

Takes: 30 min. • **Makes:** 6 servings

- 1 large egg, lightly beaten
- ½ cup dry bread crumbs
- ½ cup finely chopped onion
- ½ cup finely chopped green pepper
- ¼ cup barbecue sauce
- 1½ lbs. lean ground beef (90% lean)
- 3 Tbsp. ketchup
  Additional ketchup, optional

1. Preheat oven to 375°. Mix the first 5 ingredients. Add beef; mix lightly but thoroughly. Press about ⅓ cupful into each of 12 ungreased muffin cups.

2. Bake 15 minutes. Brush tops of loaves with 3 Tbsp. ketchup; bake until a thermometer reads 160°, 5-7 minutes. If desired, serve with additional ketchup.

Freeze option: Bake muffins without ketchup; cover and freeze on a waxed paper-lined baking sheet until firm. Transfer muffins to an airtight freezer container; return to freezer. To use, partially thaw muffins in refrigerator overnight. Place muffins on a greased shallow baking pan. Spread with ketchup. Bake in a preheated 350° oven until heated through.

2 mini meat loaves: 260 cal., 11g fat (4g sat. fat), 102mg chol., 350mg sod., 15g carb. (7g sugars, 1g fiber), 24g pro.

Chicken Tacos with Avocado Salsa

A few members of my family have special dietary needs, but these tasty chicken tacos work for all of us.
—Christine Schenher, Exeter, CA

- -

Takes: 30 min. • **Makes:** 4 servings

- 1 lb. boneless skinless chicken breasts, cut into ½-in. strips
- ⅓ cup water
- 1 tsp. sugar
- 1 Tbsp. chili powder
- 1 tsp. onion powder
- 1 tsp. dried oregano
- 1 tsp. ground cumin
- 1 tsp. paprika
- ½ tsp. salt
- ½ tsp. garlic powder
- 1 medium ripe avocado, peeled and cubed
- 1 cup fresh or frozen corn, thawed
- 1 cup cherry tomatoes, quartered
- 2 tsp. lime juice
- 8 taco shells, warmed

1. Place a large nonstick skillet coated with cooking spray over medium-high heat. Brown chicken strips. Add water, sugar and seasonings. Cook 4-5 minutes or until chicken is no longer pink, stirring occasionally.

2. Meanwhile, in a small bowl, gently mix avocado, corn, tomatoes and lime juice. Spoon chicken mixture into the taco shells; top with avocado salsa.

Freeze option: Freeze cooled meat mixture in freezer containers. To use, partially thaw meat in refrigerator overnight. Heat mixture through in a saucepan, stirring occasionally; add water if necessary.

2 tacos: 354 cal., 15g fat (3g sat. fat), 63mg chol., 474mg sod., 30g carb. (4g sugars, 6g fiber), 27g pro.

Slow-Cooked Lamb Chops

Chops are without a doubt the cut of lamb we like best. I usually simmer them on low for hours in a slow cooker. The aroma is irresistible, and they come out so tender they practically melt in your mouth!
—Sandy McKenzie, Braham, MN

- -

Prep: 10 min. • **Cook:** 4 hours
Makes: 4 servings

- 1 medium onion, sliced
- 1 tsp. dried oregano
- ½ tsp. dried thyme
- ½ tsp. garlic powder
- ¼ tsp. salt
- ⅛ tsp. pepper
- 8 lamb loin chops (about 1¾ lbs.)
- 2 garlic cloves, minced

Place onion in a 3-qt. slow cooker. Combine the oregano, thyme, garlic powder, salt and pepper; rub over the lamb chops. Place chops over onion. Top with garlic. Cover and cook on low for 4-6 hours or until the meat is tender.

2 each: 201 cal., 8g fat (3g sat. fat), 79mg chol., 219mg sod., 5g carb. (2g sugars, 1g fiber), 26g pro.

Pressure-Cooker Pork Tacos with Mango Salsa

I've made quite a few tacos in my day, but these are by far my favorite. The pressure cooker is the key to the tender pork filling. Make the mango salsa from scratch if you have time.

—Amber Massey, Argyle, TX

- -

Prep: 25 min. • **Cook:** 5 min.
Makes: 12 servings

2	Tbsp. white vinegar
2	Tbsp. lime juice
3	cups cubed fresh pineapple
1	small red onion, coarsely chopped
3	Tbsp. chili powder
2	chipotle peppers in adobo sauce
2	tsp. ground cumin
1½	tsp. salt
½	tsp. pepper
1	bottle (12 oz.) dark Mexican beer
3	lbs. pork tenderloin, cut into 1-in. cubes
¼	cup chopped fresh cilantro
1	jar (16 oz.) mango salsa
24	corn tortillas (6 in.), warmed

Optional toppings: Cubed fresh pineapple, cubed avocado and queso fresco

1. Puree the first 9 ingredients in a blender; stir in beer. In a 6-qt. electric pressure cooker, combine pork and pineapple mixture. Lock lid; close the pressure-release valve. Adjust to pressure-cook on high for 3 minutes. Quick-release pressure. A thermometer inserted into pork should read at least 145°. Stir to break up pork.

2. Stir cilantro into salsa. Using a slotted spoon, serve pork mixture in tortillas; add salsa and toppings as desired.

Freeze option: Freeze cooled meat mixture and cooking juices in freezer containers. To use, partially thaw in refrigerator overnight. Heat through in a saucepan, stirring occasionally.

2 tacos: 284 cal., 6g fat (2g sat. fat), 64mg chol., 678mg sod., 30g carb. (5g sugars, 5g fiber), 26g pro.
Diabetic exchanges: 3 lean meat, 2 starch.

Kalua Pork

Planning a tropical luau? Then this is the perfect main dish for your event. It's a no-fuss meal and easy to clean up. A Hawaiian friend shared this recipe with me while I was stationed in Pearl Harbor several years ago. It feeds a crowd and everyone loves it.
—Becky Friedman, Hammond, LA

- -

Prep: 10 min. • **Cook:** 8 hours
Makes: 18 servings

1   **boneless pork shoulder roast
      (5 to 6 lbs.)**
1   **Tbsp. liquid smoke**
4   **tsp. sea salt (preferably
      Hawaiian Alaea Sea Salt)
      Hot cooked rice, optional**

1. Pierce pork with a fork; rub with liquid smoke and salt. Place pork in a 6-qt. slow cooker. Cook, covered, on low until pork is tender, 8-10 hours.
2. Remove roast; shred with 2 forks. Strain cooking juices; skim fat. Return pork to slow cooker. Stir in enough cooking juices to moisten; heat through. If desired, serve with rice.

Freeze option: Freeze the cooled meat mixture and juices in freezer containers. To use, partially thaw in refrigerator overnight. Heat through in a saucepan, stirring occasionally; add broth if necessary.

3 oz. cooked pork: 205 cal., 13g fat (5g sat. fat), 75mg chol., 504mg sod., 0 carb. (0 sugars, 0 fiber), 21g pro.
Diabetic exchanges: 3 medium-fat meat.

Chicken Pesto Meatballs

These tender, pesto-stuffed meatballs get gobbled up in our house. They're short on ingredients, but packed with flavor. I make a double batch and freeze the other half for a busy night.
—Ally Billhorn, Wilton, IA

- -

Takes: 30 min. • **Makes:** 4 servings

- 6 oz. uncooked whole grain spaghetti
- ¼ cup dry bread crumbs
- 2 Tbsp. prepared pesto
- 2 Tbsp. grated Parmesan cheese
- 1 tsp. garlic powder
- 1 lb. lean ground chicken
- 1½ cups marinara sauce
- ¼ cup water
- Optional: Torn fresh basil and additional Parmesan cheese

1. Cook spaghetti according to package directions; drain.
2. In a large bowl, combine bread crumbs, pesto, cheese and garlic powder. Add chicken; mix lightly but thoroughly. Shape into 1-in. balls.
3. In a large skillet, brown the meatballs over medium heat, turning occasionally. Add sauce and water; bring to a boil. Reduce heat; simmer, covered, until meatballs are cooked through, about 5 minutes. Serve with spaghetti. If desired, top with basil and additional cheese.

Freeze option: Freeze the cooled meatball mixture in freezer containers. To use, partially thaw in refrigerator overnight. Heat through in a covered saucepan over low heat, stirring gently; add water if necessary.

¾ cup meatball mixture with 1 cup spaghetti: 422 cal., 12g fat (3g sat. fat), 85mg chol., 706mg sod., 45g carb. (7g sugars, 7g fiber), 32g pro.
Diabetic exchanges: 3 starch, 3 lean meat, 1½ fat.

TIMESAVING TIP

Out of dry bread crumbs? Use an equal amount of unsalted cracker crumbs or uncooked oats, or use ¾ cup soft bread crumbs. Mixing the seasonings and any bread crumbs or liquid ingredients before adding the meat helps blend the flavors with minimal handling of the raw meat.

Quinoa Unstuffed Peppers

This deconstructed stuffed pepper dish packs a wallop of flavor. I truly make it all the time, and I make sure my freezer's stocked with single-serve portions to take to work.
—Rebecca Ende, Phoenix, NY

- -

Takes: 30 min. • **Makes:** 4 servings

- 1½ cups vegetable stock
- ¾ cup quinoa, rinsed
- 1 lb. Italian turkey sausage links, casings removed
- 1 medium sweet red pepper, chopped
- 1 medium green pepper, chopped
- ¾ cup chopped sweet onion
- 1 garlic clove, minced
- ¼ tsp. garam masala
- ¼ tsp. pepper
- ⅛ tsp. salt

1. In a small saucepan, bring stock to a boil. Add quinoa. Reduce heat; simmer, covered, until the liquid is absorbed, 12-15 minutes. Remove from heat.

2. In a large skillet, cook and crumble sausage with peppers and onion over medium-high heat until no longer pink, 8-10 minutes. Add garlic and seasonings; cook and stir 1 minute. Stir in quinoa.

Freeze option: Place cooled quinoa mixture in freezer containers. To use, partially thaw in the refrigerator overnight. Microwave, covered, on high in a microwave-safe dish until heated through, stirring occasionally.

1 cup: 261 cal., 9g fat (2g sat. fat), 42mg chol., 760mg sod., 28g carb. (3g sugars, 4g fiber), 17g pro.
Diabetic exchanges: 2 starch, 2 medium-fat meat.

Beef Roast Dinner

Because this healthy dish is slow cooked, you can use budget-friendly roasts with results as mouthwatering as the more costly cuts. Change up the veggies for variety, nutrition or to suit your tastes!
—Sandra Dudley, Bemidji, MN

- -

Prep: 25 min. • **Cook:** 7 hours
Makes: 8 servings

1	lb. red potatoes (3-4 medium), cubed
1½	cups fresh baby carrots
1	medium green pepper, chopped
1	medium parsnip, chopped
¼	lb. small fresh mushrooms
1	small red onion, chopped
1	beef rump roast or bottom round roast (3 lbs.)
1	can (14½ oz.) beef broth
¾	tsp. salt
¾	tsp. dried oregano
¼	tsp. pepper
3	Tbsp. cornstarch
¼	cup cold water

1. Place vegetables in a 5-qt. slow cooker. Cut roast in half; place over vegetables. Mix broth and seasonings; pour over roast. Cook, covered, on low until meat and vegetables are tender, 7-9 hours.

2. Remove roast and vegetables from slow cooker; keep warm. Transfer cooking juices to a small saucepan; bring to a boil. Mix cornstarch and water until smooth; stir into cooking juices. Return to a boil; cook and stir until thickened, 1-2 minutes. Serve with roast and vegetables.

1 serving: 304 cal., 8g fat (3g sat. fat), 101mg chol., 533mg sod., 19g carb. (4g sugars, 3g fiber), 36g pro.
Diabetic exchanges: 5 lean meat, 1 starch.

Moroccan Lamb Lettuce Wraps

I am a huge fan of both lamb and lettuce wraps. This combination of ingredients, along with the cucumber dressing, makes a tasty slow-cooked dish. The wine and chili powder add extra flavor elements, too.
—Arlene Erlbach, Morton Grove, IL

Prep: 25 min. • **Cook:** 5 hours
Makes: 8 servings

- 2 lbs. lamb stew meat
- 1 cup chunky salsa
- ⅓ cup apricot preserves
- 6 Tbsp. dry red wine, divided
- 1 to 2 Tbsp. Moroccan seasoning (ras el hanout)
- 2 tsp. chili powder
- ½ tsp. garlic powder
- 1 English cucumber, very thinly sliced
- 2 Tbsp. prepared ranch salad dressing
- 16 Bibb or Boston lettuce leaves

1. Combine lamb, salsa, preserves, 4 Tbsp. wine, Moroccan seasoning, chili powder and garlic powder. Transfer to a 3-qt. slow cooker. Cook, covered, on low 5-6 hours, until lamb is tender. Remove lamb; shred with 2 forks. Strain cooking juices and skim fat. Return lamb and cooking juices to slow cooker; heat through. Stir in the remaining 2 Tbsp. wine; heat through.
2. Combine cucumber and ranch dressing; toss to coat. Serve lamb mixture in lettuce leaves; top with cucumber mixture.
2 filled lettuce wraps: 221 cal., 8g fat (2g sat. fat), 74mg chol., 257mg sod., 13g carb. (8g sugars, 1g fiber), 24g pro.
Diabetic exchanges: 3 lean meat, 1 starch.

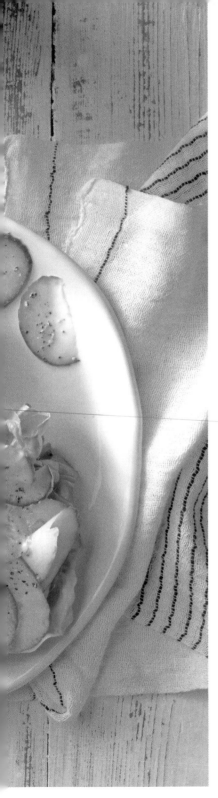

Slow-Cooker Chicken Enchilada Stuffed Peppers

Utilize leftovers and clean out the fridge by making these simple and tasty stuffed peppers. They're ideal when you're craving a warm and cozy slow-cooked meal.

—Katie Jasiewicz, Belle Isle, FL

- -

Prep: 20 min. • **Cook:** 3 hrs.
Makes: 6 servings

2 cups shredded cooked chicken
1 pkg. (8.8 oz.) ready-to-serve long grain rice
1 cup enchilada sauce
¾ cup shredded cheddar cheese, divided
3 Tbsp. minced red onion
½ tsp. ground cumin
⅓ cup water
6 medium bell peppers
  Minced fresh cilantro, green onions and sour cream

1. In a bowl, combine chicken, rice, enchilada sauce, ½ cup cheese, red onion and cumin.

2. Pour water into a 6-qt. slow cooker. Cut and discard tops from peppers; remove seeds. Fill with the chicken mixture; place in slow cooker. Cover slow cooker with a double layer of white paper towels; place lid securely over towels. Cook on low until tender, 3-4 hours. During the last 20 minutes, remove and discard paper towels; add remaining cheese and cook, covered, until melted. Serve with sour cream, cilantro and green onions.

1 stuffed pepper: 267 cal., 10g fat (4g sat. fat), 56mg chol., 364mg sod., 23g carb. (6g sugars, 3g fiber), 20g pro.
Diabetic exchanges: 3 lean meat, 1 starch, 1 vegetable, ½ fat.

Chicken Thighs with Shallots & Spinach

What could be better than an entree that comes with its own creamy vegetable side? It makes an eye-catching presentation and goes together in no time flat.
—Genna Johannes, Wrightstown, WI

Takes: 30 min. • **Makes:** 6 servings

- 6 boneless skinless chicken thighs (about 1½ lbs.)
- ½ tsp. seasoned salt
- ½ tsp. pepper
- 1½ tsp. olive oil
- 4 shallots, thinly sliced
- ⅓ cup white wine or reduced-sodium chicken broth
- 1 pkg. (10 oz.) fresh spinach, trimmed
- ¼ tsp. salt
- ¼ cup reduced-fat sour cream

1. Sprinkle chicken with seasoned salt and pepper. In a large nonstick skillet, heat oil over medium heat. Add the chicken; cook until a thermometer reads 170°, about 6 minutes on each side. Remove from pan; keep warm.
2. In same pan, cook and stir shallots until tender. Add wine; bring to a boil. Cook until wine is reduced by half. Add spinach and salt; cook and stir just until spinach is wilted. Stir in sour cream; serve with chicken.
Freeze option: Before adding sour cream, cool chicken and spinach mixture. Freeze in freezer containers. To use, partially thaw in refrigerator overnight. Heat through slowly in a covered skillet, stirring occasionally, until a thermometer inserted in the center of the chicken reads 170°. Stir in the sour cream.
1 chicken thigh with ¼ cup spinach mixture: 223 cal., 10g fat (3g sat. fat), 77mg chol., 360mg sod., 7g carb. (2g sugars, 1g fiber), 23g pro.

Steak Burritos

Slowly simmered all day, the beef is tender and a snap to shred. Just fill flour tortillas and add toppings for a tasty meal.
—Valerie Jones, Portland, ME

Prep: 15 min. • **Cook:** 8 hours
Makes: 10 servings

- 2 beef flank steaks (about 1 lb. each)
- 2 envelopes reduced-sodium taco seasoning
- 1 medium onion, chopped
- 1 can (4 oz.) chopped green chiles
- 1 Tbsp. white vinegar
- 10 flour tortillas (8 in.), warmed
- 1 cup shredded Monterey Jack cheese
- 1½ cups chopped seeded plum tomatoes
- ¾ cup reduced-fat sour cream

1. Cut steaks in half; rub with taco seasoning. Place in a 3-qt slow cooker coated with cooking spray. Top with onion, chiles and vinegar. Cover and cook on low for 8-9 hours or until meat is tender.
2. Remove steaks and cool slightly; shred meat with 2 forks. Return to slow cooker; heat through.
3. Spoon about ½ cup meat mixture into the center of each tortilla. Top with cheese, tomato and sour cream. Fold bottom and sides of tortilla over filling and roll up.
1 burrito: 339 cal., 12g fat (6g sat. fat), 59mg chol., 816mg sod., 33g carb. (5g sugars, 2g fiber), 25g pro.
Diabetic exchanges: 3 lean meat, 2 starch.

Beergarita Chicken Tacos

I was at my friend's bachelorette party the first time I had a beergarita, and I loved it! It was the inspiration for these delicious chicken tacos. I love that they have traditional taco flavors with a fun twist from the margarita!
—Ashley Lecker, Green Bay, WI

- -

Prep: 20 min. • **Cook:** 2½ hours
Makes: 6 servings

1   bottle (12 oz.) Mexican beer or 12 oz. chicken broth
1   cup thawed nonalcoholic margarita mix
1   can (4 oz.) chopped green chiles, undrained
2   Tbsp. lime juice
1   tsp. grated lime zest
1   tsp. salt
1   tsp. garlic powder
1   tsp. onion powder
1   tsp. chili powder
½   tsp. ground cumin
½   tsp. pepper
1½   lbs. boneless skinless chicken breast halves
12   taco shells
Optional toppings: Shredded pepper jack cheese, minced fresh cilantro, thinly sliced radishes and sour cream

1. Combine the first 11 ingredients in a 3- or 4-qt. slow cooker; top with chicken. Cook, covered, on low until a thermometer inserted in chicken reads 165°, 2½-3 hours.
2. Remove the chicken; shred with 2 forks. Return to slow cooker; heat through. Using a slotted spoon, serve chicken in taco shells with toppings as desired.

Freeze option: Freeze the cooled meat mixture and juices in freezer containers. To use, partially thaw in refrigerator overnight. Heat through in a saucepan, stirring occasionally; add broth if necessary.

2 tacos: 294 cal., 7g fat (3g sat. fat), 63mg chol., 627mg sod., 32g carb. (16g sugars, 1g fiber), 25g pro.

Pork Chop Cacciatore

It's hard to believe that so much flavor can come from such an easy recipe. Serve it with noodles and a simple green salad, and dinner is done!
—Tracy Hiatt Grice, Somerset, WI

Prep: 30 min. • **Cook:** 4 hours
Makes: 6 servings

6	bone-in pork loin chops (7 oz. each)
¾	tsp. salt, divided
¼	tsp. pepper
1	Tbsp. olive oil
1	cup sliced fresh mushrooms
1	small onion, chopped
1	celery rib, chopped
1	small green pepper, chopped
2	garlic cloves, minced
1	can (14½ oz.) diced tomatoes
½	cup water, divided
½	tsp. dried basil
2	Tbsp. cornstarch
4½	cups cooked egg noodles

1. Sprinkle chops with ½ tsp. salt and pepper. In a large skillet, brown chops in oil in batches. Transfer to a 4-or 5-qt. slow cooker coated with cooking spray. Saute mushrooms, onion, celery and green pepper in drippings until tender. Add garlic; cook 1 minute longer. Stir in the tomatoes, ¼ cup water, basil and remaining salt; pour over chops.
2. Cover and cook on low for 4-6 hours or until pork is tender. Remove meat to a serving platter; keep warm. Skim fat from cooking juices if necessary; transfer to a small saucepan. Bring liquid to a boil. Combine cornstarch and remaining water until smooth. Gradually stir into the pan. Bring to a boil; cook and stir for 2 minutes or until thickened. Serve with meat and noodles.

1 pork chop with ¾ cup noodles and ½ cup sauce : 371 cal., 12g fat (4g sat. fat), 110mg chol., 458mg sod., 29g carb. (4g sugars, 3g fiber), 35g pro.
Diabetic exchanges: 4 lean meat, 1½ starch, 1 vegetable, ½ fat.

Sirloin in Wine Sauce

Tender sirloin in a hearty mushroom-wine sauce is fantastic over pasta. This is one of our family's favorite dishes and one we serve to company when we want something special.
—Barbara Kamm, Wilmington, DE

Takes: 30 min. • **Makes:** 4 servings

2	Tbsp. all-purpose flour
⅛	tsp. ground mustard
1	lb. beef top sirloin steak, thinly sliced
2	Tbsp. butter
1	can (10½ oz.) condensed beef consomme, undiluted
½	cup dry red wine or beef broth
1	jar (4½ oz.) sliced mushrooms, drained
¼	cup chopped green onions
1	tsp. Worcestershire sauce
	Hot cooked linguine

1. In a large resealable plastic bag, combine flour and mustard. Add beef, a few pieces at a time, and shake to coat.
2. In a large skillet, brown beef in butter. Add consomme and wine. Stir in the mushrooms, onions and Worcestershire sauce. Bring to a boil. Reduce heat; simmer, uncovered, 10-15 minutes or until the sauce is thickened. Serve with linguine.
Freeze option: Cool beef mixture. Freeze in freezer containers. To use, partially thaw in the refrigerator overnight. Heat through slowly in a covered skillet until a thermometer inserted in beef reads 165°, stirring occasionally and adding a little broth or water if necessary. Serve as directed.
¾ cup: 258 cal., 10g fat (5g sat. fat), 61mg chol., 748mg sod., 7g carb. (2g sugars, 1g fiber), 28g pro.
Diabetic exchanges: 3 lean meat, 1½ fat, ½ starch.

Light & Easy
DESSERTS

In the mood for something sweet? These feel-good desserts are light in calories and fat. So go ahead, indulge without guilt.

Hazelnut Cake Squares

Whenever one of my daughters is asked to bring a dish to a church function, a birthday party or any special occasion, they ask me for this recipe. It's easy to prepare because it starts with a cake mix. It doesn't need icing, so it is great for bake sales, too.
—Brenda Melancon, McComb, MS

Prep: 10 min.
Bake: 25 min. + cooling
Makes: 15 servings

- 1 pkg. yellow cake mix (regular size)
- 3 large eggs, room temperature
- ⅔ cup water
- ⅔ cup Nutella
- ¼ cup canola oil
- ½ cup semisweet chocolate chips
- ½ cup chopped hazelnuts, toasted
- ½ cup brickle toffee bits, optional
  Confectioners' sugar, optional

1. Preheat oven to 350°. Grease a 13x9-in. baking pan.

2. In a large bowl, combine cake mix, eggs, water, Nutella and oil; beat on low speed 30 seconds. Beat on medium 2 minutes. Fold in chocolate chips, hazelnuts and, if desired, toffee bits. Transfer to prepared pan. Bake until a toothpick inserted in center comes out clean, 25-30 minutes.

3. Cool completely in pan on a wire rack. Dust with confectioners' sugar if desired.

1 piece: 280 cal., 14g fat (3g sat. fat), 37mg chol., 245mg sod., 38g carb. (24g sugars, 2g fiber), 4g pro.

Dark Chocolate Espresso Tapioca Pudding

I experimented with espresso powder in different dishes and came up with this chocolaty homemade pudding. I hope you enjoy it as much as I do.
—Shelly Bevington, Hermiston, OR

- -

Prep: 15 min. + standing
Cook: 20 min. + cooling
Makes: 12 servings

2	cups water
⅔	cup pearl tapioca
1	carton (32 oz.) unsweetened almond milk
4	large eggs, separated
1¼	cups sugar, divided
1	to 2 Tbsp. instant espresso powder
½	tsp. salt
¼	cup dark baking cocoa
1	tsp. vanilla extract
	Chopped chocolate covered espresso beans, optional

1. In a large saucepan, combine water and tapioca; let stand 30 minutes. Whisk in the almond milk, egg yolks, ½ cup sugar, espresso powder and salt. Bring to a boil; reduce the heat. Simmer, uncovered, until slightly thickened, 10-15 minutes, stirring frequently. Combine ¼ cup sugar and baking cocoa; stir into pan. Cook and stir 2 minutes longer.

2. In a large bowl, beat egg whites on medium speed until foamy. Gradually add remaining ½ cup sugar, 1 Tbsp. at a time, beating on high after each addition until the sugar is dissolved. Continue beating until soft glossy peaks form.

3. Gently fold a small amount of tapioca mixture into egg whites; return all to pan, whisking constantly. Cook and stir 2 minutes. Remove from heat. Cool 15 minutes; stir in vanilla. Transfer to dessert dishes. Press plastic wrap onto surface of pudding. Refrigerate until cold (pudding will thicken upon cooling).

¾ cup: 156 cal., 3g fat (1g sat. fat), 62mg chol., 182mg sod., 31g carb. (21g sugars, 1g fiber), 3g pro.

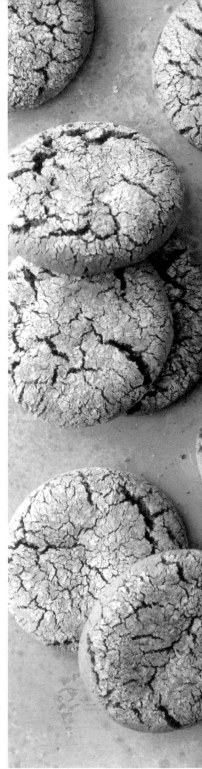

Bananas Foster Sundaes for 2

I have wonderful memories of eating bananas Foster in New Orleans, and as a dietitian, I wanted to find a healthier version. I combined the best of two recipes and added my own tweaks to create this southern treat. And with this version, it's the perfect dessert for two!

—Lisa Varner, El Paso, TX

- -

Takes: 15 min. • **Makes:** 2 servings

- 1 tsp. butter
- 1 Tbsp. brown sugar
- 1 tsp. orange juice
- ⅛ tsp. ground cinnamon
- ⅛ tsp. ground nutmeg
- 1 large banana, sliced
- 2 tsp. chopped pecans, toasted
- ⅛ tsp. rum extract
- 1 cup reduced-fat vanilla ice cream

In a large nonstick skillet, melt butter over medium-low heat. Stir in the brown sugar, orange juice, cinnamon and nutmeg until blended. Add banana and pecans; cook until banana is glazed and slightly softened, stirring lightly, 2-3 minutes. Remove from the heat; stir in extract. Serve with ice cream.

1 sundae: 259 cal., 8g fat (4g sat. fat), 26mg chol., 74mg sod., 45g carb. (32g sugars, 2g fiber), 5g pro.

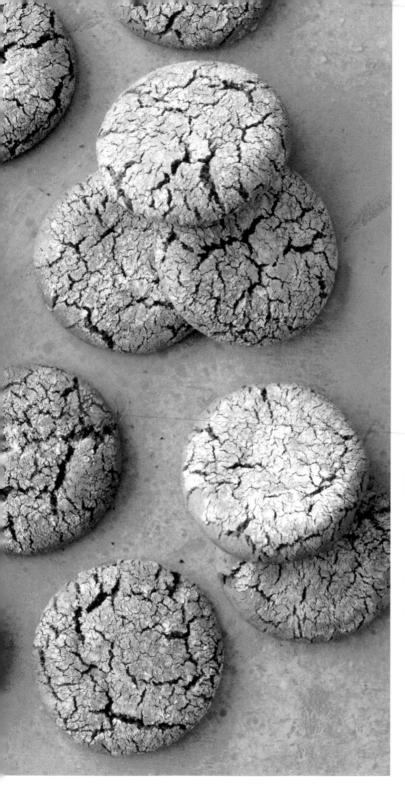

Powered-Up Molasses Cookies

These tender cookies are soft and flavorful. You'd never guess they're also lower in fat.
—Jean Ecos, Hartland, WI

- -

Prep: 20 min.
Bake: 10 min./batch + cooling
Makes: 2 dozen

⅔ cup plus 2 Tbsp. sugar, divided
¼ cup sunflower oil
1 large egg, room temperature
¼ cup molasses
2 cups white whole wheat flour or whole wheat pastry flour
2 tsp. baking soda
1 tsp. ground cinnamon
½ tsp. salt
¼ tsp. ground ginger
¼ tsp. ground cloves
3 Tbsp. confectioners' sugar

1. Preheat oven to 375°. In a bowl, beat ⅔ cup sugar and sunflower oil until blended. Beat in the egg, then molasses. In another bowl, whisk flour, baking soda, cinnamon, salt, ginger and cloves; gradually beat into sugar mixture.
2. Combine confectioners' sugar and remaining 2 Tbsp. sugar. Shape dough into 1-in. balls; roll in sugar mixture. Place 1 in. apart on greased baking sheets. Bake until edges are firm, 10-12 minutes. Cool on pans 5 minutes. Remove to wire racks to cool. Store in an airtight container.
1 cookie: 110 cal., 3g fat (0 sat. fat), 8mg chol., 158mg sod., 19g carb. (10g sugars, 2g fiber), 3g pro.

Chocolate & Raspberry Cheesecake

Fans of cheesecake won't be able to pass up this sweet treat. Each silky slice is topped with juicy raspberries.
—*Taste of Home* Test Kitchen

Prep: 25 min. + chilling
Makes: 12 servings

- ¾ cup graham cracker crumbs
- 2 Tbsp. butter, melted
- 1 envelope unflavored gelatin
- 1 cup cold water
- 4 oz. semisweet chocolate, coarsely chopped
- 4 pkg. (8 oz. each) fat-free cream cheese
  Sugar substitute equivalent to 1 cup sugar
- ½ cup sugar
- ¼ cup baking cocoa
- 2 tsp. vanilla extract
- 2 cups fresh raspberries

1. Preheat oven to 375°. Combine cracker crumbs and butter; press onto the bottom of a greased 9-in. springform pan. Bake until lightly browned, 8-10 minutes. Cool in pan on a wire rack.
2. For filling, in a small saucepan, sprinkle gelatin over cold water; let stand for 1 minute. Heat over low heat, stirring until the gelatin is completely dissolved. Add the chopped semisweet chocolate; stir until melted.
3. In a large bowl, beat the cream cheese, sugar substitute and sugar until smooth. Gradually add chocolate mixture and the cocoa. Beat in vanilla. Pour onto crust; refrigerate until firm, 2-3 hours.
4. Arrange raspberries on top of cheesecake. Carefully run a knife around edge of pan to loosen.
1 piece: 237 cal., 7g fat (4g sat. fat), 14mg chol., 576mg sod., 27g carb. (17g sugars, 2g fiber), 14g pro.

Air-Fryer S'mores Crescent Rolls

If you love s'mores in summer, you'll go crazy for this indoor riff on the campfire classic. Grab the Nutella and invite the kids to get in on the fun.
—Cathy Trochelman, Brookfield, WI

Prep: 15 min. • **Cook:** 10 min./batch
Makes: 8 servings

- 1 tube (8 oz.) refrigerated crescent rolls
- ¼ cup Nutella, divided
- 2 whole graham crackers, broken up
- 2 Tbsp. milk chocolate chips
- ⅔ cup miniature marshmallows

1. Preheat air fryer to 300°. Unroll crescent dough; separate dough into 8 triangles. Place 1 tsp. Nutella at the wide end of each triangle. Sprinkle with graham crackers, chocolate chips and marshmallows; roll up.
2. In batches, arrange rolls, point side down, in a single layer on greased tray in air-fryer basket. Curve to form crescents. Cook until golden brown, 8-10 minutes. In a microwave, warm remaining Nutella to reach a drizzling consistency; spoon over rolls. Serve warm.
1 roll: 191 cal., 9g fat (1g sat. fat), 1mg chol., 245mg sod., 26g carb. (13g sugars, 1g fiber), 3g pro.

No-Guilt Brownies

Yes, you can watch your diet and enjoy brownies, too! These light and luscious treats are the perfect cure for a serious chocolate craving.
—Rita Ross, Delta, OH

- -

Prep: 10 min.
Bake: 20 min. + cooling
Makes: 16 brownies

 3 large egg whites, room temperature
 ¾ cup 1% cottage cheese
 1 tsp. vanilla extract
 3 oz. unsweetened chocolate, melted and cooled
 1 cup sugar
 ¾ cup all-purpose flour
 ½ tsp. baking powder
 ¼ tsp. salt
 2 tsp. confectioners' sugar

1. Preheat oven to 350°. Place the egg whites, cottage cheese and vanilla in a blender; cover and process until smooth. Add chocolate; cover and process just until blended, about 15 seconds. Combine the sugar, flour, baking powder and salt; add to the cottage cheese mixture. Cover and pulse until just moistened.
2. Spread into an 8-in. square baking pan coated with cooking spray. Bake until a toothpick inserted in the center comes out clean, 20-25 minutes (do not overbake). Cool on a wire rack. Dust with confectioners' sugar. Cut into bars.
1 brownie: 117 cal., 3g fat (2g sat. fat), 1mg chol., 107mg sod., 19g carb. (13g sugars, 1g fiber), 3g pro.
Diabetic exchanges: 1 starch, ½ fat.

Healthy Peanut Butter Cookies

You need only four ingredients and one bowl for these healthy peanut butter cookies. To make this recipe gluten-free, make sure the oat bran is made in a certified gluten-free facility.
—*Taste of Home* Test Kitchen

Prep: 15 min. • **Bake:** 15 min./batch
Makes: 2 dozen

- 1 large egg, room temperature, beaten
- 1 cup creamy peanut butter
- ¼ cup oat bran
- ¼ cup maple syrup

1. Preheat oven to 350°. In a large bowl, mix all ingredients. Roll level Tbsp. into balls. Place on ungreased baking sheets; flatten with a fork.
2. Bake for 15 minutes. Remove to a wire rack to cool.

1 cookie: 78 cal., 6g fat (1g sat. fat), 8mg chol., 49mg sod., 5g carb. (3g sugars, 1g fiber), 3g pro.

TIMESAVING TIP

Peanut butter cookies can dry out fast, so store them at room temperature in an airtight cookie storage container and enjoy them within 2 or 3 days. Baked cookies can be frozen for 3 to 4 weeks.

No-Fry Fried Ice Cream

This ice cream has a crispy cinnamon coating just like the fried ice cream served at Mexican restaurants, but minus the oily mess. Make ahead of time and freeze until serving.
—Tim White, Windsor, ON

Prep: 20 min. + freezing
Makes: 8 servings

- 1 qt. vanilla ice cream
- ¼ cup packed brown sugar
- 1 Tbsp. butter, melted
- 1 tsp. ground cinnamon
- 2 cups crushed cornflakes
  Optional: Whipped cream and caramel ice cream topping

1. Preheat oven to 350°. Using a ½-cup ice cream scoop, place 8 scoops of ice cream on a baking sheet. Freeze until firm, about 1 hour. Meanwhile, combine brown sugar, butter and cinnamon. Stir in crushed cornflakes. Transfer to an ungreased 15x10x1-in. baking pan. Bake until lightly browned, 4-6 minutes. Cool completely.
2. Roll ice cream balls in crumb mixture. Cover and freeze until firm, at least 1 hour. If desired, serve with toppings.

½ cup: 216 cal., 8g fat (5g sat. fat), 32mg chol., 168mg sod., 33g carb. (20g sugars, 1g fiber), 3g pro.

Grapefruit, Lime & Mint Yogurt Parfait

Tart grapefruit and lime are balanced with a bit of honey in this cool and easy parfait.
—Lois Enger, Colorado Springs, CO

- -

Takes: 15 min. • **Makes:** 6 servings

- 4 large red grapefruit
- 4 cups reduced-fat plain yogurt
- 2 tsp. grated lime zest
- 2 Tbsp. lime juice
- 3 Tbsp. honey
  Torn fresh mint leaves

1. Cut a thin slice from the top and bottom of each grapefruit; stand fruit upright on a cutting board. With a knife, cut off peel and outer membrane from grapefruit. Cut along the membrane of each segment to remove fruit.
2. In a large bowl, mix yogurt, lime zest and juice. Layer half of the grapefruit and half of the yogurt mixture into 6 parfait glasses. Repeat layers. Drizzle with honey; top with mint.
1 parfait: 207 cal., 3g fat (2g sat. fat), 10mg chol., 115mg sod., 39g carb. (36g sugars, 3g fiber), 10g pro.

Pressure Cooker Cranberry-Stuffed Apples

Cinnamon, nutmeg and walnuts add a homey autumn flavor to these stuffed apples. Making them in the electric pressure cooker means they're ready in a jiffy.
—Grace Sandvigen, Rochester, NY

- -

Prep: 10 min. • **Cook:** 5 min.
Makes: 5 servings

- 5 medium apples
- ⅓ cup fresh or frozen cranberries, thawed and chopped
- ¼ cup packed brown sugar
- 2 Tbsp. chopped walnuts
- ¼ tsp. ground cinnamon
- ⅛ tsp. ground nutmeg
  Optional toppings: Whipped cream or vanilla ice cream

1. Core apples, leaving bottoms intact. Peel top third of each apple. Place trivet insert and 1 cup water in a 6-qt. electric pressure cooker. Combine cranberries, brown sugar, walnuts, cinnamon and nutmeg; spoon into apples. Place apples on trivet.
2. Lock lid; close pressure-release valve. Adjust to pressure-cook on high for 3 minutes. Quick-release pressure. If desired, serve with whipped cream or ice cream.
1 stuffed apple: 142 cal., 2g fat (0 sat. fat), 0 chol., 5mg sod., 33g carb. (27g sugars, 4g fiber), 1g pro.
Diabetic exchanges: 1 starch, 1 fruit.

Vegan Chocolate Mousse

My son is allergic to dairy and eggs, so I created this vegan chocolate mousse that fits within his dietary restrictions. It's also gluten free and grain free. If you're having company over, it can be prepared the night before and stored in the refrigerator.
—Sarah Meuser, New Milford, CT

- -

Prep: 25 min. + chilling
Makes: 6 servings

- ⅓ cup boiling water
- ¾ cup dried Mission figs, stemmed and halved lengthwise
- 1 cup dairy-free dark chocolate chips
- 2 medium ripe avocados, peeled and pitted
- ⅓ cup baking cocoa
- 2 Tbsp. unsweetened almond milk
- 1 Tbsp. maple syrup
- 1 tsp. vanilla extract
- ⅛ tsp. sea salt
- 1 can (15 oz.) garbanzo beans or chickpeas, undrained
- ¼ tsp. cream of tartar
  Fresh raspberries, optional

1. Pour boiling water over figs in a small bowl; let stand 45 minutes. In a microwave, melt chocolate chips; stir until smooth. Cool chocolate to room temperature. Place figs and liquid in a food processor. Pulse until a paste forms. Add avocados, cooled chocolate, cocoa, almond milk, syrup, vanilla and sea salt; pulse until pureed. Transfer to a large bowl.
2. To make aquafaba, drain garbanzo beans, reserving liquid (save beans for another use). Add drained liquid and cream of tartar to bowl of a stand mixer. Beat on high speed until stiff peaks form, 2-3 minutes. Gently fold aquafaba into fig mixture. Spoon into dessert dishes. Refrigerate at least 2 hours or overnight before serving. If desired, serve mousse with fresh raspberries.

⅔ cup: 310 cal., 18g fat (7g sat. fat), 0 chol., 149mg sod., 41g carb. (26g sugars, 8g fiber), 5g pro.

Contest-Winning Fresh Blueberry Pie

Nothing says summer like a piece of fresh blueberry pie! Blueberries are readily available where I live, so I've been making this dessert for decades.
—Linda Kernan, Mason, MI

- -

Prep: 15 min. + cooling
Makes: 6-8 servings

- 1 sheet refrigerated pie crust
- ¾ cup sugar
- 3 Tbsp. cornstarch
- ⅛ tsp. salt
- ¼ cup cold water
- 5 cups fresh blueberries, divided
- 1 Tbsp. butter
- 1 Tbsp. lemon juice

1. Preheat oven to 425°. On a floured surface, roll dough to fit a 9-in. pie plate. Trim and flute edge. Refrigerate 30 minutes. Line crust with a double thickness of foil. Fill with pie weights. Bake on a lower oven rack until golden brown, 20-25 minutes. Remove foil and weights; bake until bottom is golden brown, 3-6 minutes. Cool on a wire rack.
2. In a saucepan over medium heat, combine sugar, cornstarch, salt and water until smooth. Add 3 cups blueberries. Bring to a boil; cook and stir for 2 minutes or until thickened and bubbly.
3. Remove from the heat. Add butter, lemon juice and remaining 2 cups berries; stir until butter is melted. Cool. Pour into crust. Refrigerate until serving.

1 piece: 269 cal., 9g fat (4g sat. fat), 9mg chol., 150mg sod., 48g carb. (29g sugars, 2g fiber), 2g pro.

Fresas con Crema

"Fresas con Crema" translates to "Strawberries and Cream" in English. This refreshing dessert is wonderful when fresh berries are in season.
—*Taste of Home* Test Kitchen

- -

Takes: 10 min. • **Makes:** 4 servings

- 1   **can (7.6 oz.) media crema table cream**
- 3   **Tbsp. sweetened condensed milk**
- 1   **tsp. vanilla extract**
- 3   **cups chopped fresh strawberries**
     Fresh mint leaves, optional

In a bowl, whisk crema, sweetened condensed milk and vanilla. Divide strawberries among 4 serving dishes. Top with milk mixture. Garnish with fresh mint if desired.

¾ cup: 241 cal., 17g fat (10g sat. fat), 43mg chol., 58mg sod., 21g carb. (14g sugars, 2g fiber), 2g pro.

> **TIMESAVING TIP**
>
> Media crema table cream is a rich, unsweetened cream found in the baking aisle or ethnic food section of the grocery store. Most cremas will last for up to 2 weeks when stored in the fridge. Unopened, media crema will last 6 months or more. Creme fraiche is a great alternative if you can't find Mexican crema.

Carrot Cookie Bites

These soft cookies are an all-time family favorite. Their aroma while baking is absolutely irresistible! I'm always asked for the recipe.
—Jeanie Petrik, Greensburg, KY

- -

Prep: 15 min. • **Bake:** 10 min./batch
Makes: 7 dozen

- ⅔   **cup shortening**
- 1   **cup packed brown sugar**
- 2   **large eggs, room temperature**
- ½   **cup buttermilk**
- 1   **tsp. vanilla extract**
- 2   **cups all-purpose flour**
- 1   **tsp. ground cinnamon**
- ½   **tsp. salt**
- ¼   **tsp. baking powder**
- ¼   **tsp. baking soda**
- ¼   **tsp. ground nutmeg**
- ¼   **tsp. ground cloves**
- 2   **cups quick-cooking oats**
- 1   **cup shredded carrots**
- ½   **cup chopped pecans**

1. Preheat oven to 375°. In a large bowl, cream the shortening and brown sugar until light and fluffy, 5-7 minutes. Beat in eggs, buttermilk and vanilla. Combine the flour, cinnamon, salt, baking powder, baking soda, nutmeg and cloves; gradually add to creamed mixture. Stir in the oats, carrots and pecans.
2. Drop the dough by rounded teaspoonfuls 2 in. apart onto ungreased baking sheets. Bake until lightly browned, 6-8 minutes. Remove to wire racks to cool.

Freeze option: Drop the dough by rounded teaspoonfuls onto parchment-lined baking sheets. Freeze until firm. Transfer cookie dough balls to resealable freezer containers; seal tightly and freeze for up to 3 months. To bake, place frozen dough 2 in. apart on ungreased baking sheets. Bake at 375° until lightly browned, 10-15 minutes. Remove to wire racks to cool.

1 cookie: 50 cal., 2g fat (0 sat. fat), 5mg chol., 24mg sod., 6g carb. (3g sugars, 0 fiber), 1g pro.
Diabetic exchanges: ½ starch, ½ fat.

Grapefruit Yogurt Cake

We eat grapefruit for breakfast and in winter fruit salads—why not for dessert? Here's a sweet-tart cake that's easy, delicious and one of a kind. It's healthy, too!
—Maiah Miller, Montclair, VA

- -

Prep: 10 min.
Bake: 25 min. + cooling
Makes: 12 servings

1½	cups all-purpose flour
2	tsp. baking powder
¼	tsp. salt
3	large eggs, room temperature
1	cup fat-free plain yogurt
⅓	cup sugar
5	Tbsp. grated grapefruit zest
¼	cup agave nectar or honey
½	tsp. vanilla extract
¼	cup canola oil

GLAZE

½	cup confectioners' sugar
2	to 3 tsp. grapefruit juice
	Grapefruit wheels and fresh mint leaves, optional
	Fresh mint leaves

1. Preheat oven to 350°. Whisk together flour, baking powder and salt. Combine next 7 ingredients. Gradually stir flour mixture into yogurt mixture, then pour into a 9-in. round baking pan coated with cooking spray. Bake until a toothpick inserted in center of cake comes out clean, 25-30 minutes. Cool.

2. For glaze, mix confectioners' sugar with enough grapefruit juice to reach desired consistency; drizzle glaze over top, allowing some to flow over sides. Top cake with grapefruit and mint if desired.

Freeze option: Omit glaze. Securely wrap cooled cake and freeze. To use, thaw cake at room temperature. Prepare glaze; top as directed.

1 piece: 187 cal., 6g fat (1g sat. fat), 47mg chol., 159mg sod., 30g carb. (17g sugars, 1g fiber), 4g pro.
Diabetic exchanges: 2 starch, 1 fat.

Easy Almond Joy Chia Pudding

I like this recipe because it's easy and I can find all of the ingredients at my local market. There is no baking required, and it's served in individual jars for guests. For more flavor, add shredded coconut.
—Ashley Altan, Hanover, MD

- -

Prep: 15 min. + chilling
Makes: 2 servings

- 1   cup refrigerated unsweetened coconut milk
- 4   Tbsp. chia seeds
- 3   Tbsp. maple syrup
- 2   Tbsp. baking cocoa
- ¼   cup dairy-free semisweet chocolate chips
- ¼   cup slivered almonds

In a small bowl, mix coconut milk, chia seeds and maple syrup. Remove half of the mixture to a small bowl; stir in the baking cocoa until blended. Refrigerate both plain and chocolate mixtures, covered, until thickened, at least 6 hours. In 2 dessert dishes, layer a fourth of the white pudding, chocolate pudding, almonds and chocolate chips. Repeat layers. Serve pudding immediately or store, covered, in the refrigerator up to 3 days.

Note: This recipe was tested with Enjoy Life semisweet chocolate chips.

1 serving: 414 cal., 24g fat (8g sat. fat), 0 chol., 7mg sod., 50g carb. (30g sugars, 12g fiber), 9g pro.

Rose & Raspberry Fool

I came up with this recipe when I was going through a floral phase—I put rose or lavender in everything. This dessert is easy to make, but it's also elegant and simple to serve guests.
—Carolyn Eskew, Dayton, OH

- -

Prep: 15 min. + chilling
Makes: 8 servings

2 cups fresh or frozen raspberries
6 Tbsp. sugar, divided
1½ cups heavy whipping cream
1 tsp. rose water
Fresh mint leaves

1. In a small bowl, lightly crush the raspberries and 2 Tbsp. sugar. Cover and refrigerate 1-2 hours.
2. In a large bowl, beat cream until it begins to thicken. Add the remaining 4 Tbsp. sugar and rose water; beat until soft peaks form. Gently fold in the raspberry mixture. Spoon into dessert dishes. Garnish with mint leaves and, if desired, additional berries. Serve immediately.
½ cup: 206 cal., 16g fat (10g sat. fat), 51mg chol., 13mg sod., 14g carb. (12g sugars, 2g fiber), 2g pro.

Air-Fryer Bourbon Bacon Cinnamon Rolls

These extraordinary cinnamon rolls feature the perfect combination of sweet and savory. The bourbon-soaked bacon adds a smoky flavor, and the ginger and pecan topping makes for a crunchy, spicy finish.
—Shannen Casey, Citrus Heights, CA

- -

Prep: 25 min. + marinating
Cook: 10 min./batch • **Makes:** 8 rolls

8 bacon strips
¾ cup bourbon
1 tube (12.4 oz.) refrigerated cinnamon rolls with icing
½ cup chopped pecans
2 Tbsp. maple syrup
1 tsp. minced fresh gingerroot

1. Place bacon in a shallow dish; add bourbon. Seal and refrigerate overnight. Remove bacon and pat dry; discard bourbon.
2. In a large skillet, cook bacon in batches over medium heat until nearly crisp but still pliable. Remove to paper towels to drain. Discard all but 1 tsp. drippings.

3. Preheat air fryer to 350°. Separate dough into 8 rolls, reserving icing packet. Unroll spiral rolls into long strips; pat dough to form 6x1-in. strips. Place 1 bacon strip on each strip of dough, trimming bacon as needed; reroll, forming a spiral. Pinch ends to seal. Repeat with remaining dough. Place 4 rolls on ungreased tray in the air-fryer basket; cook for 5 minutes. Turn rolls over and cook until golden brown, about 4 minutes.
4. Meanwhile, combine pecans and maple syrup. In another bowl, stir ginger together with contents of icing packet. In same skillet, heat remaining bacon drippings over medium heat. Add pecan mixture; cook, stirring frequently, until lightly toasted, 2-3 minutes.
5. Drizzle half the icing over warm cinnamon rolls; top with half the pecans. Repeat steps to make a second batch.
1 roll: 267 cal., 14g fat (3g sat. fat), 9mg chol., 490mg sod., 28g carb. (13g sugars, 1g fiber), 5g pro.

Upside-Down Pear Pancake

There's a pear tree in my yard that inspires me to bake with its fragrant fruit. This upside-down pancake works best with a firm pear, not one that is fully ripe.

—Helen Nelander, Boulder Creek, CA

- -

Takes: 30 min. • **Makes:** 2 servings

- ½ cup all-purpose flour
- ½ tsp. baking powder
- 1 large egg, room temperature
- ¼ cup 2% milk
- 1 Tbsp. butter
- 1 tsp. sugar
- 1 medium pear, peeled and thinly sliced lengthwise
  Confectioners' sugar

1. Preheat oven to 375°. In a large bowl, whisk flour and baking powder. In a separate bowl, whisk egg and milk until blended. Add to dry ingredients, stirring just until combined.

2. Meanwhile, in a small ovenproof skillet, melt butter over medium-low heat. Sprinkle with sugar. Add the pear slices in a single layer; cook for 5 minutes. Spread prepared batter over pears. Cover and cook until top is set, about 5 minutes.

3. Transfer pan to oven; bake until the edges are lightly browned, 8-10 minutes. Invert onto a serving plate. Sprinkle with confectioners' sugar. Serve warm.

½ pancake: 274 cal., 9g fat (5g sat. fat), 111mg chol., 197mg sod., 41g carb. (12g sugars, 4g fiber), 8g pro. **Diabetic exchanges:** 2 starch, 1½ fat, 1 medium-fat meat, ½ fruit.

Must-Have Tiramisu

This is the perfect guilt-free version of a classic dessert. My friends even say that they prefer my lighter recipe over traditional tiramisu.

—Ale Gambini, Beverly Hills, CA

- -

Prep: 25 min. + chilling
Makes: 9 servings

- ½ cup heavy whipping cream
- 2 cups vanilla yogurt
- 1 cup fat-free milk
- ½ cup brewed espresso or strong coffee, cooled
- 24 crisp ladyfinger cookies
  Baking cocoa
  Fresh raspberries, optional

1. In a small bowl, beat the cream until stiff peaks form; fold in yogurt. Spread ½ cup cream mixture onto bottom of an 8-in. square dish.

2. In a shallow dish, mix milk and espresso. Quickly dip 12 ladyfingers into the espresso mixture, allowing excess to drip off. Arrange in dish in a single layer, breaking to fit as needed. Top ladyfingers with half of the remaining cream mixture; dust with cocoa. Repeat layers.

3. Refrigerate, covered, for at least 2 hours before serving. If desired, serve with raspberries.

1 piece: 177 cal., 6g fat (4g sat. fat), 41mg chol., 80mg sod., 25g carb. (18g sugars, 0 fiber), 6g pro. **Diabetic exchanges:** 1 starch, ½ fat-free milk, 1 fat.

Workweek
ODDS & ENDS

Spruce up your meals with condiments, sauces, beverages and other flavorful extras that are ready in a flash.

Lime-Honey Fruit Salad

Nothing is more refreshing than a seasonal fruit salad enhanced with this simple lime-honey dressing.
—Victoria Shevlin, Cape Coral, FL

- -

Prep: 20 min. + chilling
Makes: 12 servings

1	tsp. cornstarch
¼	cup lime juice
¼	cup honey
½	tsp. poppy seeds
3	medium gala or Red Delicious apples, cubed
2	medium pears, cubed
2	cups seedless red grapes
2	cups green grapes

1. In a small microwave-safe bowl, combine cornstarch and lime juice until smooth. Microwave, uncovered, on high for 20 seconds; stir. Cook 15 seconds longer; stir. Stir in honey and poppy seeds.
2. In a large bowl, combine the apples, pears and grapes. Pour dressing over fruit; toss to coat. Cover and refrigerate overnight.
Note: This recipe was tested in a 1,100-watt microwave.
¾ cup: 96 cal., 0 fat (0 sat. fat), 0 chol., 2mg sod., 25g carb. (21g sugars, 2g fiber), 1g pro.
Diabetic exchanges: 1½ fruit.

Cauliflower Ceviche

My 87-year-old mom showed me how to make this delicious vegetarian recipe that tastes so much like seafood ceviche. I serve it with crackers on the side.
—Beatriz Barranco, El Paso, TX

- -

Prep: 20 min. + chilling
Makes: 10 servings

- 1 medium head cauliflower, finely chopped
- 1 cup ketchup
- 1 cup orange juice
- 3 medium tomatoes, chopped
- 1 medium onion, finely chopped
- ½ cup minced fresh cilantro
- ¼ tsp. salt
- ¼ tsp. pepper
- 3 medium ripe avocados, peeled and cubed

Optional: Lemon wedges, tortilla chip scoops and hot pepper sauce

1. In a large skillet, bring 1 cup water to a boil. Add cauliflower; cook, uncovered, just until crisp-tender, 5-8 minutes. Remove with a slotted spoon; drain and pat dry. Meanwhile, stir together the ketchup and orange juice.

2. In a bowl, combine cauliflower with tomatoes and onion. Add ketchup mixture, cilantro, salt and pepper; toss to coat. Refrigerate, covered, at least 1 hour.

3. Stir in avocado cubes. If desired, serve with lemon wedges, tortilla chip scoops and hot pepper sauce.

1 serving: 129 cal., 7g fat (1g sat. fat), 0 chol., 387mg sod., 18g carb. (11g sugars, 5g fiber), 3g pro.

Aunt Frances' Lemonade

Every summer, my sister and I spent a week with our Aunt Frances, who always had this thirst-quenching lemonade in a stoneware crock in her refrigerator. It tasted so refreshing after running around on hot days.
—Debbie Reinhart, New Cumberland, PA

- -

Takes: 15 min.
Makes: 16 servings (1 gallon)

- 5 lemons
- 5 limes
- 5 oranges
- 3 qt. water
- 1½ to 2 cups sugar

1. Squeeze the juice from 4 each of the lemons, limes and oranges; pour into a gallon container.

2. Thinly slice the remaining fruit and set aside for garnish. Add water and sugar to the juice mixture; mix well. Store in the refrigerator. Serve over ice with fruit slices.

1 cup: 92 cal., 0 fat (0 sat. fat), 0 chol., 1mg sod., 24g carb. (21g sugars, 1g fiber), 0 pro.

All-Around Seasoning Mix

I always keep this mixture on hand; it's good on anything, especially grilled pork, chicken, fish and vegetables. It has a little heat, so start with a small amount and add more to taste..
—Greg Fontenot,
The Woodlands, TX

- -

Takes: 10 min. • **Makes:** 1⅔ cups

- ½ cup paprika
- 3 Tbsp. onion powder
- 3 Tbsp. garlic powder
- 3 Tbsp. cayenne pepper
- 2 Tbsp. white pepper
- 2 Tbsp. pepper
- 4 tsp. salt
- 4 tsp. dried thyme
- 4 tsp. dried oregano
- 4 tsp. ground cumin
- 4 tsp. chili powder

In a bowl, combine all ingredients. Store in an airtight container in a cool, dry place for up to 6 months.

1 tsp.: 7 cal., 0 fat (0 sat. fat), 0 chol., 120mg sod., 1g carb. (0 sugars, 1g fiber), 0 pro.

Avocado Salad Dressing

Buttermilk and plain yogurt create the base for this thick dressing, which gets its color from avocado and parsley. The mild mixture is refreshing when dolloped over a green salad.
—*Taste of Home* Test Kitchen

- -

Takes: 5 min. • **Makes:** 2 cups

- 1 cup buttermilk
- ½ cup fat-free plain yogurt
- 1 medium ripe avocado, peeled and sliced
- 2 green onions, chopped
- ¼ cup minced fresh parsley
- ½ tsp. salt
- ½ tsp. garlic powder
- ¼ tsp. dill weed
- ⅛ tsp. pepper
  Salad greens and vegetables of your choice

Combine the first 9 ingredients in a food processor; cover and process until smooth. Serve over salad. Store in the refrigerator.

2 Tbsp.: 25 cal., 1g fat (0 sat. fat), 1mg chol., 109mg sod., 2g carb. (1g sugars, 1g fiber), 1g pro.

TIMESAVING TIP

Avocado will naturally turn brown when exposed to air. If you're nervous about the dressing turning brown, add a splash of fresh squeezed lime juice.

Marinated Shrimp

My husband's aunt shared this recipe with me age ago. It's a Christmas Eve tradition in our home as well as in the homes of our adult children. But don't wait for a holiday to enjoy it!
—Delores Hill, Helena, MT

- -

Prep: 10 min. + marinating
Cook: 10 min. • **Makes:** about 3 dozen

- 2 lbs. uncooked jumbo shrimp, peeled and deveined
- 1 cup olive oil
- 2 garlic cloves, minced
- 4 tsp. dried rosemary, crushed
- 2 tsp. dried oregano
- 2 bay leaves
- 1 cup dry white wine or chicken broth
- ¾ tsp. salt
- ⅛ tsp. pepper

1. In a bowl, combine the shrimp, oil, garlic, rosemary, oregano and bay leaves. Cover and refrigerate for 2-4 hours.
2. Pour shrimp and marinade into a large deep skillet. Add wine or broth, salt and pepper. Cover and cook over medium-low heat for 10-15 minutes or until the shrimp turn pink, stirring occasionally. Discard bay leaves. Transfer with a slotted spoon to a serving dish.

1 piece: 40 cal., 2g fat (0 sat. fat), 31mg chol., 42mg sod., 0 carb. (0 sugars, 0 fiber), 4g pro.

Skillet Cornbread

This skillet bread looks like a puffy pancake but has the easy-to-cut texture of conventional cornbread. It complements everything from chicken to chili.
—Kathy Teela, Tucson, AZ

- -

Takes: 15 min. • **Makes:** 4 servings

- ¼ cup all-purpose flour
- ¼ cup cornmeal
- ½ tsp. baking powder
- ¼ tsp. salt
- 1 large egg, room temperature
- ¼ cup 2% milk
- 4 tsp. vegetable oil, divided

1. In a small bowl, combine flour, cornmeal, baking powder and salt. In another small bowl, whisk the egg, milk and 3 tsp. oil; stir into the dry ingredients just until moistened.
2. Heat remaining oil in a heavy 8-in. skillet over low heat. Pour batter into the hot skillet; cover and cook for 4-5 minutes. Turn and cook 4 minutes longer or until golden brown.

1 piece: 127 cal., 6g fat (1g sat. fat), 54mg chol., 222mg sod., 13g carb. (1g sugars, 1g fiber), 4g pro.

Crispy Baked Tofu

You'll never need another baked tofu recipe. My version is crispy on the outside while remaining super soft on the inside.
—Ralph Jones, San Diego, CA

- -

Prep: 15 min. + standing
Bake: 25 min. • **Makes:** 4 servings

- 1 pkg. (16 oz.) firm or extra-firm tofu
- 2 Tbsp. soy sauce or teriyaki sauce
- 1 Tbsp. olive oil
- 1 Tbsp. toasted sesame oil
- 1 tsp. kosher salt
- 1 tsp. garlic powder
- ½ tsp. pepper
- ¾ cup cornstarch
  Sliced green onions, optional

1. Preheat oven to 400°. Blot tofu dry. Cut into ¾-in. cubes. Place on a clean kitchen towel; cover cubes with another towel. Place a cutting board on top; gently place a large cast iron skillet on top. Let stand 10 minutes.
2. Meanwhile, in a shallow dish, whisk together soy sauce, olive oil, sesame oil, salt, garlic powder and pepper. Place the cornstarch in a separate shallow dish. Add tofu to soy mixture; turn to coat. Add tofu, a few pieces at a time, to the cornstarch; toss to coat. Place pieces on a parchment-lined baking sheet. Bake until tofu cubes are golden brown and crispy, 25-30 minutes, turning halfway through. Garnish with green onions if desired.

1 serving: 154 cal., 12g fat (2g sat. fat), 0 chol., 949mg sod., 3g carb. (1g sugars, 0 fiber), 10g pro.

Homemade Marinara Sauce

This quick and easy homemade marinara sauce is my kids' favorite. It works fantastic with spaghetti, and the kids love it in meatball subs, too.
—Cara Bjornlie, Detroit Lakes, MN

- -

Takes: 30 min. • **Makes:** 7 cups

- 1 Tbsp. olive oil
- 1 small onion, chopped
- 2 garlic cloves, minced
- 2 cans (28 oz. each) Italian crushed tomatoes
- 1 Tbsp. Italian seasoning
- 1 to 2 Tbsp. sugar
- ½ tsp. salt
- ½ tsp. pepper

In a large saucepan, heat oil over medium heat. Add onion; cook and stir until softened, 3-4 minutes. Add garlic; cook 1 minute longer. Add tomatoes, Italian seasoning, salt, pepper and sugar; bring to a boil. Reduce the heat; simmer, covered, 10 minutes.

¾ cup: 91 cal., 2g fat (0 sat. fat), 0 chol., 489mg sod., 12g carb. (8g sugars, 3g fiber), 3g pro.
Diabetic exchanges: 2 vegetable, ½ fat.

Mini Pizza Muffin Cups

The kids gobbled up these mini pizzas, and it wasn't long before they asked for more! The no-cook pizza sauce and refrigerated dough make these bites a snap to prepare.

—Melissa Haines, Valparaiso, IN

Prep: 25 min. • **Bake:** 10 min.
Makes: 8 servings

- 1 can (15 oz.) tomato sauce
- 1 can (6 oz.) tomato paste
- 1 tsp. dried basil
- ½ tsp. garlic salt
- ¼ tsp. onion powder
- ¼ tsp. sugar
- 1 tube (11 oz.) refrigerated thin pizza crust
- 1½ cups shredded part-skim mozzarella cheese

OPTIONAL TOPPINGS

Pepperoni, olives, sausage, onion, green pepper, Canadian bacon, pineapple, tomatoes, fresh basil and crushed red pepper flakes

1. Preheat oven to 425°. In a small bowl, mix the first 6 ingredients.

2. Unroll the pizza crust; cut into 16 squares. Press squares onto bottom and up side of 16 ungreased muffin cups, allowing corners to hang over edges.

3. Spoon 1 Tbsp. sauce mixture into each cup. Top with cheese; add toppings as desired. Bake for 10-12 minutes or until crust is golden brown. Serve the remaining sauce mixture with pizzas.

Freeze option: Freeze the cooled baked pizzas in a resealable freezer container. To use, reheat pizzas on a baking sheet in a preheated 425° oven until heated through.

2 pizzas with 2 Tbsp. sauce: 209 cal., 8g fat (3g sat. fat), 14mg chol., 747mg sod., 26g carb. (5g sugars, 2g fiber), 10g pro.

Homemade Tortillas

I usually double this recipe because we go through these so quickly. The tortillas are so tender and simple, you'll never use store-bought again.
—Kristin Van Dyken, Kennewick, WA

- -

Takes: 30 min. • **Makes:** 8 tortillas

2	**cups all-purpose flour**
½	**tsp. salt**
¾	**cup water**
3	**Tbsp. olive oil**

1. In a large bowl, combine flour and salt. Stir in water and oil. Turn onto a floured surface; knead 10-12 times, adding a little flour or water if needed to achieve a smooth dough. Let rest for 10 minutes.

2. Divide dough into 8 portions. On a lightly floured surface, roll each portion into a 7-in. circle.

3. In a greased cast-iron or other heavy skillet, cook tortillas over medium heat until lightly browned, 1 minute on each side. Serve warm.

1 tortilla: 159 cal., 5g fat (1g sat. fat), 0 chol., 148mg sod., 24g carb. (1g sugars, 1g fiber), 3g pro.
Diabetic exchanges: 1½ starch, 1 fat.

INDEX

1, 2, 3